CW01459834

ISBN 978-1-332-16442-4
PIBN 10103177

A JOURNAL

WRITTEN

DURING AN EXCURSION

IN

ASIA MINOR

BY

CHARLES FELLOWS

1838.

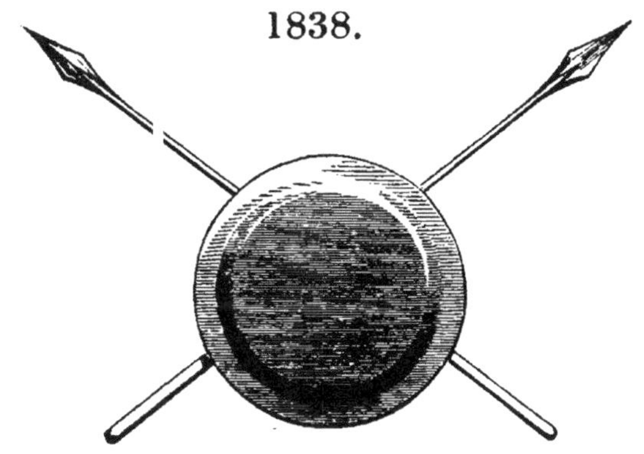

LONDON:

JOHN MURRAY, ALBEMARLE STREET.

MDCCCXXXIX.

PRINTED BY RICHARD AND JOHN E. TAYLOR,
RED LION COURT, FLEET STREET.

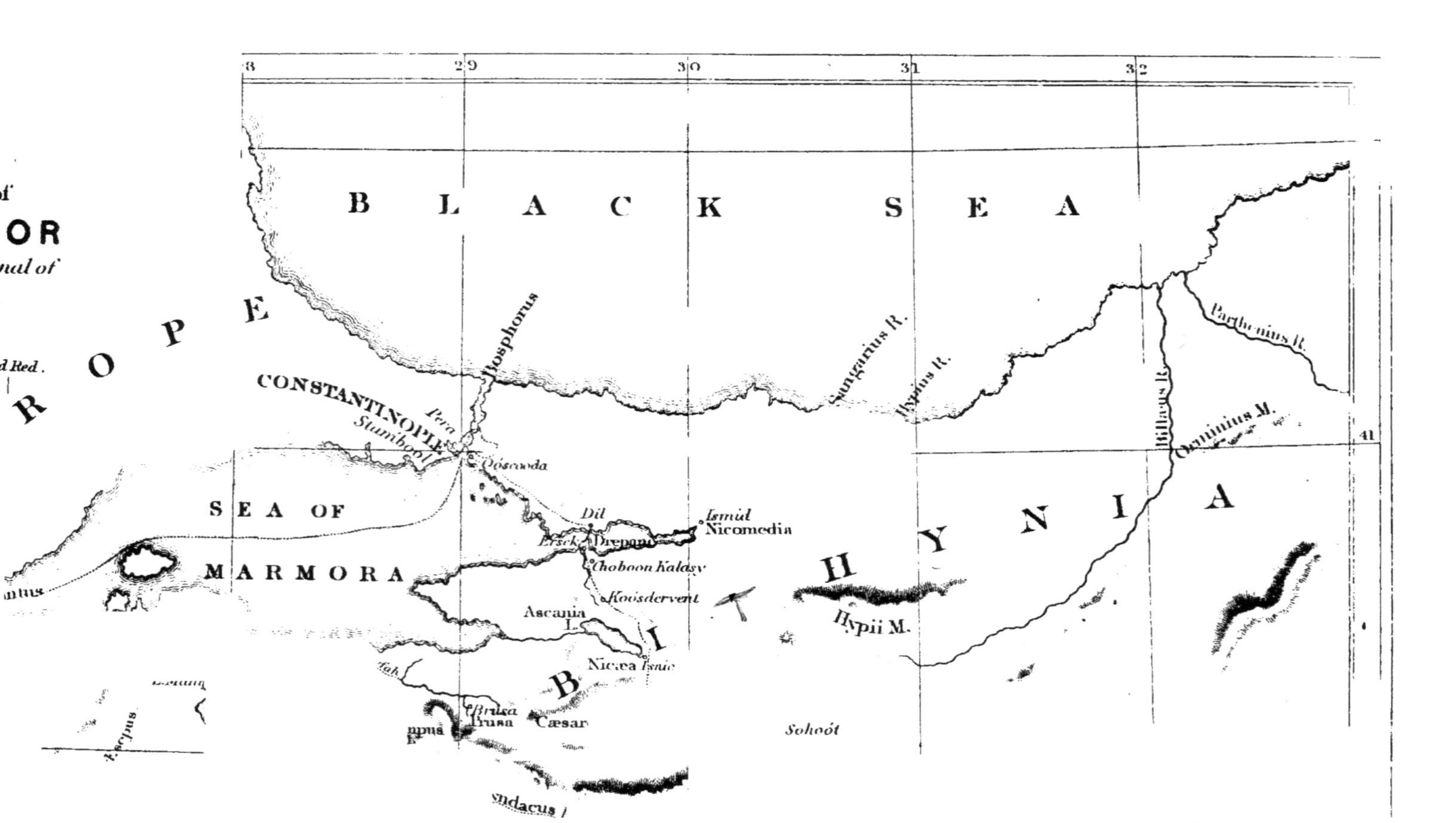

of
NOR
urnal of
rs.
lored Red.
ROPE
BLACK SEA
Bosphorus
CONSTANTINOPLE
Pera
Stamboul
Ooscooda
SEA OF
MARMORA
Dil
Ismid
Nicomedia
Ersek
Drepano
Choboon Kalasy
Koosdervent
Ascania L.
Nicæa Isnic
Brusa
Prusa
Cæsar
Sangarius R.
Hypius R.
Parthenius R.
Billæus R.
Orminius M.
Hypii M.
Sohoot
BITHYNIA
29
30
31
32
41

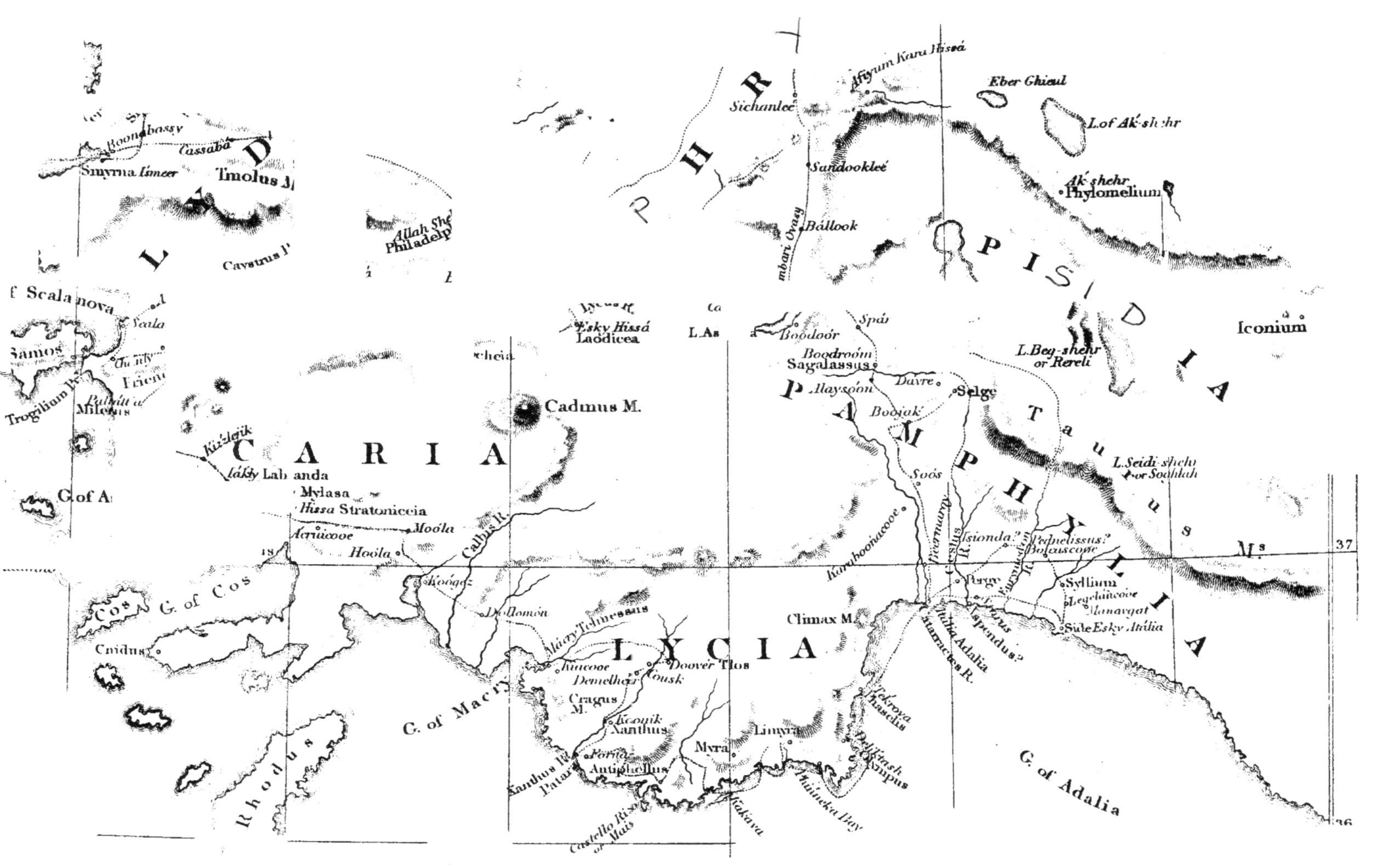
PHRYGIA
PISIDIA
PAMPHYLIA
CARIA
LYCIA
Taurus Ms
Afiyum Kara Hissá
Eber Ghieul
L. of Ak'shehr
Ak'shehr
Phylomelium
Sichanlee
Sandookleé
Ballook
Iconium
L. Beg-shehr or Rereli
L. Seidi-shehr or Soghlah
Smyrna Izmeer
Cassaba
Tmolus M
Caystrus R
Allah Shehr
Philadelphia
Esky Hissá
Laodicea
L. As
Boodoor
Spái
Boodroóm
Sagalassus
Alaysoón
Davre
Selge
Boojak
Soós
Cadmus M.
Samos
Scala
Trogilium Pr.
Miletus
Kizlejik
Iákly
Labranda
Mylasa
Hissa
Stratoniceia
Moóla
Hoóla
Calbis R.
Koógez
Dollomón
Cos
G. of Cos
Cnidus
Rhodus
G. of Macry
Climax M.
Isionda?
Pednelissus?
Perge
Syllium
Legdáncooe
Manavgat
Side
Esky Atália
Atalia Adalia
Catarractes R.
Aspendus?
Cestrus R.
Eurymedon R.
Karaboonacooe
Tlos
Doover
Cousk
Demelheer
Cragus M.
Xanthus
Patara
Antiphellus
Myra
Limyra
Kakava
Tekrova
Phaselis
Olympus
Deliktash
G. of Adalia
37
36

PREFACE.

Since my return to England from the Tour in Asia Minor which forms the subject of the following Journal, I have been informed at the Royal Geographical Society that parts of my route which lay through the Interior and Southern district of the country, and led me to the remains of important ancient cities, had not before been traversed by any European; and it is on this account alone that I am induced to lay my Journal before the Public.

The country through which I travelled is that small portion of Asia Minor (now known by the name of Anadhouly,) which lies between lat. 42° and 36°, and long. 26° and 32°, including Lydia, Mysia, Bithynia, Phrygia, Pisidia, Pamphylia, Lycia, and Caria. My route is marked in the accompanying Map.

As the most interesting period of the history of this

country was the time of its occupation by the Greeks, so the remains of their cities form now the chief attraction to the traveller. These cities, some of them of very remote antiquity, all had their origin prior to the Conquest of the country by the Romans in the third century before the Christian æra, after which time that people were nominally the possessors of the country, and the Roman taste was visibly encroaching on the Greek in works of art. About the age of Constantine, the Christians began to produce a still greater change in the architecture of the many cities of which they had possession, including the Seven Churches of the Apocalypse, piling up buildings in a style very different from the pure Greek. Next came the Venetians, whose slight fortifications, built of the remains of ruined cities, are seen on every coast and in every important mountain pass. The conquest by the present occupants, the Turks, succeeded in the fourteenth century. Their architectural works are few, and of a character so peculiar as to render them easily distinguishable from the earlier buildings by which they are surrounded.

The descendants of the Greeks, the ancient possessors of the soil, do not, I believe, now form a tenth part of the population; their costume and even language are so lost by mixture with the Turks, that these national peculiarities are with difficulty traced. The Greeks generally wear colours not so gay as those of the Turks, frequently having the turban and Turkish trowsers of black; green they are forbidden to use, that being the peculiar colour of a privileged few among the followers of the Prophet.

It will be gathered from my Journal that at the time of my arrival in the country I was strongly biassed in favour of the Greeks, and equally prejudiced against the Turks; and it will be seen in the course of the narrative how this unfavourable idea of the Turkish character was gradually removed by a personal intimacy with the people, generally in situations where they were remote from every restraint but those which their religion imposes.

Of the country which I was entering I knew as little as of its inhabitants, and this want of information may be manifest in parts of my Journal; but I have given my observations made on the spot, that the fidelity of the descriptions may not be impaired. The Drawings introduced have been selected from my sketch-book for the purpose of illustration only. Those which represent the sculptured remains found at Xanthus have been seen by the Trustees of the British Museum, and I hear that on their recommendation the Government has given directions for having these monuments of ancient art brought to this country;

we may hope therefore to see them among the treasures of our National Institution. I have added Translations of the Inscriptions which I copied on my tour, for the elucidation of which I must acknowledge my great obligations to my friend Mr. James Yates.

Had I been aware when I travelled through this district how little it was known, I should have made more careful observations of position and distance, to assist in mapping the country; and I should have devoted more time to the examination of inscriptions. I hope, however, that the partial information which I can furnish, may induce other travellers better prepared than myself for antiquarian research to turn their steps to this part of the world, which not only abounds in interest connected with early history and poetry, but is so rich in existing remains of past ages.

London, May, 1839.

CONTENTS.

CHAPTER I.

Lydia.

CHAPTER II.

Mysia.

CHAPTER III.

Constantinople.

CHAPTER IV.

Bithynia.

CHAPTER V.

Phrygia.

CHAPTER VI.

Pisidia.

CHAPTER VII.

Pamphylia.

CHAPTER VIII.

Lycia.

CHAPTER IX.

Caria.

CHAPTER X.

South of Lydia.

CHAPTER XI.

Part of the West of Phrygia.

CHAPTER XII.

Lydia.

SUPPLEMENTARY CHAPTER.

APPENDIX.

LIST OF PLATES.

JOURNAL.

CHAPTER I.

LYDIA.

Arrival at Smyrna—Costume—Description of the Town—Casino Ball—Slave-market—Manners of the People—Greek Church—Antiquities—Egyptian Customs—Departure for Magnesia—Caravan Bridge—Natural History on the way—Khan at Magnesia—Journey to Thyatira, one of the Seven Churches—Its Antiquities.

February 12th, 1838.—I AM now in the Frank town of Smyrna, having this evening set foot for the first time in Asia Minor. The whole of the Greek Islands which I have passed since leaving Syra appeared barren and uncultivated, with scarcely a tree to be seen. As we drew near the coast of Asia Minor, the Bay of Smyrna came in sight, bounded by mountains and woods, all green, rich, and beautiful. The approach to the city is very imposing, and the multitude of little boats scudding about, though not so picturesque as those of the Italian or Greek Isles, have a striking and characteristic effect, the boats being gaily painted, the men all wearing turbans, and the women concealed in white drapery.

I can scarcely believe that I am in Asia Minor, for my inn (the Navy Hotel) is just like an English public-house. I have heard the guns firing and drums beating on board the different men-of-war stationed opposite to my window, and the band of the Sapphire frigate has been playing "God save the Queen," and "Home, sweet Home."

February 13*th*.—On looking out of my window this morning, I found that I was really in the East. I beheld a whole city of Turks, a very gay scene; but the people struck me as being disgustingly fat. The variety of costume, occasioned by the different orders or sects of the Turks, is quite curious. It would be an endless task to describe the varieties, all very unlike the European; and nothing but the pencil could convey an idea of the various head-dresses. I have just seen a man with a turban, which I took for a small sack of flour placed upon his head. The women, although they contrive to have a good view of strangers at a distance, cover up all but one eye as they approach; and some are always thus ensconced, having a horse-hair mask or cowl over the upper part of the face, and the lower part concealed in the same white sheet which covers the rest of the body. The dresses are most splendidly embroidered, a Turk thinking it nothing extraordinary to give fifteen or twenty pounds for a jacket. I saw a child whose clothes must have cost sixty or seventy pounds, the embroidery being a mass of gold, and one set of clothes was put over another: the child was not above eight years old, but was probably the pet of some wealthy merchant. The expenditure of the Turks in dress is enormous, and of the Greeks also; at Syra I saw a celebrated Albanian chief of great wealth in his full dress, which I heard, independently of the jewels, was worth many hundred pounds.

Smyrna is a thickly inhabited town, and the streets are extremely narrow and dirty. The appearance of the people generally seems to me not pleasing; there is no trace of simplicity of manners, but they look as if they had always lived in the bustle of commerce. I do not like any trait in the character of the Turks which I have yet seen; what a contrast do they form to the Greeks, who appear all intelligence, and who are certainly simple and unaffected! At Syra a little boy, eight or nine years of age, acted for an hour as cicerone to our party, and on dismissing him I gave him a piastre, a coin of less value than twopence halfpenny of our money; on taking it he looked gravely in my face, and tears glistened in his eyes; he kissed my hand, and then pressed it to his forehead: it would require a far larger sum here to obtain such an expression of gratitude.

The town of Smyrna, which I have now viewed from all sides, in situation is beautiful, but in appearance is exactly like a large town of Swiss chalets. The houses are very much alike, and all of wood, with brown roofs and without chimneys. The few tiers of warehouses on the Marina or quay are whitened over, but these also are built of wood, the better to bear the shaking of the earthquakes. I do not think that there is a house more than one story above the ground-floor in the town; the ground-floor is always the bazaar or store-house, the residence being above. The churches, with the exception of the mosques, are like wooden barns, and without tower or belfry.

I have been admitted to the Casino or public rooms, where there are papers, card-rooms, and billiards, and invited to a ball there on Monday, previously to which I am to dine with our kind and attentive Consul, Mr. Brant. I have been introduced to many Europeans here; their manners are peculiar and not pleasing, displaying the caution of the English merchant, without the varied acquirements which in England are united with mercantile habits. The Frank people here, having no interest in the country they inhabit, and no voice even in the local government of the town, devote their thoughts wholly to business; their goods are all the stake they have, and even this interest is limited by the climate and government: no one has a house of value, for the frequent earthquakes place them in jeopardy; and ships of every nation are constantly stationed here, that, on any outbreak of the Turks or the plague, they may at a moment's notice put all they possess on board.

I have inquired of several gentlemen for some ruins discovered about two years ago in or near the town;

some had only heard there were such ruins, others said they were by the Castle Hill, but they had never been to that point, or not for several years past; yet the Castle Hill is not half a mile from the centre of the city, and is the only point commanding a view of the town or country; it has consequently been my daily walk.

I have been much surprised by finding really beautiful suites of rooms forming the houses of the gentry here; they consist of long corridors, opening into apartments generally of excellent proportions; all these are over the warehouses, and have no rooms above them.

The Casino Ball was extremely gay: many of the women, and particularly the middle-aged and old, wore the Greek costume, which is very elegant, although custom has prejudiced me in favour of the more compressed waist. The gold-embroidered skull-cap, the braided turban of hair blended with flowers and jewels, the velvet jacket, richly embroidered, with the gay mameluke sleeves, form a strikingly beautiful dress. The band from the Sapphire frigate, and the officers in their uniform, added to the gaiety of the room. I came away at about one, but find that most of my friends remained until five, and some until seven o'clock. I have had much attention paid to me, and can truly join with all other visitors of Smyrna in acknowledging the hospitality of its inhabitants.

Before the ball I dined at the Consul's, with a large party of English, principally officers of the army and navy. When dinner was over (at about eight o'clock) the

Governor of Smyrna sent to know if he might pay the Consul a visit, who first asked our consent, and then the Governor was ushered into the room. He takes every opportunity of showing respect to the English, and now came to request to be allowed to go to the ball with the Consul. He is an old, merry-looking fellow, but yet with the appearance of deep cunning. He was dressed for the ball in the very undress costume of the Turkish Government,—blue cloth clothes and red cap; but he was distinguished by a splendid locket of diamonds, and rings of the same stone. As soon as he had, by his interpreter, welcomed us all, his pipe-bearer handed him his pipe, which was of great value, having the mouth-piece of lemon-coloured amber, encircled with diamonds. He refused to drink wine, and persisted in declining; but, fortunately for him, rum and brandy are not verbally forbidden by the Prophet. The Chief Judge of the town afterwards called, attended by his suite. These two men are despotic, the one condemning and the other executing at his pleasure. The Governor farms his town of the Sultan, paying a certain sum for the year, and makes what he can of the taxes, fees, and fines: immense fortunes are thus made in a short time, frequently in the most tyrannical way; but the Governor's power only extends over Asiatics. Life and death are in his hands; but money will always satisfy him, and he alone has to be satisfied.

With the Slave-market I was not so much shocked as I expected, and noticed that the children seemed healthy and happy. I never saw negroes so black; their skin was bright, and looked as if it had just been black-leaded and well brushed; they had beautiful teeth, and the necks and wrists of the children were ornamented with beads; there were only thirty or forty slaves in the market, and they were all young.

The people, from their custom of sitting cross-legged, and having their feet generally bare, make much use of them. I observed the men who were working the lathe, in turning the amber mouth-pieces for the pipes, press the chisel always with the toes, which were applied as quickly and dexterously as the fingers. With all four paws together at work, they reminded me of the Sun Bears at the Zoological Gardens eating an orange. The tailors iron their work by putting one foot into the iron, and working it about, while with their hands they are arranging the plaits and braiding. The weight carried by the porters in Smyrna is wonderful; I never saw such burdens borne by men, or men apparently so able to bear them; the development of muscle in their naked legs amounts almost to deformity.

On buying a pair of slippers, I was told that last year they were not above two-thirds of their present price, but that so many workmen died during the last season, that all manufactured articles had become dearer. Fourteen thousand Turks and a thousand persons of other nations are said to have died in Smyrna alone.

The children are still brought up in national prejudices; they hoot after a European and call him Frank,

Frank-dog, and other such epithets. One little monkey gave me a smart stroke on the back with his stick, but he was soon laughed into a friendly temper. They are afraid of the consequences of their impertinence, and generally secure a retreat behind some door-way before they even call after the stranger. The men are however losing many of these prejudices. Today, whilst I was sketching, (which is an act forbidden by their religion,) several Turks came and watched me for half an hour, and expressed their delight at any new object which they recognised. I was putting in some shipping in the distance, and as I drew each vessel, although on an extremely small scale, they told me what ships they were with great satisfaction; they also recognised several views I had previously taken.

The society of an infidel is not, as formerly, shunned by the Turk, and their commercial intercourse is daily increasing; they naturally appear more suspicious of the Greek than of other nations.

The annoyances to which a Frank is subject on entering the mosques here are so great that I shall delay visiting them until I arrive at Constantinople. I see the Turks barefooted, and kneeling round the doors and in the colonnades and lobbies round the mosques; there is much devotion in their attitudes and appearance.

The three classes of people here, the Turks, Jews, and Christians, have each their own Sabbath,—Friday, Saturday, and Sunday. There is in consequence little observance of any one of the days in the town as a whole.

I have witnessed a splendid funeral of a wealthy Greek, in which all the church power was engaged, including the highest authority, an archbishop I believe. In the Greek church the dresses are more splendid than in the Romish, but the whole effect is quite in contrast. In this church there is not the slightest semblance of devotional feeling, less even than in the Synagogue worship. The priests are ordinary-looking men of the world; they sing the service in merry time, in a common but rather nasal tone, and look about them as if they were in the crowded streets instead of a place of worship. They are honest-looking men, but have nothing of the priest about them ; a long black beard seemed to be a distinctive part of their costume. There is a great deal of bowing and kissing of hands; but all the recitations seem addressed to one another, and I did not see an uplifted eye or any attitude of adoration. There is no altar, and therefore no fixed point for prayer. A candle, which is merely a waxed piece of cotton, is given to every person on entering, and they all keep their hats on during the ceremony. Celibacy is not enjoined upon the priesthood by the Greek Church; and from their appearance I should say, that they are more in their element in the noise and bustle of trade and of their families than in the offices of the church. A more different race of beings from the priests of Rome cannot well be imagined.

Camels are the only carriages in Smyrna, if I may use the expression, and you not unfrequently meet eight or nine hundred in the course of a walk. The streets are so narrow, that an European, unaccustomed to these animals, requires some nerve when walking under their necks, or standing between them and the wall, while they pass in long strings with their bulky bales of goods suspended from either side. The sheep of the country are the Cape sheep, having a kind of apron tail, entirely of rich marrowy fat, extending to the width of their hind-quarters, and frequently trailing on the ground; the weight of the tail is often more than six or eight pounds. The common pigeon here is the turtle-dove.

In all the confined seas in the Mediterranean I have observed the phosphoric light sparkling in the waves caused by our paddle-wheels; but in the sea here the boats are actually lighted by the illumination from the motion of the oar in the water; and a belt of light, some inches in width, is drawn around the boat by its motion, whilst a stream of light follows its course.

The walls of all the buildings in the upper part of the town are formed out of the ruins of ancient Smyrna; and columns, busts, cornices, and entablatures are seen built in everywhere, and mixed indiscriminately with the volcanic stone of the country. The features of the busts are generally destroyed, to satisfy the scruples of their present owners, the Turks. Hundreds of tomb-stones are constructed of the ornamental parts of ancient temples, all of white marble. The Jews have bought one hill, formed of a pile of ruins of marble, for tombs for their burial-ground. Near the town I observed a wall loosely built of stone, and thinking that it looked of a lighter colour than the common stone of the neighbourhood, I went to examine it. It was composed of what appeared to be flat stones, about three inches thick, and all of conglomerate or grout; but to my astonishment I found that the surface of every piece (some were two feet long) was formed entirely of mosaic work, with beautiful patterns in black, white, and red. There must have been hundreds of feet of this, which had no doubt formed the floor of some temple or bath in the immediate neighbourhood, probably of the Temple of Ceres, which is said to have stood here. These blocks of mosaic now form the walls of a corn-field, out of which they must have been dug, for I observed that the small pebbles in the soil were all square pieces of marble of the same size as the stones of the mosaic. Here I saw the top of an arch, with the capitals of its columns only visible above ground, and twenty or thirty feet of loose soil around it, containing the ruins of ancient art. Yet no one had been found even to remove the soil to show the proportions of the building, and this on the side of so steep a hill, that probably the rain will soon do what man has not had taste and energy to attempt: the people now prop up the soil of the hill with the capitals of columns or cornices as they are laid bare.

The spring is rapidly opening; and I have observed today a number of people with flowers tucked most tastefully into their turbans; anemone, jonquil, and iris adding to the endless variety and gaiety of the head-dress. The Greek women form their own hair, of which they have a profusion, into a turban, mixing it very elegantly with flowers, ribbon, or gauze, and generally putting at the top a skull-cap of gold embroidery. The children have many gold and silver coins suspended from the head by cords of hair; and some have their hair in twenty or thirty thin plaits hanging down the back, as it was worn by the ancient Egyptians. The edges of the eyelids also are painted by the Turkish women exactly as was done by that nation.

I have several times seen the dance so well described by Mr. Lane as performed by the dancing-girls in Egypt; the dance, music, and costume are precisely the same here.

February 21*st*,—Tomorrow I leave Smyrna for Magnesia*. I was to have started this morning, and the

* I have throughout my journal made use of the ancient names of places, as being the best known to English readers, from association both with classic and sacred history. When I have used the modern names (which alone are known to the Turks) I have endeavoured to represent the sound of the word in their language by a combination of our letters in such a manner as will not allow of more than one pronunciation; and in attempting this I have disregarded the orthography of modern maps, which give names unknown in the country, and useless to the traveller. In pronunciation I have presumed that the vowels will be sounded as in the English alphabet. In the few instances in which the *a* has to be sounded broad, as in *father*, it is put in italic.

horses were brought to the door; but the wind from the north-east, in which direction we were to travel, was so high and so intensely cold that we could not face it. Ice covers every pool, and even the streams are frozen; as the sea is dashed up by the wind upon the Marina it immediately forms a coat of ice. Walking to the south of the town I passed the Jews' burial-ground, which I before noticed, and was much struck by its appearance. It is a hill of almost bare rock, of about a mile in extent, and every level spot has a marble slab upon it. The first idea that the place gave me was its strong resemblance to the pictures of the Resurrection; thousands of tombstones cover the ground, and in as many forms; from the hardness of the rock, the grave is generally constructed above the surface, perhaps a foot high, and covered with a marble slab; but grave and slab have been continually torn up by the Turks; few remain above a year undisturbed, and they seem the stone quarry for the walls and paving in the neighbourhood. I saw several in the street near, with dates less than two years old, now torn up and used for building purposes.

Scarcely one of these tombstones is without some trace of its earlier history; many have upon them Greek or Roman letters, parts of inscriptions; and cornices, flutings, capitals, or shafts of columns may be recognised in almost all of them. I walked up the hill, and there found the quarry which the Jews had used, on the site of most extensive temples, now only to be recognised by high hills of white chippings, and long deep trenches, from which even the foundations have been greedily dug up; a lime-kiln close by had received many relics of marble too small for the purpose of tombstones.

The view of Smyrna from these heights is very imposing, and this point, as is usual in the sites of Greek temples, is chosen with admirable judgement both for seeing from and for being seen.

I have spoken with many enlightened men here, who much regretted the insensibility of the residents to the arts and sciences; but all say, "We have a glorious sun above our heads and perfect liberty." Each nation has its own idea of liberty; the Englishman's liberty extends to all those around him; exclusive liberty in a state is by him received as the proof of the worst of tyranny. I could not boast of liberty where those around me were treated as the Turkish law allows, or while the slave-market stood open in the town.

February 22nd.—Having breakfasted and packed, which latter is a serious matter with the Turks, I started from the inn at half-past eight o'clock. The first horse was ridden by a black-looking surly Turk, our guide, mounted on a saddle or pile of cloaks and padding, which was a sufficient burden for the horse without the rider; then followed the baggage-horse, bearing my canteen, tent, hammock and mattress, carpet-bag, and saddle-bags containing provisions; this appeared the slightest made horse, but was the strongest and best suited to its work.

My servant and interpreter, Demetrius Scufi*, had a most complete establishment on his saddle, of holsters (used only as bags for knife, string, etc. for the road), and long leathern cases for his umbrella and pipe; over his shoulders was slung a capital double-barrelled gun. I followed on the fourth horse, equipped as an European; having purchased for myself saddle and bridle, which articles the Turks never provide with the horses.

At nine o'clock we arrived at the Caravan Bridge, an object picturesque in itself, and highly interesting to the people of Smyrna, as it is the land-gate or entrance to the city, and all the produce of the East which is shipped from Smyrna necessarily passes over this bridge. A toll or tax upon all caravans is here levied by the Government, the payment of which gives the title to depasture the camels, free of charge, all over the Sultan's dominions. It is a common and characteristic wish of

* Demetrius Scufi was an excellent travelling servant in every department: the character of a servant in a country like this is unknown, and difficult to conceive, to those who have always travelled with the accommodations met with in Europe; it combines interpreter, cook, tailor, and valet, sportsman, secretary, and companion. Demetrius was a man of good private property, and had his house and little estate near Smyrna, and his two pleasure-horses. He travelled *con amore*, and had pursued this profession for the last fifteen years in all quarters of the globe, and had been several times to England. He was a native of Hydra, but had spent his life in Smyrna. I paid him a dollar a day, —a remuneration which, from his great knowledge of travelling and perfect honesty, I consider more œconomical than the lower price which is usually paid to an inferior person. I hope to obtain his services on any future rambles in the East.

the people to possess the value transported during one day over this bridge. The continual passing of the camels, and necessary halt for transacting the business required by the collector of the toll, make this at all times an animated scene. The Greeks also frequent this neighbourhood on their gala days, and I have here on such occasions witnessed much dancing and festivity among the lower orders.

After crossing the bridge the road increased in beauty every mile, as we traversed the valley and ascended the mountains to the north-east. For the first ten miles Smyrna, with its rich and beautiful valley, was behind us, and continually showed itself in such an attractive variety of views, that I was often tempted to stop and turn to retrace my steps over the country, which lay spread out like a map. The predicted destruction of the port of Smyrna, by the promontory formed from the deposit which the river Hermus brings down, is strongly confirmed by the view from this point. Time alone is required to complete the work, and this is constant and irresistible in its effect. The villages, in which are the country residences of the merchants of Smyrna, furnish conspicuous points of beauty in this extensive landscape. When about twelve miles on our route we halted for half an hour in a valley considerably elevated amidst the hills. The spot was beautiful, and surrounded by well-grown cypress and plane trees. After again passing a succession of hills, the rich and extensive valley of the Hermus opened before us. The descent into the valley was picturesque, wild, and in many parts precipitous. At half-past five we arrived at the ancient Magnesia, now called Manser. The rocks we passed on leaving Smyrna are limestone, although the hill on which the castle stands, and several others, are of a volcanic earth or stone, much resembling granite, and of a dark colour. As we left the valley the hills became almost naked limestone, so white and soft that it seemed to split and crumble as if it had been burnt and was ready for the process of slacking. I saw no trace of fossil remains of any kind. Suddenly, after passing a small valley near the summit, all the range of hills became of a slaty rock, reddish in colour, and so contorted, that on first seeing it at the bottom of a brook I supposed it the trunk of an old tree: but I soon found myself in a ravine, cut or worn through the hill, consisting entirely of this schisty slate, which in places was so twisted that it appeared knotted together and writhing into circles and curves in every direction; part of it is shot through with veins of beautiful white marble, varying from an eighth of an inch to some feet in thickness, entirely, I think, of the kind we call Parian. It is crystallized, sparkling at every fracture. Has not the same agency caused each of these effects? In the valley formed and still forming by the river are rolled down large stones of this red slate, tied round as it were in all directions by white cords of marble; large green-coloured stones of the same kind are also rolled from other neighbouring hills. Among the first rocks of limestone that we passed were many loose blocks of petrified vegetable substances, forming a spongy stone, as also masses of pebbles cemented by the same limy matrix; these were near streams strongly charged with particles of lime, which run in all directions, and therefore are probably not very old, nor far from their birth-place.

The fig, vine, and olive enrich this valley, surrounded by the less profitable plane, wild pear, and stone pine. I feel quite sure that the latter is the fir in its natural growth, which I never could see in that state in Italy; even when found in a wood, as is the case near Ravenna, it is always trimmed up to the top; which makes it look like an umbrella. The hills on the limestone side were green as summer, covered with clusters of a dwarf oak*, clothed with extremely small leaves, and so like a miniature holly that until I saw the acorns I fancied it of that species. There were also the juniper, the myrtle, and the oleander; but on the slate rock, although the aspect was the same, the mountains were richly embrowned with the dead leaves of the dwarf oak. The anemones of various colours, and the small dark yellow crocus, made the ground begin to look gay, but the ice was still upon all the pools, and in the evening it was intensely cold. Several times during this ride, upon the baggage getting loose on the horse, I met with instances of the civility of the Turks, who proffered their assistance with cord or whatever was wanted, and

* Quercus.

at other times offered us water, never expecting remuneration for their attention. I should mention however that on one occasion, when a man came out of a hut and begged to present me with a beautiful brace of red-legged partridges*, a species common in some parts of England, my servant Demetrius refused to receive them, and told me that presents of that kind were always dear, as the giver expected more than their value.

As we approached Manser we met many trains of natives on asses, and strings of camels, and saw every indication of a large and busy town. On the road-side were buffalos feeding, smaller than those in Calabria, and without the hump; these, although equally unamiable in their appearance, are much more tame and useful. I saw several with their calves, and others which are evidently used for milking.

The town of Magnesia lies along the foot of a fine range of hills, backed by the almost perpendicular face of a rocky mountain (Mount Sipylus), whose top is now slightly capped with snow. At apparently inaccessible places on this cliff are many entrances to artificial caves cut in the shape of doors, evidently tombs of a very early date. The town has a great number of minarets of mosques, and more and better public buildings than Smyrna. I am now in a very fine building, the public khan. It is as extensive as any Italian palace, and built entirely of stone and iron; each room is dome-

* *Perdix rufus.*

topped, with iron gratings and shutters to the windows, and an iron door, which was unlocked by a black slave with immense keys; the heavy door opened and I walked in, as if into a prison, but found it so clean, that although it offered little more than bare walls, I liked its appearance better than that of any house I had seen for months. Mats were spread on the floor, and unfolding my stores, all other comforts, together with an excellent dinner, were quickly supplied. For the first time I am lying on my travelling mattress, and surrounded by pens, ink, and paper, with my canteen for a table; but I shall have other khans to describe probably different from this, and the present may give but little idea of the accommodations in travelling in this country. Manser is a very extensive place, but the houses are wholly built of mud, and the streets here, as in all the towns that I have yet seen, are covered over from house to house with canvas, mats, or vines on trellis, shading the street from the sun; and thus the shops only are visible to the traveller, who can gain but an imperfect view of the town.

February 23rd.—From Manser we started before nine o'clock, well mounted, and travelled across the valley directly north. At two miles' distance we crossed the river Hermus by a wooden bridge, and, almost immediately after, its tributary the Hyllus, by a ferry; the latter is larger than the main river, which it joins within a furlong of the ferry. The valley over which we continned to ride must be at least twelve miles directly across from Manser, but we bore to the eastward up the valley of the Hyllus. The land is excellent, and I scarcely saw a stone during the first eighteen miles. Cotton and corn grow luxuriantly, but there are few trees except the willow and pollard poplar.

At the solitary stable or rest-house half way to Acsá, (the ancient Thyatira, one of the Seven Churches,) I found the well-coping formed of the capital of a column of white marble veined with red. A burial-ground adjoining was filled with triglyphs and columns of a similar stone, and the people said that they were brought from Sardis; but this is scarcely probable, as they would have had to be carried a very considerable distance. My informant said that within a few miles were some ruins, (from the direction, perhaps Apollonis,) and that much stone was fetched from there.

The valley along which I was now travelling inclined to the north-east, and became much narrower; at times it was intersected by the lengthened feet of the hills, on either side showing bare rocks of white marble, sometimes with veins of red, but with no appearance of the crystallization which I noticed near Mount Sipylus. Following the course of the river, the banks of which were of a white drifting sand, the *débris* of the marble, I passed over the stream, and crossed an extent of bleak, uncultivated country. Two Turks looking wild with fear stopped us, and said they had just been robbed of all their money and baggage by two men, and that three others were in the same gang. Although our importance as Europeans would be some protection, from the inquiries which would be made if anything were to befall us, nevertheless Demetrius, whose gun had already killed a couple of wild ducks and a starling, and who had loaded for more of the feathered race, at once added some buttons as bullets to his charge; I covered my watch-strings, and we all kept together to make our party appear the more imposing. We made inquiry of two other Turks, who had seen the robbers, and had in consequence made a circuit; they attributed their safety however to their show of pistols, which, like those of all their nation, were awfully large and very handsome. We passed on, and neither saw nor heard more of the robbers, who I strongly suspect never existed.

The country as we approached Acsá became very low and marshy, and seemed only occupied by wild ducks, swans, plovers, and water-hens. For some miles we passed over a paved road, for the most part of stones rounded by the rivers; but along the edge of the road, which was built up with more care, I frequently saw marble cornices and beautifully cut stones; and in the walls and burial-ground at the entrance of the town there were numerous pieces of columns, many of granite, stuck in the ground as Turkish gravestones. The scenery has been all day extremely beautiful, and the land, which is always rich, would be valuable if sufficiently cultivated, but it is much neglected. The distant mountains bounding the valleys only varied in beauty.

Within a few miles of this town I saw the trace of a

cart-wheel, and I find that such vehicles are occasionally used here in husbandry; these are the first carriages that I have seen or heard of in Asia Minor; and here there are no roads, but they carry the produce from the field to the farm, and then roll it into the town in carts, the street being made wide enough to admit them.

We arrived at Acsá at five o'clock, after travelling thirty-six miles, much of the way at the rate of six miles an hour.

This town teems with relics of a former splendid city, although there is not a trace of the site of any ruin or early building. I saw ten or a dozen well-tops or troughs made of the capitals of columns of different kinds.

In a portion not exceeding one-third of a burial-ground I counted one hundred and thirty parts of columns; and upon measuring them, and noticing their orders, I found that seven or eight distinct temples or buildings must have contributed; one Corinthian column was flat at each angle, ready for fluting, but only partly finished. The streets are in places paved with fragments of carved stone. I saw several columns of granite, some of red-veined white marble, and some of grey and white; also some small columns, or rather two-third pilasters, I fancy of a later date than the other remains, but I may be in error *.

For two miles out of the town the mouths or curbs of the wells are formed of the capitals of extremely fine Corinthian pillars, the bucket being drawn through holes cut in the centre. I was prevented from sketching many that I admired by the rain, which continued during the day.

Just before I left, the ex-governor was escorted out of the town in state by all the Turkish grandees of the place, about thirty in number, in full dress, well mounted and ostentatiously armed, producing a fine effect.

* I have since found this kind of column an unerring indication of the Christian age; it probably formed a part of the interior ornament of the church.

CHAPTER II.

MYSIA.

Journey to Sóma—Inscriptions—Proceed to Pergamus—Its Antiquities and Situation—A Khan—Natural History of the Country—Adramyttium—Assos—Its Architectural Remains—Its Tombs—Manners of the People—Alexandrian Troy—Its Ruins—Hot-springs—Stone Quarry with Columns—Enáe—Implements and Customs of the Ancients retained—Plains of Troy—Arrival at the Dardanelles—Abydos and its Antiquities.

February 24th.—TRAVELLING W.N.W. from Thyatira, we rode for several miles over low bog-land, at a foot-pace; then quitting the level we gradually ascended to a rich cultivated country, which became more picturesque as we passed over a range of limestone hills. At about twenty miles' distance a splendid and extensive valley opened upon us, in which appeared, not far off, Kírkagatch, and immediately before us Bakir.

All the Turkish towns that I have seen have, in their style of building, the appearance of Swiss villages, with the exception only of the white mosque towers; the towns before us resembled them in situation also, being at the feet of very high rocky mountains, and the valley in the front of them being bounded by another exquisitely beautiful range. I have nowhere seen valleys so wide, rich, and cultivated as in this part of Asia Minor. Cotton seems the principal produce.

Passing Kírkagatch, we kept close under the cliffs, which were of white marble, but in places stained almost scarlet with a kind of ochre, and in some places yellow, the veins or perhaps original cracks being saturated with this stain; this is evidently the source of the varied stripes in the marbles seen in the ruins in the neighbourhood. I should have been disposed to think that this is also the cause of the masses of perfectly red marble (the *rosso antico*,) which lie about in all directions, carried down by the rivers from the mountains; but that I have frequently seen these red blocks themselves veined with white.

The stone fir is extremely fine here, and the colour the most lively yet rich green that can be imagined; in the long spines are frequently seen tufts as large as a bird's nest; I opened one, and found that it contained some hundreds of full-grown caterpillars comfortably housed for the winter. The hedges are of a small kind of arbutus and jasmine, with myrtles, clematis, and other shrubs that I have before mentioned; the walnuts are magnificent, as well as the planes*, which I have not seen growing wild in any other country.

About eight miles more, making thirty-two in all, brought us to Sóma, at three o'clock, having ridden the distance in six hours. Since losing the traces of Acsá,

* Platanus orientalis.

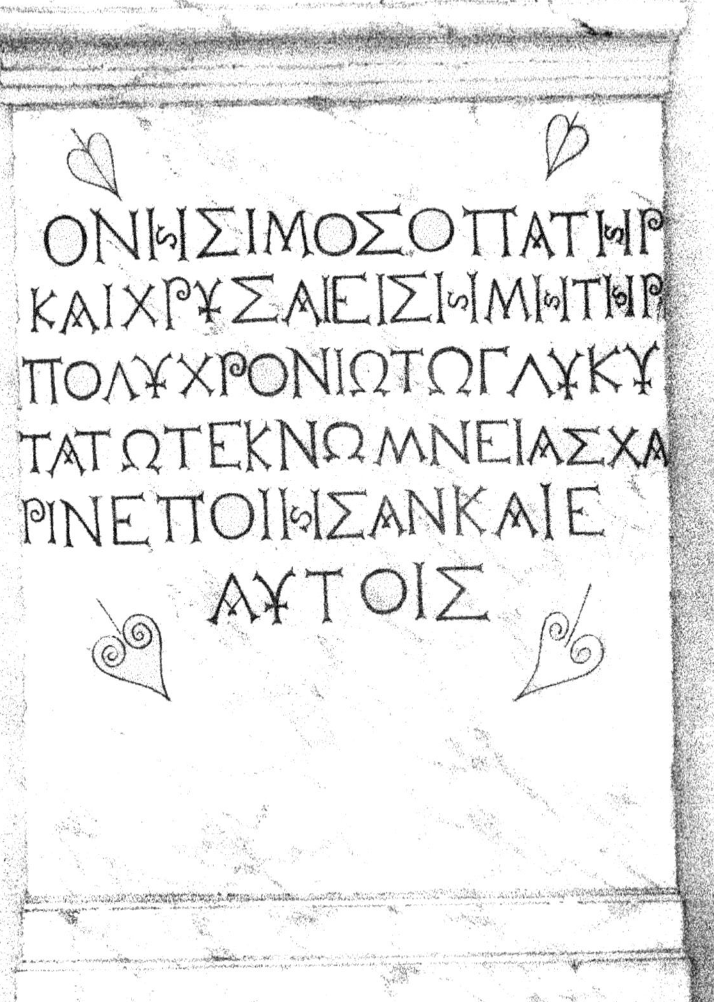

ΟΝΗΣΙΜΟΣΟΠΑΤΗΡ
ΚΑΙΧΡΥΣΑΙΕΙΣΙΗΜΗΤΗΡ
ΠΟΛΥΧΡΟΝΙΩΤΩΓΛΥΚΥ
ΤΑΤΩΤΕΚΝΩΜΝΕΙΑΣΧΑ
ΡΙΝΕΠΟΙΗΣΑΝΚΑΙΕ
ΑΥΤΟΙΣ

I have seen no relics of antiquity, even in the most certain haunts, the burial-grounds, nor are any visible in this town. I have been shown into a one-arched vault, about one hundred feet long and twenty-five wide, now used as a stable; it has three groins or projecting arches, rising on each side from as many marble pedestals, which I find are square, and let two-thirds into the wall, so as to appear like pilasters. On these are some Greek inscriptions. I have taken an impression of one by placing paper over the stone, and then rubbing the paper with a mixture of black-lead and soap. Of this I have given a copy in the annexed plate*.

I have also copied two others†.

OEYΛAEKAIMENA

EΨNOIKUTUOPCBEU
MNEIΛEXAMP////

I imagine that the building is a work of the Romans, and that these altar-shaped stones are old Greek materials used by them.

Hearing that there were some remains within three miles of this place, I walked to the spot, passing up one of the beautiful dells so peculiar to a mountain-limestone country, clothed with such planes and walnuts as

* The translation is as follows: "Onesimus, the father, and Chryseis, the mother, made [this tomb] for their sweetest child Polychronius, for the sake of remembrance, and for themselves."

† These may also have been funereal.

I never before saw. I reached at length a crow's-nest town on the peak of a rock, surrounded on all sides by mountains, and so completely shut in that I could not see the ravine by which I had approached. Probably the people had never before seen Europeans, for the whole town came out to look at us. The remains were evidently Byzantine, having stone ornaments with birds and snakes fighting, and the knotted arabesque patterns and rude carving of that age. In the street, for a horse-block, stood a marble pedestal the wrong end upwards with a Greek inscription, in form and age the same as those in Sóma.

ΠΟΜΠΗΙΟΣΙΤΟ
ΤΩΙΔΙΩ
ΕΚΤΩΝΙΛΙΩΝΑΥΤΟΥ
ΕΙΑΣΧΑΡΙΝ *

I am now in a little room in the khan at Sóma, where, on my return, I found a couple of excellent wild ducks ready for my dinner, which soon disappeared. It is about nine feet square, and is now fully furnished, though I found only bare walls. Demetrius is snoring at my feet, with his gun and saddle-bags hanging over his head; the contents of the canteen are arranged in readiness for my breakfast, and I am sitting with my canteen-box as my table, and writing by the luxurious but inconsistent light of wax candles, enjoy-

* "Pompeius [erected this tomb] to his own [son ?], at his own expense, for the sake of remembrance."

ing thoroughly the comfort of dry clothes, after having been all day wet through. My candles were purchased at Smyrna, and are "patent wax with twisted wicks," from England. Probably the wicks may have been in this country before. I understand that the people of Asia Minor find the English patent wax candles cheaper and better than their own; this is also the case in Italy.

On leaving Sóma, after a gentle rise from the valley, a new and beautiful country opened before me, not so bold, but more expanded, and surrounded by a chain of mountains. I saw the plains of Pergamus, watered by the Caicus and its tributary streams; we crossed one of them, or rather passed its source; it sprung up by the road-side so strongly, that within fifty yards it turned a mill, and was a stream a foot deep and ten or twelve wide. It is said to be tepid, but I did not stop to take out my thermometer.

The birds here are all either very bold or very tame, not moving until you are close to them. Three large eaglès sat by the road, and did not rise until we were so near that we could almost feel the wafting of their immense wings; the noise was startling, but our horses were not timid. I had never before been so near eagles at liberty, and this was on an open plain; but rocky mountains shadowed us, in the craggy sides of which these aspirants soon found their home. We had a delightful ride of seven hours and a half, about thirty-two miles, through a country so swampy with the heavy rains of yesterday that we had to travel slowly. The road varied but little in interest until within eight miles of this place, the ancient Pergamus, now Bérgama ; nor did we see even in the burial-grounds any trace of what my servant calls " old stones;" but on stopping at that point to let the horses drink, I observed that the trough was the inverted lid of a sarcophagus; and a little further on I had the baggage unpacked, and remained an hour to copy some long Greek inscriptions built sideways into a fountain.

ENANΔ
ΡΟ ΣΑΤΡΑΠΕΥΟΝΤΟ
ΣΕΓΙΠΡΤΤΑΜΙΟΣΙΣ
ΑΓΟΡΟΥΚ(ΑΤΕΥΑΣΕ
ΔΩΚΕΓΑΡΙΣΤΟΜΕΝ
ΕΙΤΙ((ΤΙΑΗΓΡΟΝ
ΕΠΟΙΚΙΣΑΙΓΡΟΣΤΩΙ
ΦΥΤΟΙΤΟΙΣΓΙΚΡΑΤΕΥ
ΑΦΥΤΕΥΟΕΝΤΙΟΔΕΠΕ
ΡΙΒΟΛΟΣΕΣΤΙΝΤΗΣΕ
ΗΣΣΓΟΡΟΥΚΥΓΡΩΝΙΚ
ΑΤΟΝΕΒΔΟΜΗΚΟΝΤΑ
ΚΛΙΟΙΚΟΓΕΔΛΚΑΙΚΙΛ
ΦΟΡΟΣΔΕΤΟΥΚΓΓΟ
ΧΡΟΥΣΟΥΣΕΚΑΣΤΟ
ΕΝΙΑΥΤΟΥ*

* This inscription appears to relate to the planting of a garden with cypresses at a certain period, and to the tenure of the garden together with dwellings annexed to it.

[ΑΓ]ΑΘΗΙΤΥΧΗΙ[ΟΙΚ]ΟΝΟΜΟΥΝΤΟΣ
ΔΗΜΗΤΡΙoΥΜΗΝΟΣΘΑΡΓΗΛΙΩΝΟΣ
ΔΕΥΤΕΡΑΙΑΛΕΞΩΝΔΑΜΩΝΟΣΕΙ
ΠΕΝΝΟΜΟΝΕΙΝΑΙΓΑΜΒΡΕΙΩΤΑΙΣ
ΤΑΣΠΕΝΘΟΥΣΑΣΕΧΕΙΝΦΑΙΑΝΕΣΘ[Η]
ΤΑΜΗΚΑΤΕΡΡΥΠΩΜΕΝΗΝΧΡΗΣΘΑΙ
ΔΕΚΑΙΤΟΥΣΑΝΔΡΑΣΚΑΙΤΟΥΣΠΑΙΔΑΣ
ΤΟΥΣΠΕΝΘΟΥΝΤΑΣΕΣΘΗΤΙΦΑΙΑΙ
ΕΑΜΜΗΒΟΥΛΩΝΤΑΙΛΕΥΚΗΙΕΠΙΤΕ
ΛΕΙΝΔΕΤΑΝΟΜΙΜΑΤΟΙΣΑΠΟΙΧΟΜΕ
ΝΟΙΣΕΣΧΑΤΟΝΕΝΤΡΙΣΙΜΗΣΙΝΤΩΙΔ[Ε]
ΤΕΤΑΡΤΩΙΛΥΕΙΝΤΑΠΕΝΘΗΤΟΥΣΑΝ
ΔΡΑΣΤΑΣΔΕΓΥΝΑΙΚΑΣΤΩΠΕΜΠΤΩΙ
ΚΑΙΕΞΑΝΙΣΤΑΣΘΑΙΕΚΤΗΣΚΗΔΕΙΑΣ
ΚΑΙΕΚΠΟΡΕΥΕΣΘΑΙΤΑΣΓΥΝΑΙΚΑΣΗ
ΤΑΣΕΞΟΔΟΥΣΤΑΣΕΝΤΩΙΝΟΜΩΙΓΕ
ΓΡΑΜΜΕΝΑΣΕΠΑΝΑΓΚoΝΤΟΝΔΕΓΥ
ΝΑΙΚΟΝΟΜΟΝΤΟΝΥΠΟΤΟΥΔΗΜΟΥΑΙ
ΡΟΥΜΕΝΟΝΤΟΙΣΑΓΝΙΣΜΟΙΣΤΟΙΣΠΡΟ
ΤΩΝΘΕΣΜΟΦΟΡΙΩΝΕΠΕΥΧΕΣΘΑΙΤΟΙΣΕΜ
ΜΕΝΟΥΣΙΝΚΑΙΤΑΙΣΠΕΙΘΟΜΕΝΑΙΣΤΩΙ
ΔΕΤΩΙΝΟΜΩΙΕΥΕΙΝΑΙΚΑΙΤΩΝΥΠΑΡΧΟΝ
ΤΩΝΑΓΑΘΩΝΟΝΗΣΙΝΤΟΙΣΔΕΜΗΠΕΙΘΟ
ΜΕΝΟΙΣΜΗΔΕΤΑΙΣΕΜΜΕΝΟΥΣΑΙΣΤΑ
ΝΑΝΤΙΑΚΑΙΜΗΟΣΙΟΝΑΥΤΑΙΣΕΙΝΑΙΩΕ
ΑΣΕΒΟΥΣΑΙΣΘΥΕΙΝΜΗΘΕΝΙΘΕΩΝΕΠΙΔΕ
ΚΑΕΤΗΤΟΝΔΕΜΕΤΑΔΗΜΗΤΡΙΟΝ

ΣΤΕΦΑΝΗΦΟΡΟΝΤΑΜΙΑΝΑΙΡΕΘΕΝΤΑ
ΑΝΑΓΡΑΨΑΙΤΟΝΔΕΤΟΝΝΟΜΟΝΕΙΣΔΥΟ
ΣΤΗΛΑΣΚΑΙΑΝΑΘΕΙΝΑΙΤΗΜΜΕΝ
ΜΙΑΝΠΡΟΤΩΝΘΥΡΩΝΤΟΥΘΕΣΜΟΦΟ
ΡΙΟΥΤΗΝΔΕΠΡΟΤΟΥΝΕΩΤΗΣΑΡΤΕ
ΜΙΔΟΣΤΗΣΛΟΧΙΑΣΑΝΕΝΕΙΚΑΤΩ
ΔΕΟΤΑΜΙΑΣΤΟΑΝΑΛΩΜΑΤΟΓΕ
ΝΟΜΕΝΟΝΕΙΣΤΑΣΤΗΛΑΣΤΩΙ
ΠΡΩΤΩΙΛΟΓΙΣΤΗΡΙΩΙ *

* *Translation.*

"May it be fortunate.

"In the Treasurership of Demetrius, on the second day of the month Thargelion, Alexon, son of Damon, declared it to be a law for *relations by marriage* [?], that the female mourners should wear clean grey cloth; that the men and boys engaged in the mourning should also wear grey, unless they prefer white; that they should perform the rites appointed by law for the departed at the latest in three months; that the men should terminate their mourning in the fourth month, and the women in the fifth; that the women, or the trains appointed in the law as a matter of necessity, should then rise from the lamentation and go forth; that the Gynæconomus, chosen by the people, should, at the purification preceding the Thesmophoria, pray for prosperity and the enjoyment of their existing possessions on behalf of those men who abide by, and those women who obey, this law, and imprecate the contrary upon those men and women who do not obey; and that the Treasurer chosen after Demetrius, bearing a crown, should inscribe this law upon two pillars, and place one of them before the gates of the temple of [Ceres] Thesmophoros, and the other before the temple of Artemis [i.e. Diana] Lochia. And let the Treasurer carry the sum expended to the pillars [or columns] in the first Chamber of Accounts."

Vegetation is rapidly bursting into life; the laburnum, which is here dwarf, is coming into leaf; the olive and fig grow wild. We met several caravans of camels, carrying cotton. Each camel carries three hundred and sixty okes, or about half a ton weight, for a day together without stopping to rest.

Pergamus, February 26*th*.—I am again in a khan, and must say that I never liked an inn half so much; it is pleasant to see all the furniture around me my own, and to feel that my room is my castle. Here the traveller finds only bare walls, with a few nails arranged for hanging things upon. When I return from the stroll I generally take, to stretch my legs after the day's ride, I find carpet, bedding, and writing-apparatus arranged for me, and a meal prepared in a room that appears well furnished; and I have no fear of leaving anything behind, for I take everything in the room away with me. In the morning, on awaking, I find my toilet around me, and the kettle boiling for breakfast. I had previously laid in a store of tea at Corfu, an article which is unknown here. Give me a good servant and a khan, and I will not wish for the bows of a landlord or the troublesome attentions of a waiter. But perhaps the novelty of the scene may influence me.

In the khan by eight o'clock all is asleep, and mine the only light burning. In the immediate vicinity of a khan is always to be seen a mosque, from whose picturesque minaret the Adán, or call to prayer, is repeated every five hours; first addressed towards Mecca, and afterwards to each of the cardinal points. The tone is very harmonious, and the words are dwelt upon with a prolonged sound, making in the stillness of the night a chant which is solemn and striking; its meaning is simple and beautiful: "God is most great!" "I testify that there is no deity but God;" "I testify that Mahomet is God's apostle! Come to prayer; come to security! God is most great: there is no deity but God!" and the voice may be heard at a great distance, the elevation being considerable and the tone powerful and distinct. There appears so much to interest in this town, that I shall spend the whole of tomorrow here.

February 27th.—I have now seen the town, and am not disappointed, never having enjoyed the excitement of discovery more than on this day. The Turks take you round, and show all they have not themselves built, calling every ruin by the simple name of the "old walls." They know nothing of traditions, for they are only conquerors here, and extremely ignorant; but I required no guide; the stupendous ruins proclaimed their builders, and their situation told who selected it. The site of the theatre is truly Greek. It embraces in its view the city, and the plains of Pergamus with its chain of mountains, and is lit by the rising sun. There is in the middle of the city a ruin of such extent that it can have been nothing less than the palace of a Roman emperor, and that worthy of an Adrian.

The river has five bridges, one of splendid masonry,

so wide that it forms a tunnel a furlong in length, upon which a portion of this great palace stands. I have been into many long and beautifully built vaults or cisterns, and several mosques and khans now occupying the buildings of the ancients. The most interesting is a mosque, from its style doubtless a church of the early Christians, in which the Epistles may have been read to the first disciples. The walls of the Turkish houses are full of relics of marble, with ornaments of the richest Grecian art. I have sketched many, but they

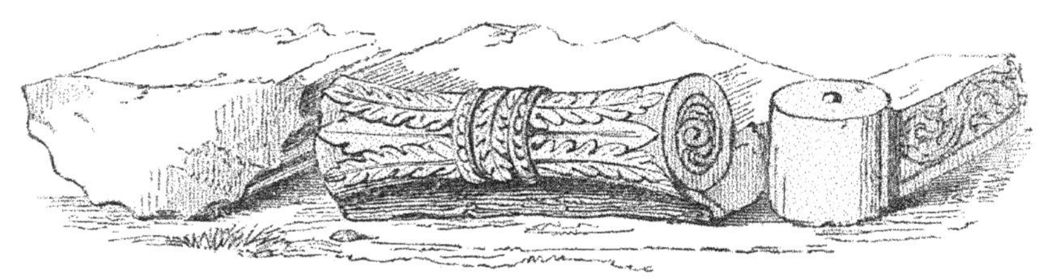

are innumerable. All the works standing are magnificent, but are not of marble, nor in a style of building showing elegance. The amphitheatre on the south-west of the castle, though in ruins, is a wonderful building. A river runs through it, and the arches, now underground, are equal in workmanship to any that I have seen. Those above have probably been as fine; but, although they now stand tier above tier, all the joints have been chipped, as in the Coliseum at Rome, and not a seat remains; the stupendous works underground will defy the exertions of the Turks to remove them. Triumphal arches and houses in ruins are to be seen in the town, with the Turks' huts among them, bearing the same proportion to them as the nests of the storks to the ruined palaces, in which they alone now reign. The burial-grounds also are full of fine relics. I have been out today from seven to five o'clock, and have quite tired myself with sketching, and should be tempted to do so each day if I were to stay a week.

The marbles found here are numerous, and are continually taken off for the museums of Europe. The French sent a vessel last year for a bath and statue, which had been for years unnoticed. I could not have imagined to what variety of uses columns may be applied; they are to be had for nothing, and are therefore used for every purpose. The modern town is as busy and thriving as heavy taxation will allow, and has seven or eight khans.

We left Bérgama at nine o'clock, and proceeded directly into the mountains towards the north, at the foot of which the town stands. On the right I saw in two places the ruins of aqueducts; these connect the hills, which are picturesque, but somewhat monotonous, resembling the Apennines north of Florence. As we ascended they became covered with the stone pine, and occasionally splendid specimens of the plane, with underwood of the dwarf oak; hyacinths of several kinds looked very gay, mixed with the anemone and pale lilac crocus. The hills were successively of limestone and what appeared to be immense mounds of sand, with very large rounded rocks on their sides, but which on reaching them I found to be of the same substance as the castle rock of Smyrna, a kind of bastard granite; it decomposes so rapidly, that to the leeward of each rock was a heap of particles similar to the sand of the whole surface of the mountain, and looking like a snow-drift. In many places these round rocks had rolled from opposite hills upon the limestone rocks, and the combination made it somewhat difficult to know whence came the sand.

Karaváren, where I am now sitting in a mud-built barn, is about fifteen miles from Bérgama, and amidst the mountains. It contains scarcely a dozen hovels; but we have travelled so excessively slowly (fifteen miles in six hours), that this is the only halting-place we can reach; it is quite a mountain village, and the management of a few goats seems to be the only care of the people.

We have been in a wood all the day, not an acre being cultivated; the cutting of timber, which the camels transport, and the herds of goats feeding, furnished, with our caravan, the only signs of life. The company of a caravan I hope in future to avoid, at all events to get ahead of it. It is a great annoyance to follow in a train of seventeen horses close behind each other; if one trips, stops to catch at the branches of the trees, or has occasion to have the baggage re-arranged, the whole cavalcade is checked. Towards the latter end of our journey I managed to take the lead, which not only prevented my feeling the interruption, but quickened the whole party. The Post in this country is established by order of the Government on all roads connecting large towns; it is used solely for the Tartars or Government couriers, and the diplomatic agents or governors communicating with the capital; the rate of charge is therefore fixed, and at the very low price of a piastre, or less than twopence halfpenny, for each horse per hour, or about four miles in distance: a small sum is added for the post-boy, and a present or *backshish* is expected by the ostlers at the stations. The charge of the post-master does not of course remunerate him, he being only an agent who obtains horses, on application of the travellers, from the farmers or people of the town, frequently paying them more than he can legally charge; he is therefore allowed by the Government a high salary, in order to indemnify him from loss. The traveller without a firman can demand horses, but the price then becomes a matter of bargain. Hitherto I have had post horses; but now, no longer travelling on a post road, there is a difficulty in procuring them, and therefore we are now to be carried for two days by horses hired, the owners of which accompany us, and generally arrange to join other parties, in order to render mutual assistance. Like all travellers in this country, my companions are so much disposed to sociability, that we form a party of seventeen, instead of only my own four horses.

Having no firman at present, which is only to be

procured at Constantinople, I am obliged to pay double the usual posting charges. When I have obtained my firman they will be very moderate, but for one person the travelling is expensive. I pay sixteen shillings a-day for four horses, and the services of the owners, who accompany me.

From the highest point of the mountain today I had a fine view of another of those productive valleys so peculiar to this country, which towards the east is watered by the Mysius, a river joining the Caicus. In most countries that I have visited, with the exception of a part of Italy, hill and valley vary every mile; but here the perfectly flat plain, of immense extent, is girt in by its mountains; detached from these ranges not a hill is to be seen.

March 1st.—By seven o'clock in the morning we had breakfasted, packed, and were proceeding through the mountains. The whole distance from Bérgama to Keméreh is occupied by the pass of the mountains. We were fourteen hours making the passage, and nearly three hours more in crossing the valley to this place, Adramít, the ancient Adramyttium. This mountain-pass is extremely wild, and occasionally beautiful; scarcely a trace of a cottage is to be seen the whole distance. About four miles from Karaváren I saw in a burial-ground several columns; and among the wilderness of immense round rocks or boulders, I observed many squared stones of considerable size; and overhead, on the peak of an isolated rocky hill, old walls of good masonry were visible. The exceedingly fine and commanding situation induced me to be on the look-out for some trace of former residents: at present the whole seemed deserted. This would appear from the map to have been the ancient Lyrnessus. At Keméreh also I saw columns and squared or wrought stones, but from the cross and other ornaments seen upon them, I fancy they must have been the relics of a later date than the Greek.

This valley of Keméreh, which is far smaller than the others I have passed, is highly cultivated and beautiful; the olive-trees are very fine, old, and numerous; and the vine is trained on trellis, as in Italy. I heard that this mode is peculiar, in Asia Minor, to this place. Here I noticed two houses built in the European style, there being nothing else European in the town. It was the dirtiest place I ever slept in; all the streets were filthy.

During this day's ride it rained in torrents for seven hours; my hood screened my body, but my legs and saddle were soaked, and a stream was running from my heels all the morning. The series of hills that we had passed since leaving Bérgama had generally been of a soft granite, while some of the intersecting ones and higher ranges were of limestone, and one part of a shining slaty stone. The granite was generally spread over the country in immense boulders; and these were so rapidly decomposing, that each had to the leeward a heap, such as I have before described as looking like a snow-drift, formed of its particles. I observed much of the *Lichen geographicus*, covering, and indeed holding together, these decomposing stones. On this soil the oak seems to spring up spontaneously, and the whole country around is covered with brushwood. The boulders being of a description of granite, and evidently igneous, I was surprised to see them intersected with horizontal strata of marble, of course the gradual deposit of waters; the marble was not crystallized. After I had been puzzling over this appearance for some time, I noticed in the same stones veins of marble shooting out in all directions. Had the substances been reversed, I should have thought the heated liquid granite might have shot into the crevices of the marble; but shortly after I saw rock with perpendicular fissures filled with marble. This led me to think that the cracks and fissures in the cooling rocks had been the receptacles for the waters filtering from the limestone, forming moulds, in which these beautiful white veins, now girting in all directions the stones washed down the river, had been cast. Having noticed these facts, I saw that the mountains were ribbed with lines of white marble, and the road afterwards became almost impeded by little walls, perhaps a foot high, of hard marble; the mould of granite in which they were cast having perished and been washed away in sand. Afterwards, in winding along the side of a mountain, we passed into richly wooded ravines, with a sandy soil, and then had to proceed round a projecting cliff of bare rocky marble.

Thus the same formation may be traced, from the striped stone on the road to the marble cliffs and the ravines, of decomposed granite rock.

The road from Adramít, a town in which no traces of antiquities are to be found, except in a few coins picked up in the neighbourhood, lay for nearly two hours through fine woods of olives, and along the sea-coast or gulf which takes its name from this town. I here saw, on a font, a marble which had been part of a handsome frieze, exhibiting the bull's head and wreath, so common in Greek architecture, and one or two fragments of columns.

We then traversed the coast through woods of the richest trees, the planes being the handsomest to be found in this, or perhaps any other, part of the world. I have never seen such stupendous arms to any trees. There were a few walnuts and pines, and the country for fifty miles was covered with olives, which still furnish the principal trade of this part of Asia Minor. The underwood was of myrtle, growing sometimes twenty feet high, the beautiful daphne laurel, and the arbutus; and these seemed contending for pre-eminence with the vine, clematis, and woodbine, which climbed to their very tops, and in many instances bore them down into a thicket of vegetation, impervious except to the squirrels and birds, which, sensible of their security in these retreats, stand boldly to survey the traveller. A kind of grape-hyacinth and the arum, added to varieties of anemones, cover the ground. I observed that the crows here are grey-bodied*, but am informed that the black crow is also known.

In the dirty khan at Adramít I had the choice of two rooms, the best of which was very offensive, having been recently filled with skins of cheese and oil. I had it swept, and a large fire made to purify it, but for nearly an hour it was not fit for me to enter; so I loitered about, and looked into the room next to my own. On a clean mat, crouching in the corner, were two fine slaves; their owner seemed very kind to them, and was feeding them with delicacies. All the slaves I have at present seen, generally from Ethiopia, are decidedly longer in the leg-joint from the ankle to the knee than any race of human beings with which I am acquainted. A person seeing the leg only would expect to find them extremely tall, but this is by no means the case.

As the post-master makes me take five horses, we have caused quite a sensation in this little village, which lies in a ravine high above the sea, another of the crow's-nest sites chosen by the early Greeks; its name is Chétme. There being no khan, I had to beg the governor of the place to extend to me the hospitality usual towards strangers, and this gave me an opportunity of observing Turkish manners. As I sat on my horse, surrounded by my little suite, and waiting the termination of the mosque service, I soon became the object of

* *Corvus cornix,* the hooded crow.

curiosity to the younger and perhaps lower persons among the inhabitants; but the elder, or those assuming any authority, passed by, merely giving me a salute in the Turkish language,—*Oōroler,* meaning 'Welcome, stranger.' Among these was the Aga, or principal man, the governor of the village, who knew I waited only to speak to him, but would not compromise his dignity by transacting his official business in the street; and we consequently had to follow him half a mile to his hut, where, on his arrival, he ascended a few steps leading to a stage or trellised platform of wood in front of the hut. His carpet and pipe having been brought to him, he sat down in state to listen to my request, making a sign to me to be seated; and during the whole interview he never uttered a word, or even looked at me. A sign was made by him to an attendant, who thereupon led us to the stranger's house, and remained as my servant. I observed that, as soon as we turned our backs, this stately Aga was on tiptoe, watching with great animation my little party as we withdrew from this ceremonious interview. Thinking that I was a *Milordos,* I suppose, he sent from his own house a handsome dinner in the Turkish style. On a large round tray of copper, tinned, was a tureen of soup, a dish of rice, and one of olives, with a supply of bread and some sweets. This Turkish title of *Milordos* is given to persons of all nations who travel without any visible motive. Who is he, a messenger of government or a merchant? The Turks can conceive no other motives for travelling; and if the stranger disowns both of these, he must be *Milordos.* To such a one particular attention is paid, and in the khan, where a small sum is demanded for the use of the room, no charge is made to *Milordos*, who is supposed to be rolling in riches; the master of the khan knowing that he shall thus obtain as a bounty double what he could demand. After food and whatever else I could need had been offered by the Aga, and accepted for me, I heard Demetrius still asking for something, using the word "*Adam*," or "*Adahm.*" On inquiring of him what he meant, he explained that he wanted 'a man' to assist him. My servant, who spoke fluently seven modern languages, said that this word was very similar in all the Eastern nations. The name "*Adam*" in our Scriptures is therefore the untranslated word "man."

March 2nd.—Our road lay by the sea-shore almost all the day. In descending from our lofty village, we saw traces in the mud of a number of wild-boars, and their ploughing for the roots of lilies and other bulbs. We shot a lark and a thrush, which did not differ from the British. Several eagles' nests were in the high cliff which formed the bold but beautiful coast. Between this and the sea lay a valley half a mile in breadth, thickly planted with olives, skirting the sea almost all the way. The hills are clothed with evergreens to their tops, and therefore vary little with the seasons; the underwood which is the most common here, and in all the country we have passed through, and which till now I scarcely recognised, is a species of the box. The beach of the Mediterranean has one peculiarity, which is seen here, as on all its shores that I have visited, namely the flatness of the stones or shingle, many being as thin as penny-pieces, and none rounded, as is commonly the case in our seas. This is occasioned by the very gradual and gentle gliding in and out of the water, by which the stones are rubbed together without being rolled over. The tide is not perceptible here; I have not in any part of the Mediterranean observed it rise more than eighteen inches, and in many places it is not felt at all. The wind is almost the only power that influences it, and in land-locked parts of course this is considerable.

This grinding of the stones destroys the shells, which in this comparatively still water are not so often washed up as in the more open seas. The only shells I saw were those of the sepia, or cuttle-fish, whose pithy cargo rides like a life-boat on the wave, and is left high upon the beach. The stones are of course of the same substance as the cliffs, namely of limestone, of conglomerate, of many kinds of igneous rocks, some quite green, but generally of a grey colour, and of a species of granite, used for all the buildings in the district.

At about six miles' distance from Beahráhm, the ancient Assus or Assos, we left the sea-side and ascended through wild rocky scenery, rich in useless vegetation. The approach to the ancient town is very imposing: we passed a small lake, and then entered a little wood of shrubs, which I found thickly interspersed with the stones and lids of sarcophagi. As we drew near to the town, its surrounding wall of beautiful Greek workmanship crossed our path, and again another inclosing the Acropolis. They are very perfect, and in many places stand thirty feet high; each stone being beautifully cut, and laid without cement. The rocks which supplied the materials of the buildings, as well as the foundation of much of the town, rise sixty or eighty feet in abrupt cliffs, each of which has had its crown of temples. The village now on the spot consists but of a few sheds, one of which is appropriated to my use.

After depositing the baggage, I took the most intelligent Turk in the place as cicerone, and went up to the ruins on the Acropolis, from which I beheld all the country round,—the beautiful island of Mytilene on one side, and the river winding through a rich meadow on the other, rising at Mount Ida, and flowing to the western coast, backed by a series of wooded hills. Immediately around me were the ruins, extending for miles, undisturbed by any living creature except the goats and kids. On every side lay columns, triglyphs, and friezes, of beautiful sculpture, every object speaking of the grandeur of this ancient city. In one place I saw thirty Doric capitals placed up in a line for a fence. I descended towards the sea, and found the whole front of the hill a wilderness of ruined temples, baths, and theatres, all of the best workmanship, but all of the same grey stone as the neighbouring rock. The annexed plate will show one of the friezes, the subject of which I cannot understand or describe; others represented bulls fighting, sphinxes crouching, and a variety of animals, well executed, although upon a coarse material. The same plate exhibits tombs, upon one of which is the following inscription:

ΑΝΓΟΕΡΚΑΔΥ
ΜΑΚΕΔΟΝΟΕ
\+ ΛΟΥΚΙ<>ΝΟΥΠΡΕΟΡ ΚΑΙΚΑΝΕΙΚΗΕ
ΠΕΡΙΟΙΚΑΙΔΙ
ΑΤΑΙΕΚΝΤΟΙΕ
ΑΡΧΕΙΟΙΕΑΠΟ
ΚΕΙΤΑΙ

The seats of the theatre remain, although, like all the parts of the building, displaced as if by an earthquake. The circumstance that the material has not intrinsic value as marble, has preserved these remains from the depredations committed on other towns near the coast; and from their appearance I imagine that the whole of the materials are scattered around, and uninjured but by age. Some immense cisterns still contain water. All the buildings were of the solid Greek style, and the friezes much ornamented. On many of the stones are deeply cut Greek inscriptions, with letters nine inches in height. I copied some, but others were too heavy to be easily moved.

PART OF FRIEZE AT ASSOS

TOMBS AT ASSOS.

John Murray London 1839.

The following are upon four scattered portions of the frieze of a temple, all of the same depth and pattern.

ΟΙΕΡΕΥΣΤΟΥΣΕΒΑΣΤΟΥΘ

ΕΟΥΚΑΙΣΑΡΟΣΟΔΕΑΥ

ΝΑΣΙΑΡΧΟΣοΚΟΙΝΤΟΣΔΟ

ΟΣΚΑΙΠΑΤΡΙΟΣΒΑΣΙΛΕΥ

The three next have belonged to a different temple.

ΟΥΟΜΟΝΩΟΥΚΑΙΤΥΜ

Σ////ΚΑΙΙΕΥΣΤΟΥΔΙΟΣΤ

ΑΙΣΑΡΙΣΕΒΑΣΤΟΙΚΑΙΤΟΙΔ

The seven following are inferior in execution.

ЄΠΙCΕΞΤΟΥΑΠΙ

ΥΑΝΘΥΠ

ΥΚΑ

ΟΛΗΙΟ

UΝΟCΤΗCΠΟΑ

ΙΠΑΠ

ΤΑΘЄΙC⌒C

I also copied a fragment of an inscription upon a stone which has been over a doorway.

ΕΚΤΗΧΠΡΟΣΟΔΟΥΤΩΝΑΕΡ
ΗΝΤΗΣΠΟΛΕΩΣΚΛΕΟΣΤΡΑ'
ΤΕΛΛΙΚΩΝΤΟΣЄΠΕ'

The only building which appeared of other architecture than ancient Greek, was constructed of the materials of the surrounding ruins, without much taste; it had an arched roof and round-topped windows. From the wall I copied a Greek inscription; the date must have been about the time of the early Christians. This town St. Paul visited.

+ ЕПІМЕΛІАЕ
ΕΛΛΑΔΙΟΥ
ΠΡΕΙΒΕΠΟ
ΛΙΤΕΥΟΩ
ΚΤΟΥΥΓЄΙΟΥΑΥΙΟΥΑΟΥΚ ΑΝΟΥ

I passed another beautiful wall in a very perfect state, exhibiting gateways of the earliest dates, as well as those of the later Greek.

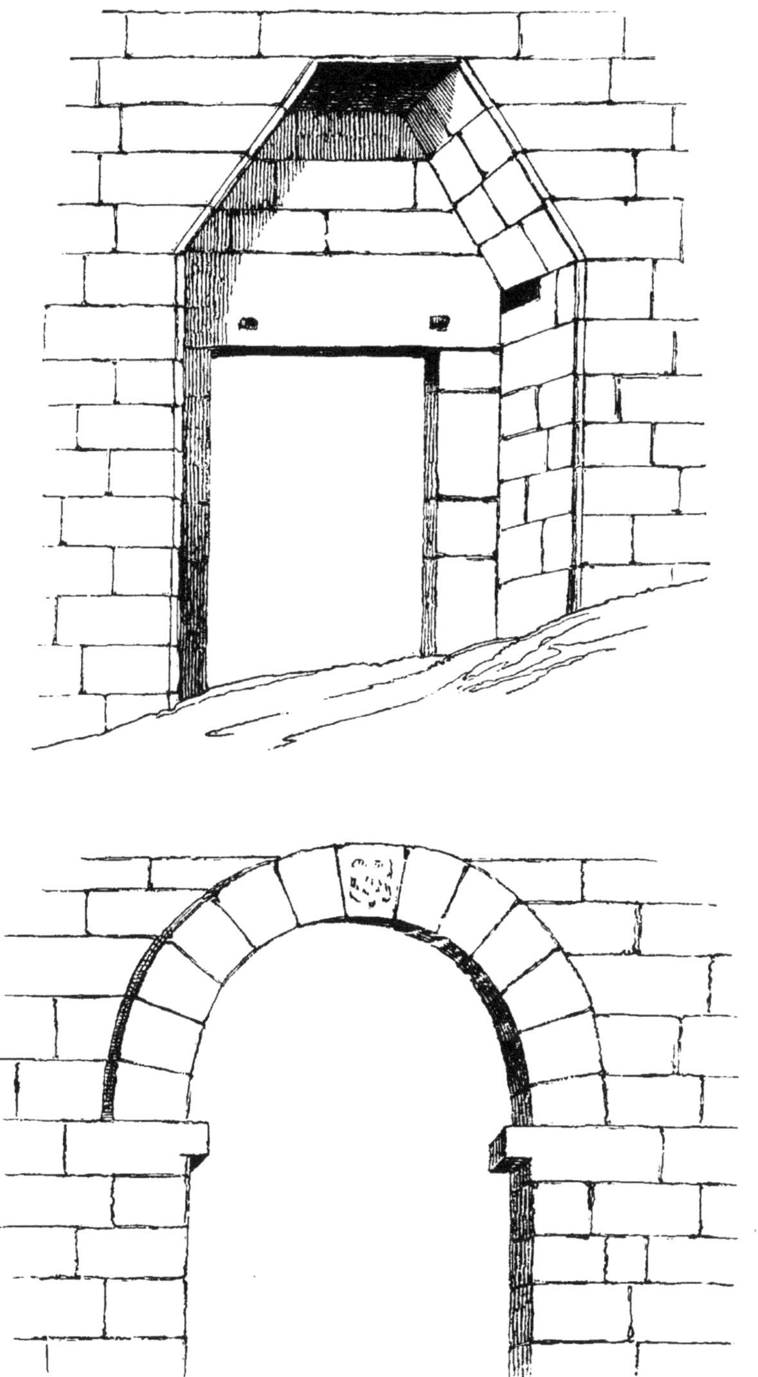

I then entered the Via Sacra, or Street of Tombs, extending for miles. Some of the tombs still stand in their original beautiful forms, but most have been opened, and the lids are lying near the walls they covered, curiosity or avarice having been satisfied by displacing them. Occasionally in the line of tombs are circular seats, as at Pompeii; but these ruins are on a considerably larger scale than those of the Roman city, and many of the remains are equally perfect. Several are highly ornamented, and have inscriptions; others are as large as temples, being twenty or thirty feet square: the usual length of the sarcophagus* is from ten to twelve feet.

My guide called every ruin an "old castle;" and even with these tombs open before him, he said that he was ignorant they were such, till an Englishman who was here six years ago informed him. He supposed the chambers, or large sarcophagi, were for the angel or spirit to wait in. The Turk's grave has a stone at the head and foot, with a turban or rag upon it, and is planted with cypress-trees. In returning to the town I found a wall of the very early and singular style called Cyclopean, considered to be older than the common architecture of the Greeks. It is here clearly proved to be so by the Greeks having repaired this wall,

* The Anglicised word *sarcophagus* is a Roman one, of not very early date. The Greek term on all tombs is *Soros*. Pliny says that a peculiar stone, found in the territory of Assos, has the property of wasting the bodies entombed in it; hence the term *sarcophagus*, meaning 'flesh-eating.'

and built over it with the beautifully squared stones of their later style.

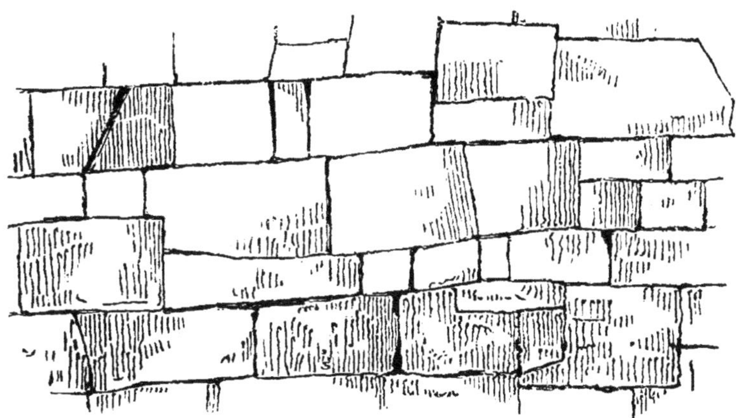

This town is perfectly open to the antiquarian, and seems preserved for his examination, appearing to have been unoccupied since its destruction, and inscriptions being exposed on innumerable stones. Many tombs of a Greek date remain unopened. There appears no trace of the Romans, nor, except in the instances I have noticed, of the Christians. The material of which the town was built not being fine, the sculpture is not of much value, but the hardness of the stone has combined with its want of intrinsic worth to preserve the inscriptions.

The Turks have no traditions of the country, and are more ignorant than can be conceived, being not only unlearned, but resolved not to learn. They call all buildings which they have not themselves constructed, whether bridge, bath or aqueduct, temple, theatre or tomb, all *Esky kalli*, " old castle." The uses of the two latter buildings are unknown to the Musselmans, and they can scarcely comprehend even visible objects. When curiosity has led them to examine my baggage, or the spring-lock of my carpet-bag, they have, after I have given a simple explanation, turned away saying, " I cannot understand." At Smyrna, the Governor and the Judge both made a tour of the Consul's dining-room, fingering everything on the sideboard, and asking questions like children.

The horses in Asia Minor are shod with plates of thin iron, thus,

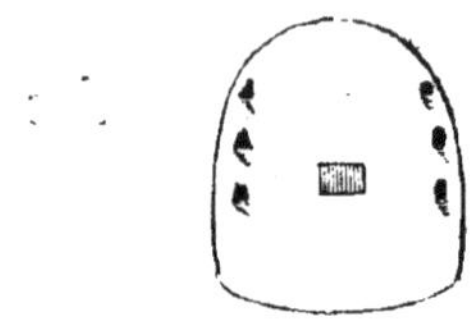

The nails project considerably, and a small square hole is left in the centre to admit air and moisture, but not large enough to catch a stone. The wear is almost wholly upon the nails, and the plate is little thicker than tin. I do not remember to have seen any specimen of ancient Greek sculpture with shoes on the horses.

The houses of the villages in Turkey seem very much alike. I have been into many, and will describe the one appointed for me last night at Beahráhm. On the outside it looked like a square box, and the inside measured from twelve to fourteen feet: it was built of stones, of all shapes, put together with mud. The roof was flat and covered with earth; a small roller, generally a piece of a column, lying on the top to make this compact, in order to keep out the wet. There was no window, and consequently light was admitted only by the door, which had no lock or fastening, except a piece of wood suspended over the top withinside, and falling down when the door shut, whilst on the outside hung a peg, with which this inside fastening might be pushed up on entering. The walls and floors were of mud, mixed with short pieces of straw; the roof was a tree laid across and boards placed transversely; the interior was black with the smoke from a large open fire-place, and on entering, the house appeared quite dark.

The lamps here are of tin or earthenware, and of the beautiful forms used by the Greeks and Romans.

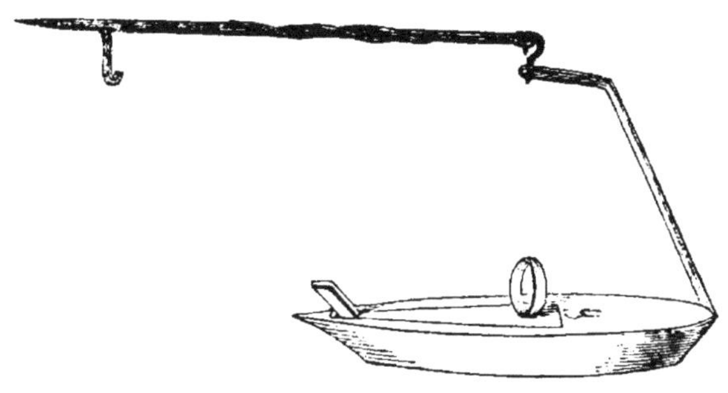

When the traveller arrives, the owner of the house, or servant appointed by the authorities, sweeps out the room and puts down a mat, the only article of furniture provided. My servant presses into the walls three or four nails, on which to hang his gun, whip, our caps, and my hood; and then places the hammock and mattress upon the carpet, whilst the canteen-box serves for table, spread with food, papers, sketch-book, or whatever I may desire. Any one who were to see the travellers' room thus occupied, would acknowledge it to be extremely enjoyable. Hitherto I have retained my English habits, am never required to smoke, and have tasted Turkish coffee but once since I entered Asia: that specimen was not at all to my liking, which will be readily believed when I describe the process of making it. Each cup is made separately, the little saucepan or ladle in which it is prepared being about an inch wide and two deep; this is more than half filled with coffee, finely pounded with a pestle and mortar, and then filled up with water: after being placed for a few seconds on the fire, the contents are poured or rather shaken out, (being much thicker than chocolate,) without the addition of cream or sugar, into a china cup, of the size and shape of half an egg-shell, which is inclosed in one of ornamented metal of the same form, for convenience of holding in the hand,—

> " Gold cups of filigree, made to secure
> The hand from burning, underneath them placed."

March 3rd.—I left Beahráhm at half-past eight o'clock this morning, and travelled until five in the evening, a distance of about thirty miles. The first part of the road lay over barren hills, and it was only in the valleys and ravines that the rich evergreens and the pink blossom of the almond, with hundreds of Angora goats browsing upon them, reminded me in what country I was rambling. On descending I came to lower hills, covered with a most beautiful species of oak, which exceeds our own in size; the acorn, or rather its cup, is exported in large quantities to Europe for dye: the planes also were enormous. I am much struck with the beauty of the trees in this country.

As we approached Doósler, about sixteen miles on our way, a range of hills lay before us clothed with little vegetation, and the valley below seemed barren, the greater part of it looking like fields covered by a flood; but as we approached I found that these expanses of waters were salt-pans. The face or cliff of these barren hills (barren from the nature of their soil,) was singularly beautiful, and strongly resembled Alum Bay in the Isle of Wight, the strata being considerably inclined, and delicately coloured in ribbons of red, grey, white, and green, of every shade, all softened by a pearly film of transparent salt, which had filtered over the face of the cliff; on closer examination I found that the whole of these colours were caused by a soft, fine, adhering sand, like fullers'-earth to the touch. The hills now became less lofty, and were entirely clothed with oak: the collecting of the large acorn and shells and the gall-nut (the formation of an insect disease) for dye employs the people for great part of the year; indeed this labour and attending the goats seem their sole occupation.

The composition of these hills is limestone, but as

we approached Alexandria Troas they became a mass of shells, with scarcely any combining earth; one of them, about two miles east of the ancient city, has many hot springs, strongly chalybeate, but my thermometer only indicated a temperature of 140°, to which the mercury rose quickly; I do not think it would in any of them have far exceeded that height, as many were only 135° and 137°, varying according to the nature of the apertures whence the water gushed. The whole of the hills that I have mentioned are surrounded on the south-east and north-east by a chain of bare craggy mountains, of the grey granite of which all the columns of the ancient city of Troas were formed. The buildings of the town were almost wholly of the stone containing, or rather consisting of masses of shells; some few were of limestone.

The site of the ancient city being now covered by a forest of oak-trees, it is impossible to see its ruins collectively; but for many miles the ground is rendered useless for agriculture by the multitude of broken stones and marbles and arches, which lie under the surface in every direction. I had fancied that the difficulty of tracing the foundation of Troy had been from the scarcity of remains, but I judge from this place that it may have been, on the contrary, from the confused numbers which meet the eye on every side. The ancient port is very interesting, and has been highly ornamented; hundreds of columns, on a somewhat small scale, lie scattered in all directions, and bristle among the waves to a considerable distance out at sea. A wall or pier also stands out in the sea, under water, causing breakers, which show its situation. The harbour is now shrunk to two small salt-water lakes. The island of Tenedos is exactly opposite, and in the distance toward the north-west is seen the island of Imbros. One immense broken granite column lies in the harbour; but I could find no trace of more, or of any corresponding parts of a temple or building.

The most striking ruins are about a mile from the sea, probably near the centre of the city; they are on an exceedingly grand scale, and contain some very fine arches of a building which must have been contained within, or have formed, a square. In one of its small arched recesses we found a man, who had long resided in this spot; he offered us milk, and was extremely communicative about himself, but knew nothing of the place he lived in; he told me that he had been a hundred years old for two or three years, and showed me some new teeth just appearing through his gums: my servant Demetrius says that he once saw a man aged a hundred and twenty with the same peculiarity. This man was a Greek, and from Roumelia; his beard was only partially grey, and he did not appear so old as other men whom I have seen, even in the course of today. The people of this mountainous district are generally extremely dark, almost of the complexion of mulattos.

The ground in every direction within the walls was strewn with carvings, mouldings and pedestals, in marble, some of which had inscriptions, generally in the Greek language; I copied the following Latin one however from a handsome pedestal *.

DIVIAVOCOAIRII
ETCOLIVIPHIIIPPENN
LORVNDEMETPRINCIPIEN
COLIVIPARIANAETRIEM
MLIICOIIXXXIIVOLVAIAR
TRIBMILITLEGXIIICIM
PRAEFETΩIOVITAIAII
SCVBVLORVM
VIII

VIC

Near the large building above mentioned is a basement story, consisting of a rectangular platform of immense stones, supported by strong arches; upon this raised site, which affords a splendid view over the whole city and the sea beyond, has evidently stood a temple. Near this is another foundation of the same kind, but semicircular, on the plan of the Temple of Venus in Rome, but smaller. In several other buildings, apparently baths or tombs, the stones are placed on their

* *Translation.*

"The colony of Apri founded by Claudius, and the colony of Philippi founded by Julius, [erect this statue to *** *** priest] of the divine Augustus, and their prince; also the colony of Parium, founded by Julius, and the tribunes of the soldiers of the 32nd cohort of volunteers; the tribunes of the soldiers of the 13th double legion; the commanders of the horse of the first wing of the Scubuli."

angles, so as to form a kind of mosaic; I have often seen this style in Roman buildings: the roofs are all arched.

I am now at Alexandria Troas, called by the Turks Esky Stámbool. The present village consists of eight or ten houses, similar to those described above: only two are occupied, one by a singular character, our host, who calls himself Consul, and talks of having been at the battle of the Nile, the other by a woman and her son; no other inhabitants are found within six miles, these being the only people who have not been driven away by the extortion of the Turkish agents.

Passing the massy foundations of the walls of the city, which at present stand but a few feet above the ground, we travelled eastwards for two or three miles, to a hill containing hot-springs. This hill looked like a honeycomb, from the number of arched buildings on its sides for baths and fountains; one or two are still used as baths by the Turks. I observed a female statue, of about seven feet in height, and without a head; it was of the finest description of white marble, but had been injured by exposure to the weather; it now lies sunk in the ground, and serves as a seat at the door of the bath. Riding towards the north-east for a mile and a half, we followed an ancient paved road from the city, and by the wayside found an immense granite column, unbroken, lying in the bushes.

I took its dimensions, which were as follow: thirty-eight feet six inches in length; the diameter of the top four feet six inches, with a cornice fifteen inches in depth; diameter of the base five feet six inches, with a moulding twelve inches broad. It was in excellent preservation; but I sought in vain for its pedestal, and wondered that its fall should not have broken it. In two hours we reached Gaicle, and thence walked to a gorge near one of the peaks of the granite range of hills, about a mile off, to see the Seven Columns. I there found in the quarry, with all their chips about them, and their parent rock within a few feet distance, seven finished columns, in form and measurement precisely like the one which I had seen on my way, and also like the column I had noticed lying on the beach at Troy,—thus making nine in all; they were, no doubt, about to be used in, or shipped from, the city, which was visible from this quarry, and distant in a straight line not above five or six miles: this at once explained the facts that there was neither pedestal for, nor fracture in, the one by the wayside, and no other remains in the city similar to the column lying in the port. A long groove was cut on the solid face of the rock in the quarry, marking out the first stage towards hewing out another similar column*.

* Dr. E. D. Clarke, in his Travels, (vol. iii. chap. vi. page 188,) says: " A short distance from the road, concealed among trees, lay the largest granite pillar in the world, excepting the famous column of Alexandria in Egypt, which it much resembles. It is of the same substance, and it has the same form; its astonishing length, as a mere shaft, without

On two adjoining summits of this range of mountains are the ruins of the towns of Criscool and Criser: I was told that the walls only of the latter remained, and that they were an hour and a half long. Riding between two of these hills we passed a woody summit, and had before us a splendid and extensive view of almost the whole of the Troas,—Mount Ida capped with snow, with the amphitheatre of mountains which range with it, encircling the valley of the Méndere, or ancient Scamander. In an hour and a half we reached Enáe, a tolerably large town, situated on the two sides of a river. I find all the maps that I have with me so incorrect, that tomorrow I shall have to make an excursion of six hours to a town which is marked on the maps two hours in a contrary direction.

March 4th.—It is Sunday; time glides away most rapidly on the tide of pleasure. I am generally on horseback eight hours a day, up at half-past six o'clock, and at night write or draw till ten.

base or capital, of one entire stone, equalled thirty-seven feet eight inches; and it measured five feet three inches in diameter at the base, and four feet five inches at the summit. It may seem to throw some light upon the origin of the Egyptian pillar. Its situation is upon a hill above Alexandria Troas. A paved road led from the city to the place where it either stood, or was to have been erected. We have therefore the instance of two cities, both built by generals of Alexander the Great, in consequence of his order, and each city having a pillar of this kind upon an eminence, outside of its walls."

It would seem that Dr. Clarke had not observed the other columns noticed in my Journal.

Having again descended into a valley, I find the buffalo, which I have not seen for the last seven days. Access to mud or water, in which they remain during the heat of the day in the summer season, with their heads only above the surface, is essential to their healthy existence; the skin, which much resembles in appearance that of the elephant, becomes otherwise so diseased that the animal pines away: their Turkish name is *Soósiger*, meaning 'water-ox.'

The women here are far more shy than in the large towns; they never leave even an eye exposed, and generally retreat into some shelter when met by a man; and if this be in the road, they turn their faces to a bush until he has passed. Sometimes, while standing at the top of my house, I have, unseen, observed fair faces; but they were all of a dumpling form, which I cannot admire, while the Greek countenance is constantly before me; their hands are always clean, but generally concealed. I have sometimes fancied their finger-ends bleeding, the henna with which they are dyed making them red, or rather of the colour of burnt sienna. As I was passing along the street, a woman hastily called out to a child of six years old, "The Ghiaour coming!" and it was snatched within the door, which she shut. This term, my servant tells me, cannot be literally translated; it means more than infidel, for which the Turkish word is *Rayah*; Ghiaour was interpreted to me to mean a man without a soul, without a God: this word is used as a bugbear to children.

In all Turkish towns are found a vast number of skeletons of the domestic animals, affording ample opportunity for studying the anatomy of the camel, cow, horse, ass, and ox; the dogs begin, and the sun and wind complete, the bleaching of the skeleton. The head of the ox alone escapes this fate; in cultivated districts it is placed on a stick, or hung on a tree, as a scarecrow. This custom prevails in Greece as well as here: the heads are always beautifully white, and retain the horns, which are in this part of the world exceedingly short and thick.

The skull, with its horns, has thus been constantly presented to the eye of the Greek artist blanched white as marble, and hence the introduction of precisely this figure in the friezes of their architecture; and perhaps the vine or clematis wreathing about the horns may have suggested the frequent accompaniment of this ornament. It appears to me the more evident that this is the real origin, from its being the skeleton of the head that is depicted. Had the figure been in honour of, or connected with the worship of, the Bull, why not have exhibited the living head, which is rarely given?

From Enáe I made an excursion to the site of Old Troy, and back, a distance of about fifteen miles. Adjoining Enáe is a mound, which, if artificial, is a colossal work. I believe it is supposed to be a tumulus, and is called Enea's tomb, connecting it with the present name of this place. The mound or tomb, whichever it may be, is now, together with the fields at its base, become a Turkish burial-ground, covered with stones and planted with the cypress. A mile below the town, the stream on which it stands flows into the Méndere, which is here a large river, equal in size to the Wye, and much resembling it in scenery; it carries down much soil, and occasionally lays waste a tract of country three times its own width. About a mile further on our route, which lay by the river, is a wooden bridge; the only other crossing at this season is by a bridge near the mouth of the river on the plain of Troy, distant eighteen miles from Old and New Troy; and in consequence, although these two places, the most interesting in this part of the country, are not far distant from each other, standing on opposite sides of the river, the traveller has to make a day's journey down the western side to Old Troy, and return, and then along the eastern bank to New Troy, and afterwards proceed to the Dardanelles. I believe at some seasons there are places in the river fordable, but there are none now. The ride is extremely picturesque: the river, with the road, generally occupies the whole of the valley, which is bounded by ranges of craggy hills richly wooded; where any inlet or hollow occurs in them, the soil is excellent and highly cultivated, exhibiting beautiful green meadows and corn-fields. Large flocks of goats, with their bells and the herdsman's pipe, give life to the scene, and climbing to the most craggy parts add to the picturesque effect.

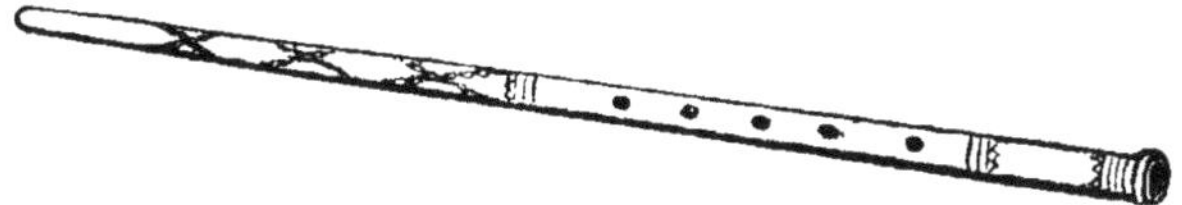

The pipe used by the shepherds in Asia Minor is a similar instrument to those found in the tombs in Athens,

specimens of which are in the British Museum; it is open at both ends, and is played by the shepherds in the manner represented on the Greek vases, by blowing sideways into it. This instrument and the lyre are sufficient evidence that the ancient Greeks, who attained a perfection in architecture and sculpture never equalled by any other age, cannot have understood the science of music.

About two miles before we arrived at Boon*á*bassy, which word means 'spring-head,' we left the river and passed over a range of hills, commanding a splendid map-view of the whole of the country where the greatest nations once contended in almost endless strife: and now nations as great, then not in being, contest the point, where lived these people whose acts for ages gave even a date to the world. The continents of Europe and Asia, as well as the islands of Imbros and Tenedos, were included in the view, the centre of which was marked by the winding course of the Scamander.

In the village of Boon*á*bassy a few relics of past days have been worked up in the mud of the hovels, but there are none to indicate the site of even a small town. This village, which is by Europeans called Old Troy, stands at the end of a chain terminating in two mountains, between which the river descends into the plains, that extend about fifteen miles to the sea. Upon one of these we rode in search of some trace of the city, of which the champions of this locality for Old Troy boast. The natives call this hill Bollhu-tepe, and some the Heights of Boon*á*bassy. We saw on the stony top of a hill (certainly very small for the site of a city) two piles of loose stones; I think it very questionable whether put together by nature or art; and if by art, a doubt may arise as to the purpose, for I have often seen in mountain districts piles as large heaped up by the villagers as a testimony of respect, upon the spot where some too adventurous brother met with an untimely end. I could not find on this or the neighbouring heights a single squared stone, or any indication of art of any age; and this is the spot fixed upon as ancient Troy. The country was beautiful, and the ride amply repaid me, affording me new information upon the geography of this district. I saw many partridges, and two eagles; one sat boldly on a tree under which we passed, looking down contemptuously upon me, and I observed his keen eye watching me continually; it was not one of the largest sort, but of the size of a small turkey.

The hills were generally of *schist* (I think geologists call it), somewhat micaceous and flaky, in colour resembling serpentine, being green when wet, and of a lighter colour when weather-worn; I judged the distant rocks, from their fractures, to be limestone: they were generally covered with vegetation. In some I observed fine veins of good white marble, and others were of mountain limestone. I first saw in the town of Enáe, in the adjoining burial-ground, and afterwards much scattered over the roads, volcanic stones, which in the former places appeared as fine hexagonal basaltic columns. I am told (but place little reliance on the report of the people here) that they come from the distant chain of Mount Ida, and from near the quarry that we visited to see the granite columns. It is probable they must be found much nearer, for the people would not take the trouble to carry them so far.

I have today had an opportunity of examining some of the agricultural implements of the country; one is used for the joint purpose of threshing and of cutting the straw. It is very primitive and curious, consisting of a thick plank of timber flat on the ground, with another smaller one inclining upwards, to which the animal is attached, for the purpose of dragging it over the corn, which is spread out on the hard rocky ground; the flat underside is stuck full of flints or hard cutting stones, arranged in the form of the palate or rough tongue of

the cow. In the one which I examined I found the teeth all made of beautiful agates, and on inquiry hear that the stones are found, chipped, and set near Béiramitch, in the mountains of the Idæan chain, a few miles from this place. The roller is the trunk of a tree, often weighted by the driver riding on it; it is dragged over the ground, but does not revolve.

The mode of winnowing is as primitive; advantage

is taken of a favourable wind, and the corn is thrown into the air. The plough, each portion of which is still called by the ancient Greek names, is very simple, and seems suited only to the light soil which prevails here.

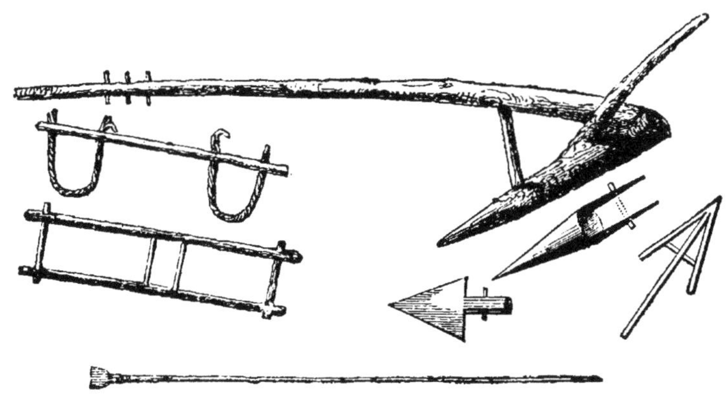

αροτρον, the Plough. *ῥυμος*, the Pole. *ὑννις*, the Share. *εχετλη*, the Handle, or Plough-tail. *μεταδα*, the Yokes. *κατρινος*, the Goad, or instrument for driving.

It is held by one hand only. The shape of the share varies, and the plough is used frequently without any. It is drawn by two oxen, yoked from the pole, and guided by a long reed or thin stick, which has a spud or scraper at the end for cleaning the share. The oxen are all small, of the size of our Scotch cattle, and either black or grey. I have not seen a red cow, nor one with long horns, in this country. The buffalos are much used in agriculture. There are very few carts here, as there are no roads: occasionally they are used to transport the crops from field to field; being sometimes of wicker-work, and sometimes without bodies, like a brewer's dray, with poles fixed at the sides to keep the load together. The wheels are of solid blocks of wood, or thick planks, generally three, held together by an iron hoop or tire; a loud creaking noise is made by the

friction of the galled axle. The harrow is a bunch of thorns. I observe it is the custom first to sow the land, then plough and brush, or harrow it. This is slovenly work, but the roots and short stumps of the maize of the last year are so much decayed that they are ploughed in, and serve as manure for the land. The spade and shovel, principally used in cutting for

irrigation, are above six feet long, and power is applied to them by placing them under the arm.

March 6th.—This morning I left Enáe, traversing the same road as on my excursion to Boon*á*bassy; and then crossing the wooden bridge, the construction of which makes this a somewhat perilous route, I travelled for about eight miles along the eastern side of the river, in a direction parallel with the road of yesterday. The rocks on this side rising more perpendicularly, less cultivation is here practicable; these rocks appeared of the same material as the opposite ones. The wild-boar leaves each morning his traces on the fresh-rooted ground, and his track in the mud on his way to the river. Wolves are also very numerous here: this may account for the number of dogs kept by the Turks, which bay at you on approaching a hut or herd of cattle. The dogs are generally of an uniform breed, much resembling the wolf in form and colour, but frequently growing to a great size, sometimes as large as the Newfoundland. The ruff of hair round the neck, and the short ears, make them handsome animals.

We now left the river, and passing a valley to the eastward ascended some hills, and were soon on the mountain opposite to the one on which we yesterday sought the tumuli above Boon*a*bassy. I came now on the same search; but here also nature appeared undisturbed by art, scarcely a stone having been moved, except by the heavy rains. There is a superstition among the Turks that a great man was buried here, and their name for the hill signifies a burial-place. The imaginary stature of this ideal person is marked by a row of stones, extending about sixteen feet. This hill and the neighbouring one were interesting, not only from the view which they command over all the classic plains to the

Hellespont, but also from the formation of the hills themselves. Of what are they composed? I should say *agate.* They contain also highly metalliferous fragments, some of apparently almost pure iron-ore; in other parts are the green symptoms of copper: every cavity seems filled with crystals of quartz; and in and over the red agate stone was a mammaliferous pearly coating. I could have selected beautiful cabinet specimens, but England is too far off for me to carry home stones in most respects similar to our Scotch pebbles: here the rock itself seemed entirely composed of that material; in Scotland I have seen it only in rounded pebbles.

Descending into the plains below I observed what appeared to be an isolated mound. At first I fancied it was a real tumulus, but on approaching I found that it was backed to the north by a long ridge of natural hills, which led me to think that it owed its origin to the ancient current of waters rather than the work of man. I find however from my books that this is asserted to be the tomb of Ilus. Proceeding north we came to a village, or assemblage of a few huts, called Shéblac, the neighbourhood of which claims to be the site of New Troy,—Ilium Novum; and here among some oaks I saw an immense number of columns, triglyphs, and the parts of many temples varying in style. They are now in a Turkish burial-ground, but I scarcely think they can have been brought there by the Turks, being too heavy for them to transport. There were besides many blocks of common stone, some squared, which would be useless in these grounds, and are evidently the remains of buildings which had stood near this spot; I could not find however any foundations, and no form is visible in the present disposition of the columns. The general style of workmanship is not of the early or finest age; the remains of inscriptions are in the Greek character, but probably of as late a date as the Roman conquest.

At a village three hours' journey beyond, called Hallil Elly, I also saw a great assemblage of similar relics, scattered over half a mile of country, some with rich carvings and inscriptions. The connexion of these with the place was more evident, for I here traced the foundations of several small temples. Both these sites are slightly raised above the general level of the plains, and consequently command an extensive view; but they are not at all similar to those usually selected for large cities by the ancients, particularly by the Greeks.

The poetical idea of the plains of Troy, the arena of Homer's battles, is frequently disturbed in passing the flat, sandy, and marshy ground, by seeing its present inhabitants,—the buffalo, with all but its head immersed in the swamps, the heron feeding in the shallow streams, and the frogs, whose voices certainly vary more than that of any other animal, sounding at different times like crying children, barking dogs, pigeons, and crows; and when in great numbers, producing a harmony almost as agreeable as the singing of birds. On the banks or sandy places the helpless tortoise is crawling sleepily along, and as we pass timidly draws in its head. They are so numerous that I often turn my horse out of the way to avoid them, although doubtless their hard shell would sufficiently protect them from injury. The dead ones lying about lose their outer shell, and become perfectly white, of a limy bone, with the horny scales scattered around.

Finding nothing of sufficient interest to detain me longer on these plains, I determined to hasten on and reach Channákálasy before evening. We therefore travelled for the next twenty-five miles at the speed of the Tartar (the couriers of the Turks), which is seven or eight miles an hour, passing over small limestone hills; and at about half the way we paused on the brow of a range of them, forming the cliffs or Asiatic frontier of the Dardanelles, at the village of Ghiaoúrcooe. The view of the entrance of the strait was so beautiful, that, favouring my own and my horse's limbs, I sat down to make a sketch.

Our Consul resides in this village, twelve miles from Channákálasy. We met his dragoman on the way, who begged that I would ask for the key of his house, and use it as my own. The residence of the Consul is in ruins, caused by the late fire. His dragoman took my name, and the following morning the Consul, Mr. Launder, came into the town to call upon me. He sat with me several hours, and offered every attention. His house has been twice destroyed by fire within a year, and from the last conflagration he only escaped with the clothes on his back, losing, among other property, a valuable library. The Sultan's government will not allow the house to be rebuilt with stone, the Turks representing the injury that would be sustained by the growers of timber and by the workmen if the houses were more durable.

One half of the town, the court end, was completely destroyed last year, but is rapidly rising again, formed entirely of wooden houses, which, while new and uniform, have a peculiar and somewhat pleasing effect, resembling the Swiss villages. A number of tents, raised upon the ruins of their houses, form the temporary shops and caffés of the half-ruined merchants. This place, which is of considerable extent, takes its Turkish name Channákálasy (meaning 'Pot Castle') from the manufactures of crockery carried on here. It is called by us the Dardanelles, which here refers to the straits alone: in the maps this town is marked as Sultana, a name known only to the map-makers.

Each nation has here its resident consul, and the strong castles on either shore make this the portal to the Sultan's capital. Several other forts above assist in completely commanding the entrance of these straits.

Having ridden with the same horses about fifty-two miles, between seven in the morning and six at night, I was ready to retire early to rest, but was so excessively cold that I could not sleep. The weather had suddenly changed, and it blew a hurricane from the north-east, making the current of the Hellespont defy the power of the steamboat which was to carry us forward. Before daylight I heard a military band passing under my window, playing very tolerably a French air. It was the first day of the Kooban Byran, one of the great feasts. The troops were going to mosque. On their return I was much amused by seeing such a burlesque upon soldiers as I should have condemned at a theatre as over-acted; the men were evidently quite out of their element in breeches and coats, which would have fitted persons twice their size, for they are all boys. Many of them were blacks: they had no collars, stocks, or shirts; their ears, and almost their eyes, were enveloped in red caps, and they were walking and talking in the most irregular manner. My appearance caused great disorder in their ranks, as they all turned round to look at an European; and as some were holding their muskets horizontally over their shoulders, some carrying them perpendicularly, a sad confusion was the consequence. The officers held their swords in one hand before them, the other being generally in the breeches pocket. I do not know whether the novelty of having such an appendage to the costume, or the cold morning, was the reason of this unmilitary posture, nor am I sure whether the troops were intended to be in lines; but as the band was playing and the officers were at stated distances, it is probable they were. Their guns were very clean and in good order; they were of French manufacture: the band did credit to their teachers, who were of the same nation.

The mosques were no sooner emptied, than the forts on either side began their thundering, and I had an opportunity of witnessing the extent of their power. They all fired immense balls of stone, generally formed of rounded sections or pieces of broken columns, two feet in diameter. I went to the top of the house to witness the firing, which was very interesting. The guns were a little diverted from the direct line across, lest each should injure the opposite fort; and the shot marked very curiously the course they took, dipping into the sea six or seven times, playing duck-and-drake, and driving up the water as if spouted from a whale; all this was seen before the report was heard, showing remarkably the time occupied in conducting sound: seven or eight balls were dancing in the sea at the same time before any report was heard, producing an extremely singular effect.

The next scene of this religious ceremony (for the firing the guns was one) I observed in walking to Abydos; numbers of people were killing sheep, and others were carrying the bodies of their sacrifice to their homes, which on this day are the scene of hospitality. Every man who can afford it kills a sheep; others receive parts from their richer neighbour. I hoped to profit by the butchery, but not a joint appeared at the bazaar, so that I had again my delicate diet of chickens and broth, and at night arrow-root. The Greeks keep Lent strictly, and it is seldom that meat can be obtained during this season.

I never felt the wind more cutting or violent than in

my walk of four miles north-east to Abydos. Of this place so little trace remains that I passed over it, and for a mile and a half beyond, and gave up the search as vain. On my return I noticed broken pottery and small stones of worked marble in the ploughed fields, at about the place where the town probably stood. Thus directed to the spot, and by seeing higher up on the opposite side of the straits the promontory of Sestos, I traced the foundation of the wall of a considerable building down to the coast. Were it not for the interest of a twofold poetic association, this spot would not have found its way into a journal or sketch-book; but, notwithstanding the strong wind, I hastily made a memorial of it.

Passing up a ravine, and ascending the hill overhanging this formerly castellated promontory, I found many remains, valueless except as leaving a trace of former inhabitants. I afterwards heard from the Consul, that a tomb was discovered a week before upon the height; but as the discoverer was a rich man, he dared not make it publicly known, as he would be taxed to any amount which the Aga chose to demand, on the excuse of his having obtained a hidden treasure. The man gave information of it to our Consul, who will be the discoverer when a prudent time has elapsed: the account he gave was that his plough struck a stone, and on raising it he found a tomb, containing a skeleton, which, when he went an hour after to examine it more minutely and privately, had crumbled to dust. His alarm at beholding this was doubled by superstitious fear.

The Greek Consul here, Signor Nicholas Vitalis, a man of great intelligence, has been fortunate in discovering a tomb, containing, I believe, the only works in terra cotta that have ever been found in this part of the country. He has discovered three specimens, and presented me with one, of which I subjoin a sketch*; they

are of high antiquity, and of considerable interest from the peculiar costume. The material is the clay now used for making crockery, and recognised as such by the particles of mica which it contains: this deposit is

* This appears to be a veiled goddess, with a polus.

brought down from the mountains of micaceous schist through which the rivers flow*.

I find it very difficult in travelling through this country to write a journal, or pursue any occupation requiring attention; for on arriving and taking possession of my room, the smoke is no sooner seen to rise from the chimney than the apartment is half filled with Turks, who, with the most friendly intention, bring their pipes and sit down, saying everything that is kind and hospitable, and watching every motion of my lips and hands. I can scarcely keep my countenance when I see them staring with astonishment at my use of a knife and fork. They watch every piece of food to my mouth; but the moment I look up, their curiosity yields to their natural politeness, and they turn away. After dinner I begin to write, and this they again watch with laughable innocence of wonder: Demetrius is obliged to give them an early hint that I am going to bed, or they would sit all night. A few years ago they would not even look at or speak to an infidel or a Ghiaour; whereas I now receive the salutation of all the gazers assembled to see me mount my horse, with its European saddle. The bridle is generally put on wrong, with the curb-chain over the nose, and the neck-strap buckled in front of the head, and the putting this right excites much curiosity. The Italian *Addio* is known to many Turks as

* On my arrival in Greece I found that Signor Vitalis had presented the other two specimens to King Otho, for the Museum in Athens, together with some coins found also at Abydos.

an expression of courtesy, and it serves on all occasions of arrival or departure, or to express obligation.

The hills along the coast of the Dardanelles are a mass of shells and sea-side rubbish, bound together with lime, forming a stone sufficiently hard for building purposes; part is of such modern formation that pieces of brick were imbedded with the shells, which would probably prove on examination to be all of the species at present found in these seas. On the coast was much sponge, but not ripe for use, the fleshy coat of the animal still covering it. The small scallop-fish is eaten as the oyster is with us, and is much esteemed: the cockle is not exactly like ours, having a darker-coloured and obliquely formed shell, but the taste is the same: both are eaten raw. Here also are excellent little oysters, but smaller than any we have in England. The sepia is much eaten here, and also a brown shell-fish, in form similar to a large snail, and larger than a pigeon's egg.

CHAPTER III.

CONSTANTINOPLE.

French Steamboat—Arrival at Constantinople—Climate—Description of the City—Bazaars—Change of Costume by the Turks—Habits of the People—Dancing Dervises—Antiquities—The Sultan—His Policy—Situation of the City.

In the evening of the 7th of March the steamboat from Smyrna, a French vessel, appeared, twelve hours after its usual time; and, being unable to face the stream and storm of wind and snow, cast anchor for the night. On the morning of the 8th, at eight o'clock, I went on board. The usual time required for the voyage to Constantinople is from twelve to sixteen hours: our passage took forty-eight; and most miserable hours they were, for it blew hard the whole time; the mingled snow and spray made it difficult even for the crew to remain at their posts. I was the only passenger in the principal cabin, which had every requisite of splendour and luxury, but no fire or stove. I was in bed almost the whole time, but never lost the numbness of cold in my feet. The captain and mate took their scanty dinner with me. I cannot like the middle classes of the French nation, particularly in travelling and in rough weather; they have little idea of cleanliness, never shaving or dressing, and often exhibit all that is disgusting in the epicure added to the German unmannerly mode of eating; but perhaps my comfortless voyage has made me hypercritical. I will therefore pass on to the pleasure of arriving on the morning of Saturday, the 9th of March, at this place, the Eastern capital,—a name which in childhood was a frequent lesson in my copy-book, and from which I now date my letters,—Constantinople, or, as it is called by the Turks, Stámbool. On landing I observed vast numbers of porpesses, which seemed to threaten to upset the light boats or caifes which swarm on the water. The Turks always squat at the bottom of these boats, which are very like canoes, but to the European, who sits higher or stands, they are a dangerous conveyance.

March 13*th*.—I have now been four days in the city, and each day the snow has continued to fall, and the wind is still north-east. On my noticing the severity of the weather, the people say, "Yes, we always have this weather at this season;" and, both from the state of vegetation and the accounts given by residents here, I am persuaded that we English are strangely mistaken with regard to the climate of this country, as well as of Italy, fancying from the great heat of the summer that there is no cold season. I am told that the winters here are extremely long and severe, and that the use of fur is greater than in any part of northern Europe; every person, male or female, rich or poor, being clothed in fur, varying from the richest sable to the most common skins. The houses are certainly built for a warm season; but Dr. Millingen, a resident here for many years, with whom I conversed about the climate, says very truly that it is easier to obtain artificial heat than cold; the people can warm themselves in winter, but could not cool an European-built house in summer.

The snow has not prevented my ramblings, but all my associations of luxury and sunshine with the East, which have hitherto accompanied minarets, are, like the vegetation here, folded in the bud: in a warmer atmosphere they may expand. I can only speak of the substantial features of the city, and must leave its gayer colouring to poets, or those who may visit it during a more genial season.

The streets of Constantinople are certainly better than those of other eastern cities, but I know none in Europe that I can mention to convey an idea sufficiently bad even for the best of them. In some a carriage may be, and occasionally is, dragged along, but the partial pavement renders it unsafe. The conveyance for ladies is drawn by a single horse or ox, led by a man, the body swinging like a hammock; yet I know not what danger there can be, for there is not width to allow of the carriage being upset; and as the ladies sit at the bottom, they cannot be jolted from their seats. The wheels and body are all carved and gilded, and hung with drapery of gay colours; but these carriages are not numerous;

for besides the above objections to their use, all the districts of the city—Pera, Galatea, Constantinople, and the Seraglio Point, or Golden Horn,—being situated on a series of hills, the greater number of the streets would be impassable for such a conveyance. For all commercial purposes connected with the shipping the water must be crossed, therefore boats are used with more advantage than carriages, and the fares are very low. Horses stand in the streets for hire, as hackney-coaches with us.

The mosques are prodigious masses of building, piled together without plan or reference to outward effect. But the elegant minarets are redeeming features, and render the general effect almost beautiful, especially when backed by a clear horizon. The proportion which the mosques bear in size to all other buildings is so colossal, that this alone renders them imposing: in fact there are no other public buildings, unless the bazaars may be so called. These are delightful places of amusement, through which you may walk perhaps for miles, generally under cover of a kind of arched vault. From the outside, or from any neighbouring hill, they look like a series of ovens or dome-tops rising from flat roofs. In these covered streets or bazaars camels and asses have free passage; and on either side are shops, or shop-boards, with the vendors on their knees, or leaping about like frogs over their various wares, which are arranged in the manner most tempting to those fond of gay colours and gaudy embroidery. The trades generally are in separate compartments, each having its bazaar: the one for ancient arms, or rather armour of all ages, is quite a museum; but the articles generally sold are clothing and ornaments of a costly kind, and these are very dear.

The people in the East spare no expense in dress. They wear a garment for a great length of time, but it would ruin an active-bodied, weather-braving inhabitant of northern Europe to dress as they do here. Their furs, shawls, arms, and embroidery are each a little fortune, and not kept as holiday-clothes, but worn daily. The price of a travelling-cap of lambskin from Persia was eight pounds: a piece of material of cheap imitation Persia shawl, for a dressing-gown, was seven pounds ten shillings; an embroidered tobacco-bag, four pounds; and yet the buyers of these things count their paras (about four to a farthing), and spend little except in dress.

The bazaars for spices, scents, drugs, and dried fruits have each their peculiar and often pleasing perfume. That for shoes forms one of the gayest marts; not a pair of black ones is to be sold. I see "Day and Martin" advertised, but this must be for the Frank population alone, who do not frequent the Turkish bazaar for the purchase of shoes.

The lambskins of which I spoke are generally from Astracan, but are produced in most of the southern countries. I have seen some of inferior quality in the south of Italy; the peculiarity of the most valued is that the wool is of close, firm little curls, and the colour glossy black: this is obtained by the following process. A short time before the ewé lambs she is killed, and the lamb extracted; the skin never having been exposed to the atmosphere, the wool retains the closeness of its curls. Should the skin happen to be purely black the prize is great, its value being about a guinea, while the sheep and lamb alive would not be worth three shillings. In Italy the lamb is dropped before it is sacrificed for its skin, in consequence of which the value seldom exceeds a few shillings; this is done probably in order to preserve the mother, whose life is there of more value than in Asia Minor or Persia.

The change to European manners and costume is far from becoming to these people, and the painter cannot but regret it; many years must elapse before the new dress and habits will harmonize with their character. The mere substitution of trousers for their loose dress interferes seriously with their old habits; they all turn in their toes, in consequence of the Turkish manner of sitting, and they walk wide and with a swing, from being habituated to the full drapery; this gait has become natural to them, and in their European trousers they walk in the same manner. They wear wide-topped, loose boots, which push up their trousers: Wellington boots would be still more inconvenient, as they must slip them off six times a day for prayers. In this new dress they cannot with comfort sit or kneel on the ground, as is their custom; and they will thus be led to use chairs, and with chairs they will want tables. But were these to be introduced, their houses would be too low, for their heads would almost touch the ceiling. Thus by a little innovation might their whole usages be unhinged.

The change that has been introduced shows the wonderful power of the Sultan over the people; all has apparently been done by example, and by the influence of that universal power *fashion*. The Turk, proud of his beard, comes up from the province a candidate for, or to receive, the office of governor. The Sultan gives him an audience, passes his hand over his own short-trimmed beard; the candidate takes the hint, and appears the next day shorn of his honoured locks. The Sultan, who is always attired in a plain blue frock-coat, asks of the aspirant for office if he admires it; he of course praises the costume worn by his patron; whereupon the Sultan suggests that *he* would look well in it, as also in the red unturbaned fez. The following day the officer again attends to receive or lose his appointment; and to promote the progress of his suit, throws off his costly and beautiful costume, and appears like the Sultan in the dull unsightly frock. A regimental cloak may sometimes be seen covering a fat body inclosed in all the robes of the Turkish costume, the whole bundle, including the fur-lined gown, being strapped together round the waist. Some of the figures are literally as broad as long, and have a laughable effect on horseback. The saddles for the upper classes are now generally made of the European form; but the people, who cannot give up their accustomed love of finery for plain leather, have them mostly of purple or crimson velvet embroidered with silver or gold, the holsters ornamented with beautiful patterns. The horses are small, but very good and showy. Every gentleman in the street is on horseback, with one, two, three, or four servants, according to his rank, walking by his side, one carrying the pipe.

I witnessed the very curious religious ceremony of the Dervises,—a most extraordinary sight. There is no doubt that it has high antiquity as a religious ceremony, and the performance is not so laughably ridiculous as I had expected from descriptions and pictures. There were fifteen dancing at the same time, and during the whole service of prayers and dance I never saw more signs of devotion; the dance indeed appears to be a religious rhapsody. The performers generally continued to turn

during three or four minutes, then bowed, and almost

immediately recommenced turning; during the whole time the eyes appeared closed, and the peculiar effect was given by the perfect fixedness of the body, head, and arms. They assumed a certain position, and I could with difficulty perceive the movement of their feet, and almost felt at a loss to account for the rotatory motion given to the figure. These Dervises are a very small sect, and although followers of the Prophet, they are quite distinct from the rest of the Mahometans; they have here a little privileged convent. I hope to learn more of their history. David danced before the altar, the Chinese dance during prayer, and many pagan nations have had the same custom. The music accompanying the ceremony is simple and monotonous, and performed on a long pipe and a tabor or drum.

Constantinople has a few standing relics of antiquity,—an aqueduct, still carrying water to a part of the town, and one or two iron-bound columns, which have suffered more from fires than from age. It has a fine obelisk, brought by the Romans from Egypt; the pedestal has been carved by the Romans, in the style of a rather base age: on the lower part is a chariot-race, sculptured in a better style and apparently of an earlier school. This is unconnected in subject with the upper part. One of the most curious remains is the "Cistern of a Thousand and One Columns;" it is subterranean, and is now used as a silk factory. It is a chamber supported by columns, bearing arches of Roman brick from one to the other. I counted two hundred and thirty standing, and I cannot see how a greater number could have been placed here. Perhaps from their form each may be considered as composed of two columns, one above the other; the two are visible: but even should

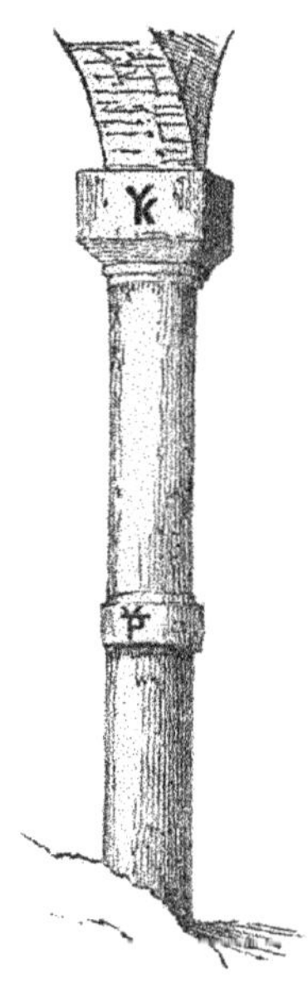

another joint or portion be below the level of the floor of earth, still the number would fall short of this eastern appellation. Of this term, as applied to indefinite numbers, there are many instances; amongst others, the 'Thousand and One Nights', and a mass of ruins of Christian churches called the 'Thousand and One Churches'. But, whatever be the origin of the name, it is certainly a very curious place, and from its great height and depth, can have been nothing but a cistern. I have copied some singular characters, cut deeply on most of the granite pillars, apparently at the time of their erection, sometimes upon various parts of the capitals, sometimes upon the junctions of the columns. Each of the groups in my copy is taken from a separate column. I think they are Phœnician or Byzantine; perhaps they may be only numbers or monograms. I hope that, from this notice of them, others may be enabled to decipher them. The capitals are of the cushion kind, precisely the shape of the cap worn by the Armenians in this country.

ЄKL ♡ AƆC ЄKL ЄKL

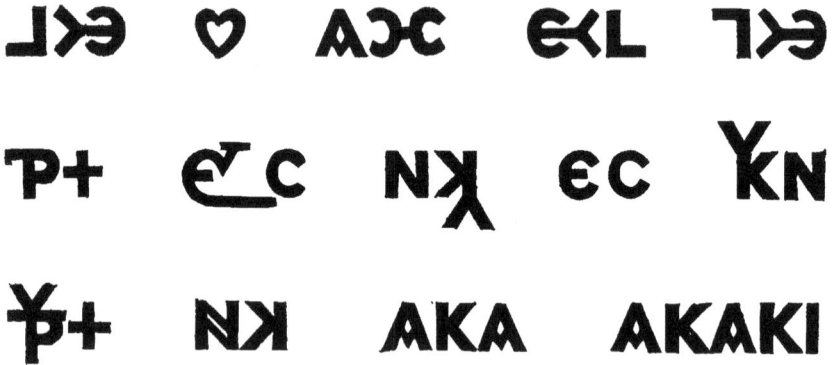

P+ ЄC NK ЄC YKN

P+ NK AKA AKAKI

The mosques contain many marble pillars, and sarcophagi from ancient cities; the latter are now used as cisterns; but these marbles have been transported from all parts of Asia Minor, and can only be looked upon as remains of the country at large.

I have said that the people here eat a kind of shell-fish like a snail: I find it is a snail, and not a native of the sea, although sold by the fish-dealers. This morning I saw a dozen hampers of them; the well-known tender-horned inhabitants were gently peeping forth, but an occasional shake given to the hamper made them retire into their shells; the large brown kind I have before mentioned is the most common, but the people here also eat the more delicate small ones; as they are not considered meat, they add to the limited fare of the Catholics during the fasts. It is now Lent, and hence the greater display of them in the streets. The snail found in the chalk-pits near Epsom, and said to have been introduced into England nearly a century ago for medicinal purposes, appears to me of precisely the same species*.

Among the hospitable presents that I have frequently received on my journey, was a simple preparation of cream used in this country, and made from the milk of the goat or buffalo, which I have not very much liked; but here it is made of cow's milk, and is so excellent that I give the receipt. It is called Kymac, which means scum. Take a pan of new-milk, let it stand on a stove or near a fire, to simmer, but not boil; a thick scum will form over it, which must not be broken; when this is well formed, set the whole by till the next day to stand for cream, and it will be found that the cream has saturated and adhered to the spongy under-part of the scum: this coating, nearly half an inch thick, may be taken off, and doubled or rolled up; it will keep for some days, and is excellent with fruit or coffee, and good with

* Helix Pomatia.

anything. The people here seem to use it as a substitute for butter, which latter is supplied entirely from Russia; but neither here nor at Smyrna have I ever tasted it fresh or good. The butter is low-priced however, and used profusely in cakes and pastry, of which great quantities are consumed. There is a kind of curd or cheese, which is pressed and sold in skins; it is spread upon or eaten with bread, but has a sourish unpleasant taste. I have also occasionally seen as a luxury a description of whipped cream, which is eaten as butter: it is white and opake, and not greasy. Butter, I believe, was never made by the ancient Greeks*.

The Turks are by no means a dirty people; their hands, feet, and faces are always religiously kept clean. I know no European country where there is so little annoyance from offensive impurities in the streets. I do not remember ever seeing a Turk spit: what a contrast to the manners of France, Italy, and Germany! Yet none smoke more than this people, but they smoke in a cleanly manner, always with a mouth-piece; so that the pipe never enters the lips, and may therefore be, as it often is, without indelicacy handed to a friend. I have never made a trifling purchase without my servant taking the pipe of the shopman while he attends

* "Butter was unknown to the ancient Greeks; they have no word which expresses an idea of it: *βουτυρον* signifies cheese, or coagulum of cow's milk," (Beloe's Herodotus, book 4. ch. 3.)—a very good description of the substance I have named as made by the present inhabitants.

to me with his wares. When there is any question about price, a pipe is handed, and the parties sit down to smoke, and consider the difference between them; this has often happened to me in making bargains for horses. But the Turks in their dealings are generally fair, and their claims for increased price seem always made with reason and justice.

It was my intention to have started hence yesterday, the 15th of March, but a new commander-in-chief and head of police having been just appointed, it was necessary to obtain the signatures of the new officers to my firman, which is just sent home,—a prodigious document, for ensuring to me every personal accommodation and assistance on my journey. There is another for obtaining horses, and a third to be used on a new road opened only a few months ago.

I have seen the Sultan today: he is certainly, cousidering the people whom he governs, one of the most wonderful men of the age. That reform should be carried into effect, with even dangerous rapidity, among a people ten years ago considered incapable of change, and whose religious habits, education, ideas, and very nature were all opposed to change, and that the whole of these reforms should have been introduced so quickly, show that the Sultan has not only a powerful mind to plan, but an equal energy to effect, such astonishing changes. Within these five or six years, upon his going publicly to mosque, as is always the custom, he was shaded by plumes and dressed in all the cumbrous robes and jewels associated with eastern pomp. At that time it was scarcely safe to look up as he passed; the offence of pointing at him was repressed by summary punishment, and report says that the scimitar was seldom long idle in its scabbard. Now, on the contrary, he wears a red cap, or fez, with a star in front, and a military European blue cloak over a plain blue uniform. He rides on an European saddle, and retains none of his former state, except the fumes of incense rising from a censer swung by a page who precedes him. When I saw him he was attended by thirty or forty officers on horseback, all in the same plain uniform, and he rode for about three quarters of a mile along the street lined on either side by soldiers: a band played as he approached. In fact no feature of the ceremony would have appeared extraordinary in any European capital; and there was scarcely an individual among the thousands that attended, who had not completely changed costume, manners, and almost opinions, during the last few years. In the seraglio the ladies show their faces when attended by their music, drawing, and French masters; and in so doing at least three offences against the Mahometan law are committed;—that a man should be admitted into the harem, that women should be unveiled before men, and that Mahometans should be taught to imitate natural objects and to speak a foreign tongue.

Curious instances are shown however of the difficulty of subduing the prejudices of an ignorant people. One very unpopular reform which the Sultan had to effect, in the formation of his troops, was that of their wearing *braces*, a necessary accompaniment to the trousers: and why? because these form a cross, the badge of the infidel, upon the back: many indeed will submit to severe punishment, and even death, for disobedience to military orders, rather than bear upon their persons this sign, hostile to their religion. No one can appreciate the difficulty of making the first change among this people, without knowing their character: succeeding changes will follow with comparatively little opposition. It is amusing to see the longing after old habits, which have become in fact the very nature of the older people: their beards are rather concealed than cut off; and, in spite of the plain blue frock-coat, I often see beneath it costly embroidered vests. This habitual indulgence in variety and extravagance of dress, it will require time to subdue.

The Sultan does not appear to be above fifty years of age; he has a short, trim, black beard, sits extremely well and upright on his horse, and looks as if he would in the natural course of life see many more years of change. He is suspected of being a Christian; and certainly his exertions are doing far more than any other means now at work to remove the superstitions of Mahometanism; and these reforms may perhaps prepare the way for further changes in the religion of the people. Here the barriers of the Mahometan law are falling fast, and there is now as much religious freedom in this as in any city in the world. There are many picture-shops, and portraits of the Sultan are seen exposed in all of them, and this by his command. The devices on the embroidered clothes and the painted ceilings and fronts of houses now represent flowers, guns, and flags,—objects in nature or art,—which is a direct violation of the laws of the Koran; but it would be endless to relate the changes in progress here. It is for this reason that the villages and interior of the country are more interesting to the traveller; there the change is scarcely perceptible, the natural manners and character of the people remaining undisturbed. In Constantinople the turban and the variety of head-dresses, which I have before described, are comparatively unseen, every one wearing the red cap; and the character of the people is changing as quickly as the costume.

The weather is now very fine, but still bitterly cold. I cannot face the north-east wind to make an excursion up the Bosphorus to the Black Sea. The straits, as far as I have seen them, are exceedingly beautiful; the continued ravines or sheltered dells on either side, with palaces and villas down to the water's edge, are rich and picturesque, and present a contrast to the bare hills above them.

The natural situation of Constantinople is lovely, and appears designed for the site of a great city. I know no capital which covers so many and such steep hills, and to this peculiar character it owes the whole of its beauty; indeed I have never seen a city so picturesque, viewed from every point around. The activity among the people, both on land and water, is amusing; they seem like bees, and their city somewhat resembles a hive. The boats completely speckle the water, and as I have watched them at a distance, they appeared to me stationary; but hundreds succeed to hundreds, moving in all directions, yet from their similarity producing the effect of fixed objects. In London the tides and the stream of the Thames influence the course of vessels upon it, but these waters have more the appearance of a lake, with equal traffic from all sides. I can frequently count from my window six or seven steamboats; their introduction is recent, as is also the opening of a bridge, built to unite Pera with Constantinople; it was to form a drive for the Sultan from one palace to another. The bridge is already passable, but the streets leading to it are not yet formed.

It is said that few persons remain a week in this city without witnessing a fire; one broke out yesterday, but before I could reach the spot it was subdued. The largest houses are frequently burnt down in the space of ten minutes, being entirely constructed of a very inflammable wood. The fire-engines are numerous, but, having to be transported on men's shoulders, they are small. The English, French, and Dutch ambassadors' palaces, all in Pera (the district of the city where the Franks live), are in ruins, and their respective governments are tardy in rebuilding them. The ambassadors reside at their country-houses, twelve miles distant.

CHAPTER IV.

BITHYNIA.

Departure from Constantinople—Burial-ground—New Road—Dil Ferry —Manners of the People—The Country—Natural History—Arrival at Nicæa—Its Remains—Discovery of Inscription—Pass of the Mountain Léfky—Vizier Khan—Power of the Firman—Sohoót.

Saturday, March 17th.—We left Constantinople this morning at seven o'clock, but were detained at Oós-cooda, the opposite town on the Asiatic side, waiting for horses, until ten.

These Turks are luxurious fellows; the post-master left word that he had waited for us until past eight, and was then at his bath; and as he had to sign my post firman, I was obliged to wait patiently till he had completed his toilet. A governor is never to be seen until after eleven in the morning, being in his harem, which, with his bath and mosque, occupy much of his day.

For some miles on the way, after leaving Oóscooda, on either side of the road were burial-grounds, whose groves of cypress-trees give a striking feature to hills otherwise uninteresting; but the view from them of the city, and its splendid situation, will always reward the traveller who may visit them. The whole line of our journey skirted the eastern shores of the Sea of Marmora, and passed the series of islands ending with Prince's Isle; but the chain of eminences is continued by a similar isolated rocky hill upon the coast, and three others which carry on the range towards the north-east, diminishing in size towards the end of the curve, until the termination is marked by the small brown rocks opposite the entrance to the Bosphorus from the Sea of Marmora. The shore is somewhat monotonous, from its continued undulations, and has no village, or even trees, to give it interest, the whole line of country being for the most part barren. Much of the land is capable of better cultivation, but the greater part would always prove unprofitable.

There is one feature in this country which is very striking, but more so to the Turks than Europeans,—a new road, or rather *a road*; for this is, I believe, the only one in Asia Minor. This splendid line, extending at present as far as Ismid, a distance of about sixty miles, was designed by the Austrians, and bears their character even to its rails, barriers, bridges, and mileposts, all being striped with diagonal lines of black and white. I speak of the design of the road only, for at present it is formed merely of the natural soil of the country, which is far too rich, even in this part, to make carriage-roads without the assistance of M'Adam. It will require a long time to complete such an undertaking; and indeed it is wonderful how much has already been done, opposed as the work has been by the strong stream of prejudice. The regulations of the road are quite completed; for instance, I was charged for two carriages, one for myself, the other for my luggage; but on asking for them, was told that at this season they could not run upon the road, on account of the mud; the charge was however the same, and I was to take horses instead. I soon came to a barrier, and was asked for my post firman, which was to be signed, being in fact nothing more nor less than a passport, an instrument hitherto unknown in this country. The road is also divided into posts, at which we change horses, having had three sets in the space of thirty-three miles: this may appear an advantage over the usual course of taking post-horses for the day or journey, but we found (perhaps owing to the people's inexperience, or natural slowness,) that more than an hour was lost at each post in re-packing the luggage upon the fresh horses.

It was nearly seven o'clock in the evening when we arrived at Dil Ferry, a solitary house on the sea-coast, containing one very large room, or caffé, but little resembling an European one. We took possession of our corner, and were as usual independent of the other company, which consisted of eight or nine people, boatmen, boys, and post-guides. These people were until ten o'clock highly entertaining, and afterwards all lay down in different parts, and I hope slept; one poor man had a sad asthma, and six dogs and two cats were until five in the morning continually exerting their vocal powers at the door, making such a confusion of noises as I scarcely ever heard.

The opinion that I formed of the Turkish character from my first observations of their manners was a totally mistaken one. All their taciturnity and dignified appearance is assumed, more particularly in the higher classes. This I have had frequent opportunities of observing in the khans and coffee-houses, and in my own rooms each evening, as well as among the innumerable companions by whom we are joined on the road. Sociability is here carried almost too far, all travellers joining company, and forming a sort of caravan,—a custom which originates probably in the necessity of protection.

I certainly never met with more determined *wits* than among the lower classes of the people here, in whom the national character is most easily read. Though in perfect ignorance of their language, I have been so amused by their inimitable acting and buffoonery, and by their games and even childish tricks, that I have laughed until they fancied I understood them, and began to talk to me: my servant was interpreter on these occasions, and their observations and repartees were so pointed, that he hesitated in literally translating them to me. In the coffee-room last night game succeeded game, all ages joining; and one man, who was unwittingly made the laughing-stock of the party, having had his face blackened while sleeping, took the joke in excellent humour, and enjoyed it as much as any of the party.

The games are generally very simple, perhaps almost childish: no species of gambling is known. Our postillion today, the ugliest and most unprepossessing fellow I ever saw, headed us for forty-eight miles on horseback, whistling and hooting after the baggage-horses with as much animation and noise as a huntsman. On our halt for half an hour in the middle of the day, I counted a crowd of people around us, nearly thirty in number, who were all taking the most ridiculous interest in our party, and joking with my servant and guide. On seeing me look at my watch and map, and then at my compass, one of these bystanders said something in a very significant manner, which I learned was, "Ah! you can tell anything that *is*, but you cannot, with all your things, say what weather we shall have tomorrow." The remark was quick, and showed a readiness of thought; but what I would more particularly notice is their love of buffoonery and sprightliness of manners; the boys are constantly saying something smart, that makes my servant laugh, and he in his turn with his whip makes them scamper off.

In the morning I was up at six o'clock, and by half-past on board the boat which was to ferry us to the opposite long neck of land stretching out from Ersek, the ancient Drapane. There we had to await the arrival of horses, for which we sent to the village of Ersek, lying about two miles off inland. After sketching the view to the east of the Gulf of Nicomedia (now Ismid), and rambling along the flat, swampy promontory, I examined the shore, which was entirely formed of shells mixed with weeds, drifted lightly in, and but little broken. I saw no shells but of the common kinds. The echini were very numerous, with many varieties of the scallop, muscle, and cockle; and there were masses, almost amounting to little rocks, of the worm-like cases of the serpula, which are so often seen attached to the shells of fish.

Several of the plants were curious. I observed the butcher-broom* as a common shrub, and a species of asparagus† sometimes growing to the tops of the high trees as a creeper. There are water birds here of all kinds; snipes abound, and the stork builds undisturbed on every public eminence. Why does it always select for this purpose the most public spots, the top of a chimney, a pump, or the trees in the centre of the court-yard of a khan or public square? It makes a loud chattering noise, entirely instrumental, with its bill, at the same time throwing its head back with a graceful curve; it does this as an indication of pleasure, and generally on the return of the mate.

At the bottom of the shallow clear water, on either side of the road, I saw the tortoise; but I suppose the early morning was too cold for it to venture out of the water, as I have seen none on the land today. On passing through the small village from which the horses had been procured, I traced for half a mile its ancient towered walls; and the tombs and paved water-road

* Ruscus aculeatus. † Asparagus acutifolius.

gave the usual indications of the site of an ornamented city, and supplied now its only memorials.

Ascending gradually to the hills we forded the river above twenty times, in preference to passing through the stiff mud of the roads: the guides generally seem to avoid the common track, which is always the most impassable. The scenery now became wild and beautiful; one isolated hill, round which the river flowed, I observed, had its summit surrounded with a wall, apparently a Roman work; eight or ten circular towers were still standing. The Turkish name is Chobon Kálasy ('Shepherd's Castle'), and it has probably been a little fortified town. The hills are of a slaty limestone, and are much veined with marble. On the opposite side of a little brook, not four yards from us, lay a dead horse by the side of the stream. The party which were feeding upon it were enjoying their meal greatly: two eagles were perched upon the body, whose heads were continually diving between the ribs; on the neck were three crows, and at its head and eyes were two magpies; another eagle, quite satiated, was wiping his bill against the hoofs. So intent were they all on their meal, that even the noise of our horses and our shouts caused only the last-mentioned guest to take flight, which he did with much dignified composure. The smaller birds heeded not the eagles, nor did the eagles notice us.

Today I saw several specimens of that beautiful bird the hoopoe, which is new to me in its wild state. It perches on the trees, gliding among the branches as silently as the woodpecker, and is here extremely bold; my servant has several times marked it to a small tree, which he has approached, and even beaten the branches; failing to start it he has returned, thinking it gone, when the bird has flown from the tree with a flight similar to that of the blackbird. The hills are almost wholly mounds of rich earth; indeed the soil is so deep, that where they are at all abrupt the rains have burst the surface and formed landslips; for twenty miles the country was but scantily cultivated, and had little timber, although capable of producing anything. At Koósdervent (the 'Pass of the Girls') the mulberry is much cultivated, this district supplying the best silk sent to Brúsa, the great mart for silk manufactures.

Leaving this place we passed through underwood and shrubs, all evergreens, and to the eye of an Englishman the richest that could be. There were the common and dwarf daphnes, the blossom of the latter scenting the air; many varieties also of the laurestinus, and among them the strawberry-tree*, whose luxuriant foliage and beautifully clean and oriental stem distinguished it above its rivals. It grows so large and plentifully as to be the principal firewood, burning rapidly with a great blaze. Amidst this perfect garden,—for beneath our feet were violet, hyacinth, and anemone, in great variety,—the most beautiful view opened before us, not grand, but of perfectly lovely beauty. In the extreme distance was

* Arbutus Unedo.

the snowy range of Olympus, and before it a series of fine mountains, with their feet bathed in the most placid of lakes, the ancient Ascania, which is about ten miles long and four in breadth. At the southern end of the lake, beautifully situated, stood the ruined towers of the many times famous Nicæa. Beneath us, sloping from our feet to the edge of the lake, was a highly cultivated and rich valley. We were still twelve miles distant from the town of Nicæa, and every turn we made in the descent only varied the beauties of the scene. After a ride of about forty-six miles, we arrived before six o'clock, on the 19th of March, at the ancient Nicæa. Entering through a hole in the walls of this famed and fated city, we had still another mile to travel through fields and mulberry plantations before we arrived at the village of Isnik, a small place standing within the walls, which form a circuit of four miles around it. As I passed on to this village everything has shown such variety of interest that I have determined to rest a day here.

March 20th.—Seldom have I had a harder day's work than in attempting to see and comprehend this ruin of ruins. The points of the greatest interest are the relics of its earliest age; little of that date now remains standing in its original form; but the grandeur and peculiar beauty of the arts among the earlier Greeks cannot be concealed even in the broken materials. Three square towers and their connecting walls are evidently built out of the ruins of one magnificent temple, which probably stood on or near their site. The stones, which are of white marble, are so well squared, that, although put together (probably by the Romans) without cement, the joints are generally too close to admit the blade of a knife between them. Each stone is also grooved along the edge, as if a line of metal had concealed the joint; the face of the stone has still a polished surface, whilst the groove is left scarcely smooth, showing the mark of the tool. If this groove were filled with

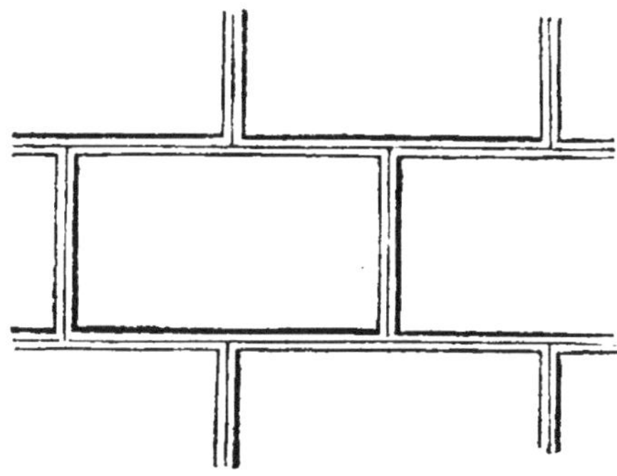

metal, the building must have combined splendour with simple grandeur. Temples in Sacred History are described as glittering with gold, perhaps from this mode of covering the joints. The cornices are of wreaths of acanthus leaves, with bold dentals and the usual Corinthian ornaments; but an idea of the whole building can only be formed from the grand scale of the blocks, and the highly-finished workmanship of the detached fragments. Other parts of the walls are composed of the relics of apparently an earlier age,—immense stones cut to fit into each other, without the attention which was paid in later ages to the horizontal courses: these would rank as Cyclopean. Again, some parts of the walls are entirely Roman, being of brick, and with arches built in the most substantial style; while others are formed of marbles of a much less pure age, in which the cross (always found among the ornaments) and the ill-proportioned figures and letters in the inscriptions give them the date of the earlier Christians. On three of the towers in the walls of the city are three similar inscriptions*: I subjoin a copy of one of these.

+

ΠΥΡΓΟϹΜΙ
ΧΑΗΛΜЄΓΑ
ΛΟΥΒΑϹΙΛЄ
ωϹЄΝΧω̄Α
ΤΟΚΡΑΤΟΡΟЄ

ΕΤΟΥϹ STIS

In other parts of the walls are many inscribed marbles, built in, without regard to their inscriptions, some sideways, some reversed.

* The sign of the cross is prefixed to all three. The translation is "The Tower of Michael the Great King, Emperor in Christ" To the first one the date is added, viz. the year of the world **STIS**, i. e. 6316.

ΟΝΗΣΙΜΟΝ
ΟΝΗΣΙΜΟΥΤΟΝΑΓΑΘΟΝΙ ΡΑΝ
ΙΔΙΕΥΣΛΝΙ ΑΚΑΠΥΜΝΑΣΙΑΡΧΗ
ΣΑΝΤΑΕΝΔΟΣΟΣΚΑΙΕΣΤΙΑΣΑΝ
ΙΑΤΟΣΥΝΕΔΡΙοΝΜΕΤΛΛΟΙΡΕΤΠΟΣΚΑΙ
ΔΟ///ΔΗΔΟΣΕΟΣΕΚΑΣΓοΓΕΡΥΣΛΣ
ΗΑΤΠ/////////ΣΣΑΡΑΣΚΑΙΡΞΑ///Α
ΗΝΜΕΓΙΣ ΗΝΑΡΧΗΝΕ///ΑΡΧοΝΟΝ
ΑΡΙΣ Ι ΑΙΝΕΤΙΑΝΟΥΑΜΜΙΑΝΟΥ
ΚΑΙΠΑΥΛΕΙΝΙΑΝΟΥ Ι ΡΥΦΩΝΟΣ
ΡΑΜΜΑΤΕΥΟΝΤΟΣΑΥΡΣΥΜΦΟΡΟΥ
ΚΑΙΚΟΥΝοΣΔΙΑΒΙΟΥΑΥΡΣΤΕΦΑΝΟΥ*.

The following is another inscription which I copied from a stone built into the wall.

ΚΕΙΛΙΑΡΧΟΝΛΕΓΙΔΓ~ΙΔΤΕΜΙΝ
ΧΕΛΙΑΡΧΟΝΛΕΓΙΕ~ΕΠΙΤ+
///ΟΝ~ΣΕΒΕΠΑΡΧΕΙΑΣΓΑΛΛΙΑΣ
///ΚΥΙΤΑΝΙΚΙΣΕΠΙΚΕ//////ΝΣΟΝ
ΕΠΙΤΡΕΠΑΡΧΕΙΑΣΙΜΥΣΙΑΧ
//////ΣΚΑΤΟΕΠΙΤΡΕΠΑΡΧΕΙΑΣ
///ΑΚΗΣ~ΕΠΙΤΡΔΟΥΚ~ΕΠΕΑΡ

* *Translation.*

"Onesimus, son of Onesimus the good, who arranged the pic-nic parties, who presided with high reputation over the Gymnasium, and gave at his own house a magnificent entertainment to the Synedrium, and * * * * Aristænetianus Ammianus and Paulinianus Trypho being archons, and Aurelius Symphorus Cæco being scribe, during the life of Aurelius Stephanus."

////ΑΣΔΑΛΜΑΤΙΑΣ~ΚΑΙΙΣΤΡΙ
//Σ~ΕΠΙΤΡ^ΔΔΟΥΚΗΝΑΡΙΟΝ
ΑΛΕΞΑΝΔΡΕΙΑΣ~ΤΟΥΙΔΙΟΥ
·ΔΟΓΟΥ
+ΛΟΥΚΗΝΟΣ∘ΑΡΧΕΔΑΟΣΤΟΝ
ΟΥΦΙΛΟΝ//ΑΙ//// *

I observed two fragments of basso-rilievo, probably part of a frieze, equal to the marbles of the Athenian Parthenon, but much mutilated; they were three feet deep, and one of them nine feet long, the other fragments shorter. The cornice on the lid of a sarcophagus, built into the wall as material, bore an inscription †.

* *Translation.*

" Caius Lucanus Archelaus at his own cost [commemorates] his friend * * * * * Chiliarch of the 14th double Legion, Chiliarch of the 15th Legion, the Emperor's Steward over the province of Aquitanian Gaul for the Census, Steward over the province of the Lower Mysia, Steward over the province of * * * * *, Ducenary Steward over the provinces of Dalmatia and Istria, Ducenary Steward of Alexandria."

† " Paulinus son of Aulius lived seventeen years. Farewell."

These three Stones lie in a

ΙΚΑΙΣΑΡΙΜΑΥΡΚΛΑΥΔΙΟ ΕΥΣΕΒΕΙ ΕΥΤΥΧΕΙ ΣΕΒ

ΝΚΛΗΤΩΚΑΙΤΩΔΗΝΩΤΩ ΡΩΜΑΙΩΝΗΛΛΜΙ ΟΤΑΤ

ΕΔΛΕΙΟΥΜΑΚΡΕΙΝΟΥΤΡΕ ΣΒΕΥΤΟΥΚΑΙΑΝΤΙ ΣΤΡΑ

No. 1. 3

Inscription upon Stones which hav

Part of Inscription formed of projecting

John Mu

roadside. *This Stone lies on the ground near*

Κ ΗΣΕΞΟΥΣΤΑΣΤΟΔΕΥΤΕΡΟΝΑΝΘΥΠΑΤΩ ΠΑΤΡΗ ΠΑΡ

ΣΤΗΚΑΤΑΡΙΣΤΗΝΕΙΚΑΙΕΩΝΠΟΔΙΣΤΟΤΕΙΧΟΣΕΠΙΤΟΥΛΑ

ΟΥΣΕΒΚΑΙΣΑΜΙΟΥΑΝΤΩΝΙΝΟΥΤΟΥΛΑΜΠΡΛΟΓΙΣΤ

3   No. 2.

he top of a Gateway at Nicaea.

The carvings generally were of a baser age. There were several statues the size of life, and one colossal head, a Medusa, placed over a gateway, probably in its original position. Four gateways, of which the north and south-east are the most important and perfect, are standing in the middle wall (for the town is partly inclosed by a small outer Turkish wall), and upon these are portions of inscriptions, but purposely so much erased that I did not copy the few lines remaining. Each has also had metallic inscriptions, the holes in the marble for attaching them now only remaining to indicate the shape of the letters. At the two principal arched entrances were immense gateways of a square form, built of very large stones. I was much interested in one of these from seeing a stone (No. 2. in the annexed plate) near the spot, which I was sure from its form must be the fellow stone to one containing part of an inscription (No. 1.) that I had seen over the gateway; and if so, its under side would probably have another portion of the same inscription. I soon collected a number of men, and for a few pence had the stone turned over, and discovered the characters as fresh as if just cut. The men seeing me refer to a book said, "Yes, the Franks know by their books where all the writing and gold are concealed;" always fancying that we search for inscriptions to find treasure. We certainly did find a small coin, but only four hundred years old, probably of the time when the stone fell, for the coin was exposed beneath it. Searching about I found by the road-side three other stones (Nos. 3.), lying on the sides of a ditch, and all inscribed in the same style of character as that over the gateway. Judging that they might complete the inscription, I took copies and drawings of all*.

Upon one of the towers of the wall an inscription rudely formed with tiles is built in edgeways, as represented in the annexed plate. The name "Theodorus" appears, and the whole is probably of Christian date.

In the midst of the half-buried ruins of the ancient city are some curious remains of an early Greek theatre. The avenues, out of which are large chambers or vaults, now all subterranean, are built of descending arches tending to a centre, probably at the area of the theatre. The workmanship is extremely good, and is colossal, the stones being some nine, and others fourteen, feet in length. Entering with lights, we saw that many of these chambers much resembled each other, and that they were all extremely perfect. We encountered thousands of bats, flying towards the entrance in a cloud; and as

* The translation of this inscription, thus completed, is as follows:

"The very splendid and large and good city of the Nicæans [erects] this wall for the autocrat Cæsar, Marcus Aurelius Claudius, the pious, the fortunate, august, of Tribunitial authority, second time Proconsul, Father of his Country, and for the Sacred Senate and the People of the Romans, in the time of the illustrious Velleius Macrinus, formerly Consul, Legate, and Lieutenant of the august Cæsar Antoninus, the splendid orator."

The portion of inscription upon the stone marked No. 1. has been published by Von Hammer, "Umblick auf einer Reise nach Brussa: Pesth, 1818." p. 185.

they rushed out we were obliged to crouch down, to prevent their striking our faces, or with the flapping of their wings extinguishing our candles.

A very small church still stands within the present town, which, from its mosaic floor and ceiling, may probably be of the date of St. Mark's at Venice, or rather of the Byzantine age.

Every fence, step, trough, or paving-stone is from this quarry of art; many fragments of good sculpture are also built into the houses. Without the walls is a

Roman aqueduct, which still supplies the town with water from the neighbouring mountain.

In the lake are the remains of a port or landing-place; and judging from the foundations seen in the depths of this clearest of water, these works must have been extensive. I have taken several sketches of the exquisitely beautiful scenery of this neighbourhood; but they cannot give an adequate idea of the natural features of the country, although of the architecture they may.

On the morning of the 20th of March at eight o'clock I left Nicæa, passing up the valley behind the town towards the south-east, where the hills were covered with short underwood of evergreens, but without timber; the valleys were but scantily cultivated, principally for the growth of the mulberry-tree. We gradually ascended for about twelve miles, when, almost without being aware of it, we reached the summit of a ridge of hills. As the view on approaching Nicæa was calm, rich and beautiful, so was this craggy, rocky and bold. I had before seen nothing so wild and romantic in this country: before us, as we descended through a gorge in the rocks worthy of the Alps, the ranges of mountains rose into rugged points, reminding me of the scenery in Savoy. The view here was extremely grand, and perhaps rendered more so by the sublime effect attending a stormy day, the heavy clouds rolling apart, and thundering along the broken chains of mountains, many of the higher peaks being shrouded with clouds.

The ranges of mountains all yield up their rivers to the Gallus, which bears them on to the ancient Sangarius. The strata of the limestone rocks are here much contorted, and are often perpendicular, appearing like colossal ruins; if seen foreshortened, they resemble the aiguilles of Switzerland. The town of Léfky stands near the junction with the Gallus of one of the principal rivers, which has its source in the lake by the ancient Cæsareia, while its recipient flows directly from Olympus.

Leaving Léfky at two o'clock, we again ascended a range of hills, which changed the scene by opening to our view a highly picturesque but much smaller valley, with its river, and bold and almost perpendicular range of cliffs, attainable only by the eagles, whose nests we saw on the broken crags. Around us the rocks were covered with a beautiful flower, looking like a kind of dwarf stock*. Fifteen miles brought me to this place, Vizierkhán, which I reached by half-past four, Demetrins having ridden forward with the firman to obtain accommodation, which is here afforded, as it was at Nicæa, in the house of a Greek family. At present I cannot overcome the feeling of intrusion and obligation, and therefore am not so independent as at a khan; but this mode has many advantages, and one is allowing me more time to write and draw, as I am freed from the intrusion, amusing though it be, of the Turks, and from the gossiping which they carry on with my servant whilst he is cooking. I find he is stored with thimbles, needles, and scissors; and by presents of them he makes himself very popular with the young people of

* On showing a drawing of this plant at the Linnean Society, without naming in what country I had been rambling, I was at once told, that it was a plant peculiar to the sides of Mount Olympus in Bithynia, and had never been heard of elsewhere,—that it was the *Arabis purpurea*.

the families with whom we stay, and I generally profit by eating the fruits given to him in return. He received yesterday a quince, but so large that I did not recognise the species; it weighed, I should think, a pound; I am to have it cooked *à la Turque.*

Vizierkhán has its name from an immense khan founded for the Hággi, or pilgrimage to Mecca. On examining the stone of this building I have been much puzzled. I had seen on entering Léfky, in a wall of loose stones, one which, like the rest, was of a pale greenish colour, but contained beautiful specimens of fossil shells quite protruding from it; there were a scallop or two of different sizes, and a kind of snail or round shell, all of the same colour as the stone. I called Demetrius back to look at them, and to show him the difference between these shells and those which we saw at Troy, which were themselves imbedded in lime. Thinking fossils might be common, I did not dismount from my horse. On proceeding I found the rocks in the neighbourhood of the same colour, and thought they were of a greenish limestone, or perhaps sandstone; but I now find that the khan, the only stone building in this village, is formed of the same material, and that it is an igneous rock, not stratified, and speckled throughout with green schisty particles. How comes this to contain shells? I have described the stone in the wall at Léfky to the post-guide, and he is to send it after me by the first Tartar coming.

March 21*st.*—Quitting Vizierkhán, which we did this

morning by six o'clock, we again continued our ascent amidst mountains of the same bold and craggy character, the only vegetation being shrubs, amongst which the berries of the arbor vitæ scented the air with their peculiar perfume. The smell reminded me of painting in oils, and my servant exclaimed, "What a strong smell of castor oil!" We at length reached a summit, which I expected would be quite sterile, but found a fine cultivated country, the sloping hills clothed with the mulberry, and the plains with corn; and this continued with little change for about twelve or fifteen miles, until we arrived at the town of Sohoót.

Here I had to wait two hours for horses; and after piling my baggage under a wide-spreading plane-tree in the open space in the town, my servant accompanied me in search of antiquities. On my suggesting the possibility of the unguarded luggage being stolen during our absence, he replied that the Turks might not steal, their religion forbade it; that the things were quite safe, and the more so from their being left exposed. During this time I was the lion of the place. One of the chief persons begged me to tell him the hour; and his watch and others (if there were any others in the town) were doubtless regulated by mine, which I had set by guess some weeks before whilst I was watching the sun sink into the sea.

Two very anxious-looking men came to ask me to prescribe for their friend, who was sick, and wished me to go and see him; my servant assured them that I was no doctor, and advised me not to offer even simple medicines, as if the man grew worse it would be attributed to me. His case was simple, and I have no doubt I could have cured him; but I have not much compunction for not having attempted it, as his disorder had been caused by eating too much of a not very wholesome dish called Youghoot. This food is very common here, and generally liked by Europeans; it resembles lemon cream, but is made of commoner materials, namely new milk with a little rennet, turning it to a curd, which is not pressed, but eaten in the consistency of jelly; this dish is served up at all times, and with various accompaniments. Sometimes for œconomy a little of a former making is kept to leaven the new batch.

CHAPTER V.

PHRYGIA.

A Forest—Oneóenoo—Singular Caves—Mountains and Table-lands—Curious Geological features—Kootáya—Extraordinary Rocks—Expedition to seek Doganlu—Customs of the People—Æzani—Its Antiquities—Inscriptions—Habits of a Private Family—Delicacy of the Manners—Departure for Altuntash—Sichanleé—Sandookleé—Dumbári-ovasy—The Plague—Catchíburloo.

After leaving Sohoót, we came upon a less productive country, and the rocks, protruding through the scanty underwood, were of volcanic production, a kind of grey-coloured basalt, or lava. In about an hour we entered a forest, extending for some hundreds of miles to the north-east, till it reaches the shores of the Black Sea. In crossing this part of it, we rode through woods of oak, fir, and plane, with a great variety of underwood, for about twelve miles. On the ground, among the dead leaves of the oak, sparkled the most fresh and gay-looking flowers; the commonest, which tinged the banks with a beautiful reddish lilac, was the cyclamen*; and there were the snowdrop, primrose, the

* C. coum.

beautiful dwarf hyacinth, the yellow, blue and lilac crocus, with many others.

On quitting this forest we crossed a valley, and saw at a distance of about four miles, under the cliffs or ranges of mountains, the town of Oneóenoo, (meaning a " Place of Caves,") so called from some caves in the cliffs overhanging the town. The situation appears very damp and unhealthy, and the perfectly flat valley, which is almost a swamp, seems to be the possession of plovers and wild ducks. The situation is strikingly like that of Magnesia, but the Hermus is wanted to drain the meadows in front. The ground here is so high that it appears to receive no waters but from the heavens, a source which latterly has been very liberal.

Oneóenoo is a long village immediately under the face of the rock, and is overhung by two immense arches or caves, which at a distance I had no doubt were artificial, the forms of the huge arches being so perfect.

This evening I ascended to them, and extremely curions they are. The whole rock is of marble, veined with red, but shivered into innumerable cracks as if by heat. The caves are evidently natural, although at an early age of the Turks perhaps, or in the time of the Christians, the fronts have been fortified by strong walls, parts of which still remain. The caves communicate with one another, and from their size and dryness, as well as commanding situation, they must have been an excellent substitute for a castle. Through several small cavities or fissures in the rock of the caves, water had at a remote period filtered, forming a semi-transparent crust of stalactite. While in the cave I was surprised at hearing distinctly people talking and dogs barking as if close to the entrance, but on going to the front of the cave, I perceived that the sounds came from the village beneath. The effect of this immense ear or sounding-board was as powerful as a whispering gallery; and perhaps this peculiarity might have been an advantage in times of war or alarm.

Several fragments of columns, altars, and other remains were built into the walls of the houses in the town, but the principal material used was lava or scoria, of nearly every colour; many of the spongy holes being filled with a white crystallized substance similar to that which I have seen in the basaltic columns at Staffa.

March 22nd.—On leaving the town, before we began the ascent of the mountains to the south, we passed a pond or small lake, the temperature of which was shown by steam rising from the water; it was supplied by some hot-springs which rise at the foot of the cliff. After ascending for a quarter of an hour, I looked back to the valley we had left, surrounded by its little range of low hills, and saw over them to the north-west Olympus covered with snow, at a distance in a straight line of at least ninety miles; but the elevation here is very great. We continued the ascent for an hour, and I fully expected to find myself on a barren summit, and then to descend into more eastern climes; but what was my surprise on reaching the top at seeing before me meadows and cultivated land for twenty miles, and a series of gentle hills and undulations beyond, still bounding the view! These table-lands are a peculiarity in this country, and materially affect its climate. Yesterday I rode through a garden of flowers, today I have in forty miles seen nothing in bloom except the yellow crocus. The country is some weeks later than that of my yesterday's ride, and many weeks later than that of the north-western parts over which I have lately travelled. In ascending we passed up a craggy marble steep, down which had rolled many rounded pieces of lava and blocks of red marble of the kind so frequently seen in combination with the white marble, and came to a small hill of the serpentine schist, like that near Enáe. For fifteen miles we rode over this table-land, almost the whole being in pasture, and here, in this wild and high country found a burial-ground, consisting only of a few graves, but several of them marked by columns or cornices, and one by a richly carved pedestal or altar, with the following inscription.

ΑΓΑΘΗΤΥΧΗΘΕΟΙϹΟΕΙΟΙϹΚΑΙΔ
ΚΑΙΟΙϹΗΡΟΦΙλ
ΠΑΠΑΕΥΧΗΝ

ΑϹΙΧΑΕΚΑΙΑϹΚΧΙΙΠΑΕ
ΟΙΑϹΚλΗΠΑλΑΤΥΠΟΓ
ΚΟΥΡΝΑΕΤΗΝΟΙ *

Of the carving on each side I could see but little, those parts being sunk deep into the earth; but a figure with wings which was on one side, led me to believe this fragment of Christian date.

All the hills before me presented in form the same appearance, and I was the more eager to approach them as the stones on the land were of a singular chalky, soapy appearance. I had reason here to regret my slight knowledge of geology, as I feel confident that more scientific observers would find much that is extremely remarkable. I believe that the whole of this district is marble or limestone, as I have already described the mountain at Oneóenoo; and the country which we have crossed since leaving it, a distance of forty miles to the north-west of this place, (we are now at Kootáya, the ancient Cotyæium,) appears of the same character, and but little varied. In elevation it is still on the high plains,

* These fragments may perhaps be rendered as follows:

" May it be fortunate.

" Herophilus [erected this according to the tenor of his] vow to the gods, to divine and just persons. Asilas and Asclepas, Sons of Asclepas, Citizens of Curnaetos."

and the boundary hills generally appear white and flat table tops, much and very conspicuously stratified. The

intervening matter having perished, the stratum remains almost a shelf; and towards the foot of the hills are slopes of the debris from the softer parts, forming unpicturesque heaps, apparently of lime. I observed another appearance in the distance, which was extremely singular; the background was a stratified cliff or hill, and the lower shelf of these strata, which stood on a soft hill of the white loose substance looking like lime, was surmounted by a number of pointed sugar-loaf rocks, and in other

places by lofty rocks perforated with caves, having artificial forms, although from their appearance I judged them to be natural openings to caves within equally natural; a deep river intervening prevented a closer examination of them.

The whole of this immense district appears to be agate or chalcedony, the strata varying beautifully in appearance. The prevailing kind is of a flinty opaque white; the next proportion is of a transparent white, deepening to almost the black appearance of our flint, and in every shade; it has, like flint, the property of emitting light. Another large portion varies from yellow to orange, and is sometimes opaque and sometimes transparent; and again another is of a pink tinge, shaded into red. In the white, similar gradations lead to a green hue. I have brought away specimens of each, but I do not exaggerate in saying that the road and rocks were all glittering with many-coloured agates. The softer parts look as if burned or calcined, like lime, and when wet form a kind of mortar. My ride of forty miles has probably not extended across the whole of this field of chalcedony. In some instances the stones of this substance were themselves striped, and in one or two I saw them in nodules like flints. It cannot be that the whole should be a bed of chalk, containing flints of various kinds, although the appearance of the country led me at first to suppose that this was the case. I do not know that any scientific geologist has traversed this region, but I hope that it may have been visited by Mr. Hamilton during his recent excursion. If I were to indulge my own speculation, I should ask if heat, which by the scattered lava, hot springs, and various appearances is shown to have been so active an agent here, may not have produced the different effects on the various textures of marble which I have noticed. May not the most soft or limy parts have been calcined, and by exposure to moisture decomposed? May not the more stalactitic or aqueous parts have partially withstood the heat, and by its action have only been somewhat hardened and crystallized? And may not this have been the case also with the red portions of the marble, which are always the hardest? I must notice that the strata are all apparently horizontal. Before entering this singular plain, I likewise observed, after leaving Oneóenoo, that the hard baked cliffs were pierced in all directions with veins of a crystallized marble, or perhaps of this same agate-like substance.

We soon entered another plain, much resembling the one at Oneóenoo; and on the opposite side, again under a cliff, stood the large town of Koot*á*ya. The plain is traversed by a considerable river, the ancient Thymbrius, which, like the Gallus, falls into the Sangarius. To enable me to judge of the elevation of our present position, I asked the name of a snow-mountain in the south-west, and found it was Baba Dagh, the ancient Mount Cadmus, at a distance, as appears by the map, of about one hundred and ten miles. There is another pile of the sugar-loaf aiguilles, which I have before described, not far distant from this town; I shall therefore remain here in order to visit them, and also to rest, or rather to vary my occupation.

March 22nd.—I have today closely examined these hills, and am amazed, but no longer in doubt. The whole of the white limy or chalky matter forming them, and which is stratified with chalcedony, is a volcanic dust, the lower being more purely tufa, the higher more mixed with the shattered fragments of various kinds of broken stone; but far the greater part is pumice-stone, and all appears massed or washed together by a rush of waters. The curiously shaped points are almost wholly of pumice, which may account for their being less decomposed. I have filled my pockets with specimens, but the varieties of appearance caused by volcanic heat are endless. The peculiarities of this country are so striking, that I hope, with my collected specimens and such explanation as I can give, to gain information respecting it from my geological friends*.

May not one fancy oneself, upon the granite range of Olympus, Caucasus, or Taurus, as on the side of a

* I am sorry to find that Mr. Hamilton has not seen the line of country which I have taken; I heard however from my servant, who has travelled much eastward of this part, that the peculiarities continue the same; and I find that in a district near Cæsarea, perhaps three hundred miles to the eastward, Mr. Hamilton thus describes, far better than I have been able to do, the singular features of a similar country. "'In the ravine near Tatlar and in the valleys of Utch-hissar and Urjub, the tuff has been worn into cones from one hundred and fifty to three hundred feet high. They are principally detached from the sides of the valleys, but are connected at the base; and are in

cauldron pouring forth the boiling matter, which as it subsides forms its scum of agate and froth of pumice? May we not suppose that after a lapse of ages, volcanic heat bursts forth again, shattering the crust; that it afterwards slumbers and coats itself with its agate scum; and again bursting forth, that at last its own productions become its prison-walls? For thousands of ages has this region stood deserted; not even a shell remains as a record of past life, while all the world around has been clothed with vegetation and peopled with animals, whose fossil dead have formed mountains. At length the germs of vegetation, borne on the wings of the wind, have strewn the barren dust, already softened with rain; and it has been clothed with trees and verdure. Then did man, wandering from the southern east, take possession of this new world, making dwellings for himself in its caves of soft dry pumice, and feeding on the spontaneous fruits around him. But I must not waste paper and time in speculating further on what may have been, but note down what now is.

These peculiar, pointed rocks are hollowed like a

some places so numerous and close together that they resemble at a distance a grove of lofty cypresses. Where the cones occur on the sides of the valleys, they exhibit every stage of development, from the first indication of a mound near the summit of the slope, to the full-formed cone at the bottom. In the valley of Urjub some of them are capped by a mass of hard rock, which projects like the head of a mushroom.' The production of these cones the author ascribes to the action of running or atmospheric water." (Proceedings of the Geological Society, No. 56, vol. ii.)

honeycomb with sepulchral caves, many leading from one to the other by flights of steps, and all having small recesses scooped out of the sides, probably for urns containing the ashes of the dead, and little holes abôve each for a lamp or small offering; in some of them slight traces of architectural ornaments remain. In these, near Koot*á*ya, the debris has so far buried the points, that several of the chambers are not above the level of the mound at their base. In one of these tombs I saw above twenty holes or receptacles for the dead bodies, forming a series of bins or troughs around the cave. These are now used as mangers, the place being converted into a stable, holding fifty or sixty beasts. A fire lighted in the centre has blackened the whole of the flat roof, which still retains the marks of the pickaxe used in its formation.

March 24*th.*—Here I was misled by the misnomers of the map-makers, which have been followed in the books written by travellers. I asked for Doganlu, or, as the "Useful Knowledge" maps term it, Dooanlu, but no such place was known. With compass, map, and guide-book however we started, leaving the luggage behind. Our course lay up the valley towards the south-east, and at about seven miles crossed a river, and soon after passed the little village of Arrácooe: we proceeded in the same direction through a country scarcely varying in any respect from our route since we left Oneóenoo, vegetation being as yet stationary; not a flower was to be seen but the half-starved yellow crocus springing from the brown grass, and the goats were browsing on the dead leaves of the stunted oaks, or on the branches of the arbor vitæ and juniper.

At the distance of twenty miles from Kootáya we entered a valley, also filled with the singularly formed pointed rocks of the pumice-earth, and for eight miles passed through a continued cemetery, the rocks and the ground being perforated by thousands of caves. Each of those which we entered had others above and below it, and the road sounded hollow from the excavations. A sound like this indeed is always heard in trotting over this kind of soil, but here the effect is stronger, and must be caused by caves underneath. The most important group of these pumice-rocks forms a hill, which has the appearance of a castle standing at the end of a plain, and that idea is conveyed by the Turkish name, Gurjare Kálasy. In one or two of these caves were the remains of architectural ornaments cut in the rock: a few scattered columns, door-frames, and pedestals were seen in the valleys in the neighbourhood, but they had more the appearance of having formed parts of the cemeteries than of having been the remains of ancient towns.

On making inquiries of the peasantry, I learned that the neighbourhood was full of ruins, which appeared from their description to be all of tombs: at about two hours' distance to the east, they said, there were remains, which must be marble sarcophagi, some broken, but others not yet opened.

We continued our route to Dooaslán, which is called in the maps Doganlu; this name is also erroneously given by the writer of the "Modern Traveller" to a place described as near Kásru Khan, which latter village is twenty-eight miles distant from this misnamed Doganlu. In the place of this name he describes some interesting inscriptions on the rock, which I learned are at the village of Yasilíchia (a name signifying "Writing on the Rocks"), about eight miles N.N.W. of Kasru Pasha Khan, near Ghumbat. This error has occasioned us a ride of fifty-six miles, which with much difficulty we accomplished upon the same horses, returning to Kootáya by ten o'clock the same night.

On our return we were obliged to stop to feed the horses at the little village of Arrácooe, seven miles from Kootáya. Here we rested for an hour and a half, and had an opportunity of noticing the simple and hospitable customs of the country. A traveller had just arrived; and as the village, consisting only of a few huts, was too small to have a governor, the inhabitants have a house for strangers, which is as good as any in the place, although without windows: one end of the room forms the stable, accommodating six horses. The traveller who had arrived before us was at prayers; but no circumstance ever disturbs Mahometans at their devotions, when they appear completely abstracted. I delayed to enter until the traveller rose, when the prayer-mat was hung up and he gave me the usual salaam. I was beginning to make my meal upon the food we had with us, when in came nine people each bearing a dish. A large tray was raised on the rim of a corn-sieve placed on the ground, in the centre of which was put a tureen of soup, with pieces of bread around it. The stranger, my servant, and a person who seemed to be the head man of the village sat round the tray, dipping their wooden spoons or fingers into each dish as it was placed in succession before them. Of the nine dishes I observed three were of soups. I asked why this was, and who was to pay for the repast; and was informed that it is the custom of the people, strictly enjoined by their religion, that, as soon as a stranger appears, each peasant should bring his dish; he himself remaining to partake of it after the stranger has fed,—a sort of pic-nic, of which the stranger partakes without contributing. The hospitality extends to everything he requires; his horse is fed, and wood is brought for his fire, each inhabitant feeling honoured by offering something. This custom accounts for the frequent recurrence of the same dish, as no one knows what his neighbour will contribute. Towards a Turkish guest this practice is perfectly disinterested, but from an European they may possibly have been led to expect some kind of return, although to offer payment would be an insult. The whole of the contributors afterwards sit down and eat in another part of the room.

Instead of waiting till the horses had fed, I had determined to walk forward to Kootáya, but was deterred

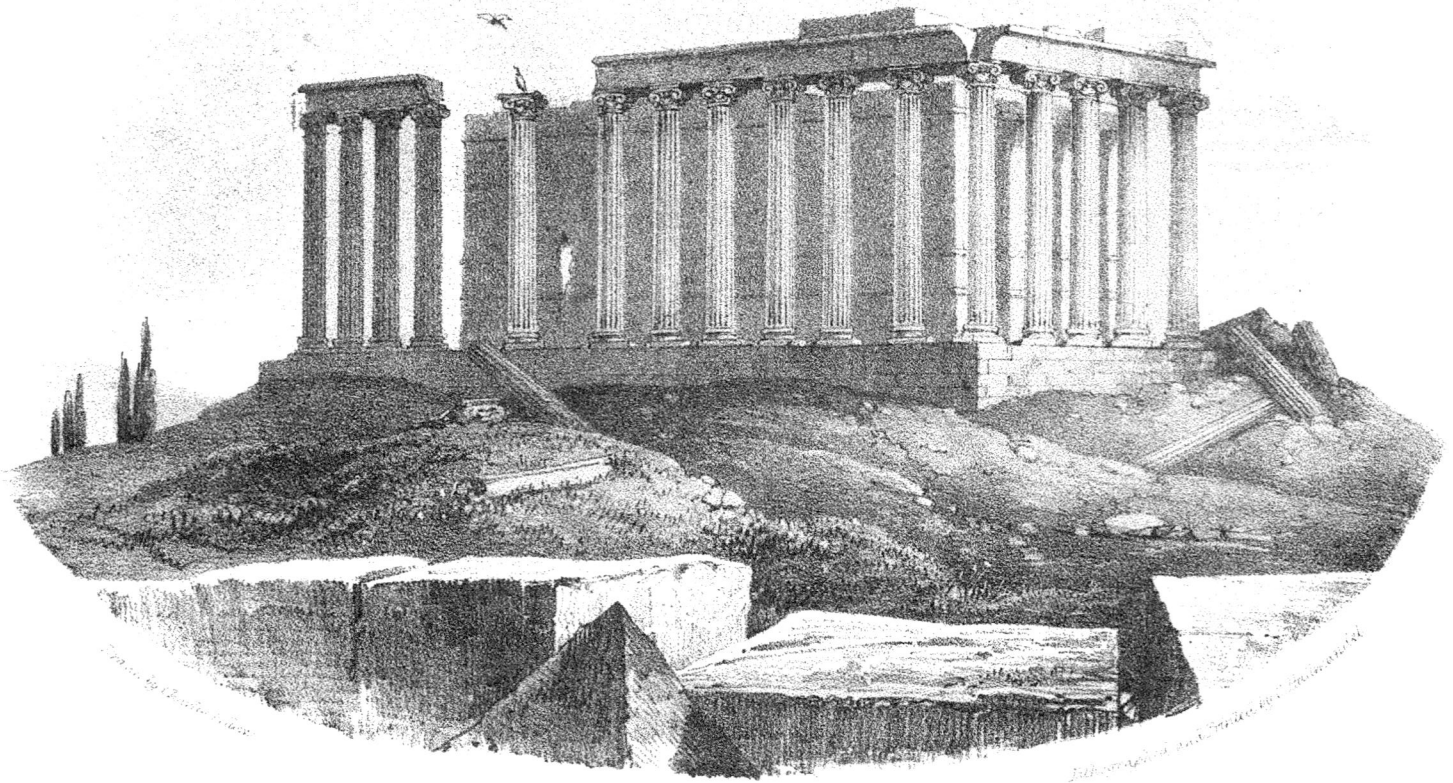

IONIC TEMPLE AT ÆZANI.

by its being dusk; for having no lanterns, we could not have entered the town without incurring the penalty of the law which prevails here, as in all Turkish towns, for the prompt apprehension and imprisonment of any person found in the streets without a light after dusk.

March 25th.—This morning I left Koot*á*ya for Tj*á*den, in order to see the ruins of Æzani; and the distance being thirty-six miles, I arranged to return on the following day. Our route lay west-south-west, and the country through which we passed presented the same geological features, except that much of our track the second day lay at an elevation of probably two thousand feet above the plain of Koot*á*ya. In several places were strata of slate, some almost white, and generally too much shivered by heat to be used for the purposes to which we apply it in Europe. The road was wild and overgrown with stunted oak and juniper, and had nothing of interest about it, not a village or house for the first thirty-two miles. When we arrived at Hágicoóe, my horse strained his shoulder, and I left him with the guide, whose horse I took across the plain to Æzani. The sight of a temple which I passed in the twilight made me long for the morning, to examine the numerous and comparatively perfect remains which I saw in every direction.

The modern village consists of a few huts, and is as straggling as most other Turkish villages. We were as usual shown to the stranger's house, which I will describe as a specimen of this kind of building, and as displaying the manners of the people, which, as I advance into the interior of the country, are becoming more simple. My arrival in the place was generally known before I reached the stranger's house, which had a wall of loose stones piled round to mark the extent of the premises, the whole of the stone employed being fragments of worked marble. The house was of mud mixed with straw, about seven feet high, with a flat roof of earth grown over with grass, and a chimney, but no window. We passed through the stable into the smaller apartment within, which had walls of bare mud, and a wide open chimney, admitting scarcely sufficient light to enable me to see the interior. I was closely followed by three men, each with a contribution of fire-wood, small fir-trees, which they placed up the chimney, out of the top of which they protruded; and these being set on fire, in a few minutes gave to the little room a most cheerful appearance, and showed the floor matted, and on either side of the fire a carpet, cushion, and pillows, looking very clean and comfortable. As we had no bedding or canteen with us, we fared as strangers, and my cloak was the only additional furniture.

We asked for something to eat, and in a short time appeared, dish by dish, a curious but very good dinner. Three of the peasants brought bowls of soup; four others dishes of eggs, some fried with little pieces of meat, others with butter, or simply poached. We had also an excellent pelaf, turnep-radishes scraped like horseradish, and sweets made of honey; and another sweet made from the dried grape, which is commonly used in Turkey as a substitute for sugar: it is the raisin stewed until the moisture evaporates, and this treacly substance remains. The dishes were left but a short time on the tray, and were taken off by the sons of my hosts who attended upon us. As soon as the tray was removed, the carpet was swept, lest any crumbs should have fallen, it being a religious law never to tread on food. The same mode of eating was observed by the younger party, who afterwards sat down to the meal in another part of the room, finishing each dish in rotation; then the whole party sat down round the fire, some with their pipes, talking and telling the simplest tales of commonplace occurrences, the scene of which was of course always their own village. My inquiries were for coins and relics, which were hunted for in every child's toy-place or old wall where they had been noticed. Each person produced his fancied treasure, which he had preserved because some Frank had before given money for such things. They know nothing of the value or uses of our purchases. I heard of a beantiful Greek statue being sold by them for five shillings, and two bronze vases for eight shillings; and yet they were boasting of the large sums such things produced. My servant bought thirty or forty Greek coins, some of silver, at an average of three farthings each; and I obtained at an equally cheap rate the foot of a statue and some bronze handles.

I think I have not mentioned that the light generally used in this part of the country, even in the large town of Kootáya and the other towns through which I have passed, is a chip of the fir-tree. The people make a wound in the tree, which draws the sap to that part, and the tree is then cut for fire-wood, reserving this portion filled with turpentine for candles. I was surprised to find how long they burned; during a meal a piece is placed between two stones, and it burns with a large flame and a black smoke for half an hour. At Æzani they brought some of this resinous wood to light our fire; and when any one of our party quitted the room, he with his large knife (a weapon which all carry) split off a slip, which served him for a candle. We met people in the streets at Kootáya carrying them; but the rich use tallow-candles, in the excellent and elegant lantern of the East made of folded paper.

In the morning my breakfast-table was furnished with the very good brown bread of the country, and with a kymac and a large supply of milk; for my servant they brought a meal of soup, etc., which he with a party of six enjoyed: this hospitality appears from habit, and perhaps from its religious obligation, to have become a part of their nature. The Frank however, when he is so treated, may mostly find one of the younger of the party, who, whilst holding a stirrup or the horse's head at parting, is quite ready to receive a present, which probably exceeds the value of the articles consumed.

by Charles Fellows. Lithographed & Printed by C. Hullmandel.

T ÆZANI.

I had heard of the recent discovery of Æzani, and, having been told that it was a small Roman town of the time of Adrian, I felt comparatively little interest about seeing it. But I now find from its architecture that it appears to be a purely Greek city, though perhaps afterwards possessed by the Romans, as there are some few Latin inscriptions. The architecture is entirely Greek, except the tombs, many of which appear to be of a more recent period than the public buildings. The situation of the town is not so striking as the Greeks generally choose, but it has its gentle hills, one of which was its Acropolis, crowned with a very highly finished Ionic temple, No. 6. in the following plan.

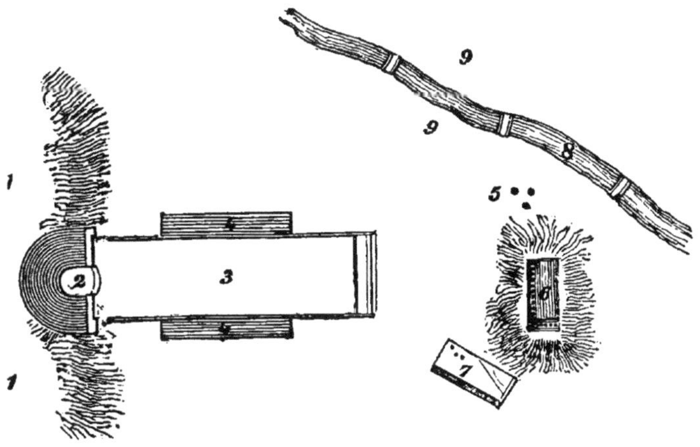

Eighteen columns, with one side and end of the cella, are still standing. In the interior of the latter are four long inscriptions, one in well-formed Greek characters, and apparently as old as the temple; of this I took a copy.

ΑΟΥΙΔΙΟΣΚΟΥΙΗΤΟΣΑΙΖΑΝΕΙΤΟΝΑΡΧΟΥΣΙΒΟΥΛΗΙ
ΔΗΜΩΙΧΑΙΡΕΙΝΑΜΦΙΣΒΗΤΗΣΙΣΠΕΡΙΧΩΡΑΣΙΕΡΑΣΑΝΑ
ΤΕΘΕΙΣΗΣΠΑΛΑΙΤΩΙΔΙΙΤΡΕΙΒΟΜΕΝΗΠΟΛΛΩΝΕΤΩΝΤΗΠΡΟΝΟΙΑΤΟΥ
ΜΕΓΙΣΤΟΥΑΥΤΟΚΡΑΤΟΡΟΣΤΕΛΟΥΣΕΤΥΧΕΕΠΕΙΓΑΡΕΠΕΣΤΕΙΛΑΑΥΤΩΔΗ
ΛΩΝΤΟΠΡΑΓΜΑΟΛΟΝΗΡΟΜΗΝΤΕΩΤΙΧΡΗΡΟΕΙΝΔΥΟΤΑΜΑΛΙΣΤΑΤΗΝ
ΔΙΑΦΟΡΑΝΥΜΕΙΝΚΕΙΝΟΥΝΤΑΚΑΙΤΟΔΥΣΕΡΓΕΣΚΑΙΔΥΣΕΥΡΕΤΟΝΤΟΥ
ΠΡΑΓΜΑΤΟΣΠΑΡΕΧΟΜΕΝΑΜΕΙΞΑΣΤΩΦΙΛΑΝΘΡΩΠΩΤΟΔΙΚΑΙΟΝΑΚΟΛοΥ
ΟΩΣΤΗΠΕΡΙΤΑΣΚΡΙΣΕΙΣΕΠΙΜΕΛΕΙΑΤ//ΠΟΛΥΧ//ΟΝΙΟΝΥΜΩΝΗΑΧΗΜΚΑΙΥΠοΨΙ
ΑΝΠΡΟΣΑΛΛΗΔΟΥΣΕΑΥΣΕΝ ΓΑΟΩΣΕΚΤΗΣΕΠΙΣΤ//ΗΣΗΝΕΠΕΜΨΕΝΠΡΟΣΜΕ
ΗΑΟΗΣΕΣΘΕΗΣΤΟΑΝΤΙΓΡΑΦΟΝΥΜΕΙΝΠΕΠΟΜΦΑΙ ‾Σ‾ΕΙΑΑΔΕΕΣΠΕΠΩΤΩΕΠΙ
ΤΡΟΠΩΤΟΥΣΕΒΑΣΤΟΥΟΠΩΣΓΕΟΜΕΤΡΑΣΕΠΙΤΗΑ ΕΞΑΜΕΝΟΣΕΚΕΙΝοΙΣ
ΠΡΟΣΧΡΗΣΗΤΑΙΤΗΝΧΩΡΑΝΔΙΑΜΕΤΡΩΝΚΑΚ ΝΥΗΕΙΝΓΕΝΗΣΕΤΑΙ
ΚΑΙΕΚΤΩΝΙΕΡΩΝΤΟΥΚΑΙΣΑΡΟΣΓΡΑΜΜΑΓ ΕΔΗΛΩΚΑΟΤΙΟΔΕΙΤΕ
ΛΕΙΝΥΠΕΡΕΚΑΣΤΟΥΚΛΗΡΟΥΚΑΤΑΤΗΝ ΦΑΣ ΗΣΛΝΗ
ΜΕΡΑΣΛΑΒΗΤΕΤΗΝΕΠΙΣΤΟΛΗΝΕΚΑΕ
ΧΩΡΑΣΤΕΛΕΣΕΗΝΑΜΗΠΑΛΙΝΤΙΝΕΣ
ΒΡΑΔΕΙΟΝΑΠΟΛΑΥΣΑΙΤΗΝΠΟΛΙΝΤΗ
ΓΕΝΩΝΤΑΙΑΡΚΕΙΓΑΡΑΥΓΟΙΣΤΟΜΕΧΡΙ
ΦΑΔΕΚΑΙΤΗΣΠΡΟΣΕΣΠΕΡΟΝΕΠΙΣΤΟ
ΜΟ//ΕΓΡΑΦΕΝ ΕΡΡΩΣΘΑΙΥΜΑΣΕΥΧ *

There is another inscription in inferior Greek characters, and there are two in badly cut Roman: on the outside of the cella also are three or four more; but my time having been spent in taking sketches and in visiting the other ruins, I could only copy one of these, which I subjoin (page 144). Moreover the weather was so cold, and the snow falling so fast, that I had difficulty in putting anything on paper.

* *Translation of Inscription at page* 142.

"Avidius Quintus to the Archons, the Council, and the People of Æzani sendeth greeting.

"The dispute carried on during many years about the sacred territory which was anciently dedicated to Jupiter, has by the forethought of the very Great Emperor been ended. For, after I wrote to him explaining the whole matter and inquired what was to be done, he prescribed two things which may best tend to extinguish this difference for you, and to diminish in the view of a benevolent citizen whatever is difficult to be performed or discovered in the affair, viz. a principle of equity, in conjunction with care in the public administration of justice, things which will put an end to your protracted contention and your spirit of reciprocal suspicion; as you will see from the epistle which he sent to me, and a copy of which I have just sent to you. And I have sent directions to Deespepus, the steward of the Emperor, to select proper surveyors, and to employ them in measuring the said territory."

ΟΑΡΧΩΝΤΟΝΠΑΝΕΛΛΗΝΩΝΚΑΙΙΕΡΕΥΣΘΕΟΥΑΔΡΙΑΠΥΠΑΝΕΜΗΝΙοΥ
ΚΑΙΑΓΩΝΟΘΕΤΗΣΤΩΝΜΕΓΛΛΩΝΠΑΝΕΛΛΗΝΙΩΜΚΔ[...]ΙΑΣΩΝΚΑΙΟΙ
ΠΑΝΕΛΛΗΝΕΣ ΤοΙΣΕΠΙΤΗΣΑΣΙΑΣΕΛΛΗΣΙ ΙΧΑΙΡΕΙΝ
ΜΟΥΛΠΙΟΝΑΠοΥΛΗΙΝΕΥΡΥΚΛΕΑΤοΝΑΙΖΑΝΕΙΤΗΝΦΘΑΝΜΕΝΗΔΗΚΑΙΣ
ΕΤΕΡΩΝΓΡΑΜΜΑΤΩΝΜΑΡΤΥΡΙΑΣΤΗΣΠΑΡΗΜΩΝΗΕΙΩΚοΤΕΣΕΠΕΣΤΜΡο
ΤΕΣΥΜΕΙΝΤΕΑΥΤοΙΣΥΠΕΡΑΥΤοΥΚΑΙΤΗΙΠΑΤΡΙΔΙΚΑΙΤΩΙΜΕΤΙΣΤΩΙΑΥΤΟ
ΚΡΙΤοΡΙ ΔΙΚΑΙοΝΔΕΗΓΗΣΑΜΕΘΑΚΑΙΤοΥΚΡΑΤΙΣΤοΥΙΛΙΑΣοΝοΣΠΑΡΑΛΛΒοΝ
ΤοΣΓΗΝΑ ΧΗΝΜΑΡΤΥΡΗΣΑΙΑΥΤΩΙΤΑΑΥΓΑΕΠΙΕΙΚΕΙΛΤΕΚΑΙΑΙΔΟΙΠΑΣΗΙ
ΚΕΧΡΗΜΣΝΩΙΠΕΡΙΤΗΝΠοΛΙΤΕΙΑΝΤΩΝΣΥΝΠΑΝΕΑΗΝΩΡΚΑΙΤοΑΣΙΩΜΑ
ΤοΥ[...]Λ‿ΧοΝΑΥΤΩΙΑΝΩΘΕΚΑΙΑΠοΓΕΝοΥΣΕΠΙΜΑΛΛοΝΠΡοΑΓοΝΠΕΝοΙ[...]
ΔΕΙΩΝΚΑΙΠΡΑΤΤΩΝΔΙΑΤΕΤΕΑΕΚΕΠΑΡΑΠΑΝΤΑ[...]οΙΤΗΣΣ[...]ΝΕΑ[...]ΝΕ
ΚΡοΝοΝ

ΕΡΡΩΣΘΑΕοΜΑΣΕΥΧοΜΑΙ*

At the foot of the Acropolis, which is for the most part artificially raised upon fine substantial arches of massive stone similar to the vaults of Nicæa, stand several pillars of another temple (No. 5. in the plan of the town given at p. 141); and between these and the river is a single column, now occupied by the nest of a stork, four similar ones having been just removed and used in the erection of a Governor's house at Kootáya. On a hill towards the north are the colossal foundations of another temple (No. 7.), which from the many splendid fragments of Corinthian columns and friezes scattered around, I have no doubt was of that order. Still further to the north-east stands a hill (No. 1.) covered with tombs, and hollowed out from the side of it is a beautiful Greek theatre (No. 2.); the seats still remain, and such a mass of the materials, that the whole might

* *Translation of Inscription at page* 144.

"The Archon of the Panhellenes, and Priest of the god Hadrian Panhellenius, and Director of the Games at the Great Panhellenia, Jason, and the Panhellenes, to the Greeks of Asia send greeting.

"By the testimony contained in another letter of ours we have already expressed our regard for Marcus Ulpius Apuleius Eurycles, citizen of Æzani, having written both to you on his behalf, and to his country, and to the very great Emperor. The most excellent Jason having accepted the archonship, we have thought it right to renew this testimony, inasmuch as he has always evinced courtesy and great modesty in the administration of the * * * * * and this resolution we pass to the honour of his forefathers, preferring more especially his descendants on account of what he persevered in doing during the whole period.

"Farewell."

probably be put together again. A splendid frieze of lions, in every attitude, with trees in the background, cut in bold basso-rilievo, appears to have surrounded the building. The proscenium is similar in form to others that I have seen, and probably contained equestrian statues like those found at Herculaneum, as the pedestals are still remaining; the form was this:

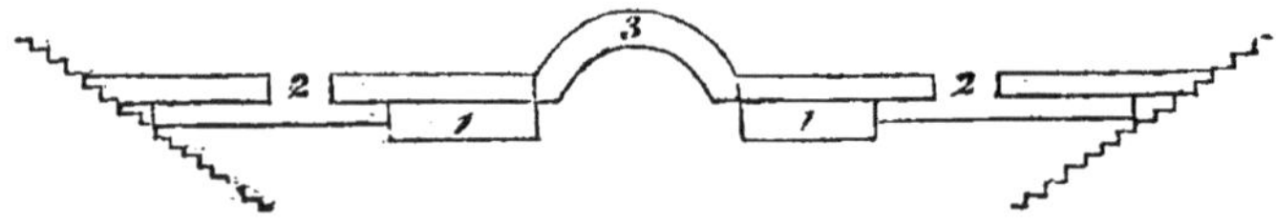

1. The pedestals. 2. The doors in the proscenium. 3. A large opening in the middle of the proscenium, commanding a splendid view from the theatre along the stadium (No. 3. in the former plan) to the city, with its Acropolis and many temples.

On either side of the stadium are the ranges of seats for the spectators, rising one above the other (No. 4.), forming an avenue for the view from the theatre. These seats are raised upon fine stone arches, which served as the entrances to the stadium.

There are still standing three bridges across the river (No. 8.) which meandered through the city (No. 9.), its banks having been lined with finely ornamented masoury. The subjects of the ornaments in the architecture of the city, which are abundant, are taken from sports and games. Panthers, lions, dogs, eagles, and Bacchanalian figures are carved in the friezes. Among these are many fronts of tombs sculptured as doors, with panels and devices, having inscriptions*.

I copied another inscription from a similar doorway.

ΩΜΙΑΜΑΡΣΥΑΜΝΗΜΗΣΧΑΡΙΝƎ///// †

The following had formed part of a frieze over an entrance, probably of a temple.

ΚΑΙΑΡΤΕΜΙΔΙΚΑΙΤΟΔΗ/// ‡

Another was cut on the front of a pedestal, which now

* Perhaps, "Crito to his brother Julius Lucianus, in token of remembrance."

† "To Omias, son of Marsyas, in token of remembrance * * *"

‡ "And to Diana and * * *"

stands near a small building serving as the mosque for the present inhabitants of the village.

ΚΟΥΑΡ
OLKAIϹA
ΓΟΥΡΝΕΙΝΟϹ
ΟΝΗϹΑΑΔΕΛΦω
ΙΝΗΜΗϹΧΑ
ΡΙΝ*

Upon the top of this pedestal the muezzin ascends to cry the hour of prayer, as from the minaret.

I saw no trace of the tombs or architecture of the Christian age, nor of any walls or fortifications. From the character of the architecture I should judge that this had been a small town devoted to amusement; I could not hear of any mineral or peculiar waters, or I might have fancied it to have been a Cheltenham of the ancients. I have seen no place so little plundered or defaced by the people of after ages, and much information might be gained here to interest the antiquarian.

At one o'clock we set out to return; and being our own guides, and in a country without road and with so few marked features, it was no easy matter to find the way. The tracks through the woods are innumerable, for the road is changed at each season as the swamps become passable; many of them are only the tracks of the woodcutters. Steering by compass however we took the right course, but the delay in climbing the hills

* "Quartus and Saturninus to their brother Onesas in token of remembrance."

in this steeple-chase mode of travelling caused us to be benighted.

Were I disposed to dwell upon personal annoyances, I might here relate our ride of twenty-five miles against a strong wind from the north-east, and getting thoroughly wet through with cold rain, which was succeeded by a heavy fall of snow: darkness came on, and we were compelled for the last ten miles to trust ourselves entirely to the guidance of our horses, being unable to distinguish the stones from the streams, many of which wound down the steep craggy rocks over which we were riding. In this manner we had to cross and re-cross thickets and swamps. But it was in our favour that our horses were approaching home; and at last we found to our great joy, that an object which in the darkness we had fancied to be a curiously shaped rock, was the wall of the citadel of Koot*á*ya. As it was ten o'clock when I arrived, wet through and miserably cold, I asked to be allowed to undress and have tea by myself, instead of in the presence of eight or nine friends of my host; my request was granted, but one or two of the sons were directed to remain with me, that I might not be lonely. My servant told me afterwards that the good gentleman was much hurt at my request, attributing it to my dislike to the society around him.

There is little to be said of Koot*á*ya. Through its streets run several rivulets, which carry away the remains of animals, often a nuisance in Turkish towns: the streets are wide, and the houses better built than usual.

Today I borrowed the only thermometer in the town (the one I have with me not being of sufficiently extensive scale) for the purpose of ascertaining the elevation of this country. I find it to be great, as I judged from the vegetation and climate it would be. The plain of Kootáya is about six thousand feet above the sea, and the hills we passed over on our way to Æzani are perhaps two thousand feet higher.

At Kootáya I have been residing in the house of a private gentleman, and have witnessed the manners of his family. On my firman being presented to the Pasha, he sent me to this house, the residence of the principal merchant, an Armenian. He was from home at the time, but I was put in possession of the place of honour, or raised floor in the principal room, which was painted like the coat of a harlequin, and surrounded with cushions; the floor being entirely covered with Turkey carpets and Persian rugs, which gave the rooms an appearance both of comfort and wealth. This house may be considered as a specimen of the house of a Turk equally as of a Greek, both being of the same construction. The family were numerous; three of the children of my host immediately surrounded me, one of them, a little girl about six years old, very pretty, and evidently the pet of the family: two sons afterwards appeared, who were men thirty years of age. The little girl told me many things, which, as she did not understand English any more than I Turkish, it was in vain for me to attempt to answer otherwise than by signs;

whereupon she very gravely left me, and going up to my servant inquired if "*Franky*" had a tongue, for he never spoke to her, although she had told him everything. Refreshments were brought in, and shortly after arrived the master of the house, a fine handsome man, who saluted me with great respect, and regretted that I had dined before he came home, but arranged that I should take my meal with him the next day. In the evening he had many visitors, and sent for a Neapolitan quack doctor in compliment to me, saying that he spoke European languages. The doctor and the other guests sat until twelve o'clock: how often I wished them away, that I might go to bed! I did not know a word that was said, but had to receive the compliments and farewells of each guest, the purpose of whose visit was evidently to see the European. My servant, who is at his request called in the firman my dragoman, made himself very entertaining, and was in consequence a welcome guest; for the people are delighted to be talked to, and have not the slightest idea of the luxury of being alone. They are extremely sociable, and never read or write, which renders them very dependent upon each other for amusement. I longed to be alone, even in the den-like rooms of a khan, that I might write, draw, and go to bed; but this was impossible whilst every eye was watching, although with the most refined politeness, my slightest movement. If I was by chance left alone for five minutes, an apology was made, or the children sent in that I might not feel lonely. At breakfast two of the sons watched every mouthful, until I literally could hardly swallow my food; and all this attention proceeded from politeness. I dislike this system of being lodged with a private family under the authority of a firman, and, having once availed myself of it, shall return to my former custom of occupying empty houses or khans, rather than be the forced and probably unwelcome guest of a stranger, as I am here.

During my toilet I saw that the sons were watching every act, and anticipated every wish, except their absence. I quite dreaded the *tête-à-tête* dinner with the head of the house, neither of us understanding a single word of each other's language. When the time arrived, the father entered with his pet child, who was sent to kiss my hand, or put it to her lips and forehead; the father, respectfully saluting me, took his seat on the opposite side of the tray, which was placed on a little stool about six inches high. We each had a plate, knife, fork, and spoon, the three former being seldom, and then with great difficulty, used by my *vis-à-vis*. When the soup, which stood in the middle, was uncovered, my host, having arranged a napkin over his breast and pulled up his sleeve, set the example of dipping into the tureen, and then I did the same, wishing that it was nearer to me. After each dish he saluted me by passing his hand to his breast, mouth, and forehead,—indicating the devotion of heart, lips, and head to my service: the eldest son, who waited most humbly upon us, watched my movements as closely as a dog expecting its share of every mouthful. A dish of brain-fritters succeeded; chickens, birds (which we had shot), pelaf, and sweets followed. When our formal meal was over, the son brought a basin, having a false bottom like an inverted colander, at the top of which lay a

piece of soap; also a water-ewer, and a towel handsomely embroidered with gold. The basin was first presented to me, and the son continued to pour water through my hands; my host made a longer ceremony of it. In the operation of washing is seen a strong instance of the delicacy of this nation; so great is their horror of anything unclean, that by the contrivance above referred to they avoid even the sight of the soiled water, into which among other nations the hands are repeatedly dipped. In the fonts at the mosques the water always trickles through the hands from the tap of a cistern, thus avoiding the inconvenience of the former mode, which requires the assistance of a servant in washing the hands. After we had completed our meal, two of the sons, the child, and my servant ate theirs at the lower part of the room, attended by numerous servants. The sons alone are privileged to wait upon their father, filling his pipe, presenting his coffee, and sitting looking at him for hours together; and they never all leave the room while he remains. A servant seldom or never enters the apartment unless to attend to the fire.

The cooking is excellent, and nothing objectionable is met with in it; no garlic of Italy, sour greens of Germany, or unknown compounds of France. The kymack is excellent here, and is fully an inch thick; I see it sold in the bazaars in plates, as our cream-cheeses are, scantily scattered over with carraway seeds. The bread is all good, but the common bread is peculiar in appearance, being as thin and soft as a Derbyshire oat-cake: meat, eggs, etc. are brought to table wrapped up in it, in the manner in which fish is folded in a napkin; its taste is the same as that of the other bread, being made of pure wheaten flour. I observe that many persons here form this bread into a kind of cone, which serves as a spoon or fork in eating their almost liquid food, thus keeping their fingers clean.

On Tuesday, March 27th, I left Koot*á*ya for Altuntash. The road was toward the south, and very like the one to Æzani, there being not the slightest change in the nature of the soil or its produce. We passed over various hills, descending frequently to cross a rapid river, whose course showed that we were gradually attaining a higher elevation; and at thirty miles' distance we entered the extensive plain in which the few huts of Altuntash stand. This perfectly level plain must be at least fifty miles long and twenty wide, and these extensive flats occur perhaps six thousand feet above the sea. The spring has not yet arrived; a few men are at work ploughing, but the country has at present the appearance of the Downs at Brighton during the winter, there being not a tree to be seen.

Birds of endless variety, many of them unknown to me in England, form the only objects of interest to the traveller. I observed partridges with black heads, wings and legs, brownish backs, and white breasts; another bird with a forked tail (probably the pratincole); a species of plover, very different from the one common with us, which also is here seen in myriads; a little bird with white body and black wings and head*; the red duck, and flocks of geese, ducks, snipes, and other water-fowl. I found here the common cuckoo at an earlier season and in colder weather than it meets on its visits to England. I counted a hundred and eighty storks† fishing or feeding in one small swampy place not an acre in extent. The land here is used principally for breeding and grazing cattle, which are to be seen in herds of many hundreds.

The village of Altuntash consists of a number of large

* Muscicapa leuconotus, or White-backed Flycatcher.

† Ciconia alba.

flat-roofed huts and cattle-sheds, on the tops of which are placed stacks of provender in the form of large haycocks. The people sit and indeed spend much of their time upon the tops of the buildings, probably on account of the frequent floods and the dampness of the ground, as well as because from this slight elevation they can command a view of the whole plain with their herds of cattle. Here I had the usual present of kymack, in the middle of which was an excellent honeycomb. My servant went out to shoot birds, and at breakfast-time brought back six starlings for dinner, and three rare birds, which he has since skinned for stuffing; among them are the spur-winged plover* and a grey hawk.

March 28th.—The road for thirty-six miles beyond this village was only varied by being still more dreary; we have scarcely seen a single tree, and not a flower. The stalks of last year's opium crops and the brown grass covered the earth, partly concealing the stratum of opaque agate-stone, which on some of the most elevated parts of the hills varied to veins of a hard, burnt, slaty substance. On entering the village of Sichanleé all the walls are of grey scoria or lava, the same as I observed near Léfky and Oneóenoo; here are also rocks rising with crags, formed by the perpendicular strata, such as I noticed on quitting the range of Olympus. I am now on the range of Taurus. My route has hitherto been directly across this table-land, entirely of volcanic

* Charadrius cristatus, or Crested Plover.

production, for above one hundred miles, besides travelling thirty miles east, and as far west, without seeing its bounds. Sichanleé is another village consisting only of a few cattle-sheds, and has its plain of thirty miles in width extending before it.

March 29th.—Another day's ride of forty-four miles has been still more dreary, with not a flower and scarcely a tree in the whole distance. For the first ten miles I passed a series of hills formed of a variety of loose stones, principally of grey lava, then a long plain with no vegetation at present springing, the land being used only for rearing cattle and growing poppies for opium. The town of Sandookleé stands at the end of a plain, backed by the high and now snow-covered mountains of the Taurus range. The branches of the chain which have crossed our road are of a spurious kind of granite very similar to that at Pergamus, which country also I judged to be volcanic, after having seen it from the range of mountains at the back of the city looking towards the north-east. I have mentioned finding at Enáe many basaltic columns, and that the agates used in the straw-cutting machines were brought from the neighbourhood, or from the other side of the mountain, which I know to be granite; this may probably bring Ida also into the range bounding to the north-west, the immense tract of volcanic production. I shall be heartily glad to leave it, and to reach a climate more genial both to vegetable and animal life.

I am now writing in a room in Bállook, the most

dreary of villages. Tomorrow I shall descend, and expect to find a great difference in the season; a month ago the trees were bursting into leaf in the west country, and above two months since at Syra the corn was beginning to show the ear, whilst here they have only in a few places now begun to plough and sow.

I am at this moment sitting at dinner, stared at by fourteen Turks, all complimentary visitors, who have watched every mouthful I have taken, and are now secretly looking at and talking of me. I was so much annoyed at Altuntash the night before last by this custom of the country, and by the repetition of it by the people again appearing the next morning early with cream and honey as an excuse for remaining to see me dress, that I determined to put a stop to it, at the risk of offending them, rather than have a number of men waiting to see me turn out of my bed; and I gave directions to my servant accordingly. On inquiring afterwards how he had kept them out, I found that he had represented me as unwell, and not able to bear the talking; and thus both I and my servant were left to pursue our occupations undisturbed. These people are so sociable that no one is ever alone, and I believe that I must occasionally represent myself as an invalid, in order to get time for writing and the other occupations of a traveller.

March 30th, Catchíburloo (meaning Goat-country).—I have travelled another day thirty-six miles, and am still in the mountains, having scarcely seen a tree the whole way; the road lay over a series of gentle hills and long valleys bounded on either side by high mountains, covered with snow, their summits of marble and of a porous weather-beaten limestone, stratified and cavernous. The long plain of Dumbári-ovasy (the Buffalo-plain) has several villages along its line, placed on the declivity of its bounding hills, and all known by the general name of Dumbári; we passed through one, and I inquired for ruins, but none were to be heard of. I rode to the burial-ground, as the best index of the age of the neighbouring places, but no "old stones" were to be found there. I noticed a number of newly-formed graves, two then open ready for the dead; and on turning round, saw assembled a multitude of people advancing towards me; as they approached the graves they paused to pray, setting down two biers. They probably formed the whole population of the place, perhaps with the addition of friends from the neighbouring villages. I soon learned that the plague had been some time in the valley, and that the persons whose bodies were now brought for burial had died that morning. Hearing this I did not cross over to another village opposite, although I understand several relics of an ancient town exist there. The next burial-ground we passed had also a long row of newly-formed graves. The plague had visited Sandookleé, the town we had passed at the head of the valley two months before; finding however, on my approach to this place (Catchíburloo), that no case had occurred here for a month,

I have not thought it necessary to pitch my tent, allowing my servant, who is rather an alarmist, to ride forward and inquire into the state of the village.

Without discussing the causes of the disease, I will notice the seasons and situations in which I meet with it. The country I have passed is certainly from five to six thousand feet above the sea, the first part of the road being by no means damp or swampy. The whole country is very thinly inhabited, and has at this season no vegetation, for the winter is not yet over; the ground each morning is covered with white frost, and a sharp easterly wind prevails. I have seen no part of Asia Minor more cleanly, or where the streets are freer from animal remains. The earth is a porous limestone, and the water seems excellent everywhere. I have remarked the bread for its peculiar goodness; it is made wholly of wheaten flour; the pelaf is here, as in other parts, the general food. On entering the first village, where I found the plague raging, I noticed to my servant that I thought it unlikely we should find ruins there, for the houses appeared built in the fields, the streets had spaces of grass, and each house was detached; the whole village standing on the gentle slope of the hill, with no rivers or water in sight.

While waiting for horses this morning, I climbed up the rock in the town to see the lake anciently called Ascania and its scenery, which is very beautiful. Whilst contemplating the view, looking down upon the village just under me, I saw twenty or thirty people assembled there. From a house near to the one I had occupied they brought out a body and carried it to the grave. They buried it without coffin, and I observed the body bend when lowered into the grave; this might have been caused by the washing in warm water which took place at the door of the house. The man had died in the night, and I was not sorry to see our horses loading and at the door, where I found my servant in great alarm, and anxious to escape from the town.

CHAPTER VI.

PISIDIA.

Journey to Sparta—Reception of a Governor at his Province—Honesty of the People—Singular Pass of the Mountains—Alaysoón—Ruins of Sagalassus—Natural History.

My maps are very incorrect as to the direction of the lake and town of Boodoór. I noticed the surrounding localities on my way to Sparta, which lay to the south-east, over a range of limestone mountains variously acted upon by volcanic heat; some parts cracked into small atoms, others split into slabs like flagstones, having a wavy surface, as if caused by water, similar to the stones in the Weald of Sussex: a great portion is broken into flakes resembling slaked lime, and there are many hills of sand; washed stones also of all kinds, with much volcanic production, are scattered around. The valley of Sparta is beautiful compared with the country through which I have lately passed; the season here is a degree forwarder, and the almond-trees are just coming into bloom; at Smyrna and on the western coast two months since they were nearly out of blossom. No other vegetation is yet bursting, but the walnuts and magnificent planes must be beautiful in their season. I have been much annoyed by travelling in advance of a Governor of this district, whose Tartar or courier has just preceded me, securing thirty-four horses; and until they were supplied I could not have mine; but after a few hours' delay I have always obtained them. On entering this valley we found thirty or forty of the principal inhabitants waiting the arrival of their new Governor, to escort him across the plain, about three miles, to the town. Among the group of full-dressed Turks sitting on the ground, with their gaily-caparisoned horses feeding by their sides, were about a hundred young lambs and kids, which on the first appearance of the cavalcade were to be slaughtered, and presented to the Governor, each by its owner, with a view to secure the favour of the new despot.

The town of Sparta is better built than any I have before seen in this country, perhaps owing to the use of stone in the construction of the houses; but it is the stone as washed down the hills, and not hewn; and an inner plastering of mud is added to fill up the crevices. Many of the houses have large gardens filled with trees, which give the town the appearance of a wood. Streams of water run through most of the streets, and the town being on the declivity of the mountain, there are many mills erected upon them. I lodged about a mile up one of these rivers, at the house of the owner of a mill, a man of considerable property, quite a character; having been a slave some years in Moscow, he fancied he had seen all Europe, and that England and France were parts of Russia; indeed I find that this people generally know no distinction between the various European nations.

Few traces of antiquity are found here: from a rich Corinthian cornice I copied the following inscription, which was evidently of a later date than the work of the frieze.

ΥΠΕΡΜΝΗΜΗΕΚΑΙΑΝΑΠΑΥϹΕѠϹΠΑΥΛοΥΕΠΙΚЅΔΙΟΥΑΝΕ
ΚΤΙϹΕΝΤΟΝΝΑΟΝΤѠΝΑΡΧΑΝΓΕΛѠΝΙΝΔЅΓ *

I had great difficulty in obtaining hòrses, owing to a Pasha passing through Sparta to Adalia; but after a delay of three hours, by half-past nine o'clock I was on my way to Alaysoón. I notice the following incident as illustrating the character of the people. About three miles from the town my servant found that his greatcoat had fallen from his horse; riding back for two miles, he saw a poor man bringing wood and charcoal from the hills upon asses. On asking him if he had seen the coat, he said that he had found it, and had taken it to a water-mill on the road-side, having shown it to all the persons he met, that they might assist in finding its owner; on offering him money, he refused it, saying with great simplicity that the coat

* "For the commemoration and the repose of Paul Epicadius: he built the temple of the Archangels." The last five letters may mean the date.

was not his, and that it was quite safe with the miller. My servant then rode to the house of the miller, who immediately gave it up, he also refusing to receive any reward, and saying, that he should have hung it up at the door, had he not been about to go down to the town. The honesty perhaps may not be surprising, but the refusal of money is certainly a trait of character which has not been assigned to the Turks.

The road to Alaysoón was most singular. For eight or nine miles it lay up the bed of the river, on each side of which the mountains rose abruptly. The ravine was at first monotonous, but afterwards assumed a bold and highly interesting character: the rocks are generally of marble, and some of common limestone, with veins of marble running through them in all directions; the whole of the mountains are stratified, and thrown about in the wildest manner. But the most singular features in this district are the mountains of volcanic dust, which I saw at ten miles' distance, looking as if they were smoking; this appearance being caused by the sand, which with every little wind is blown into clouds, and carried into the air and along the valleys. Out of these hills rise jagged points of marble rocks, each of which forms a nucleus of the drifting sand. This dust occasionally almost blinded us; and I observe that the people ride with their faces covered with handkerchiefs, or wait till the cloud of dust has passed. The whole of this light sand or dust is tufa, the dust of the pumice-stone, and a volcanic production; the decomposed lime has in many parts mixed with this tufa, and formed hills of Roman cement: perhaps nature first suggested this invention to the Romans, and we have learned it from their works. Pieces of pumice-stone were united by this cement, so as to form cliffs and cavernous rocks some hundred feet in height. It seemed to me that there was here every variety of volcanic substance, from the white and light pumice-stone to the metalliferous black basalt. The material of which these sand-hills are composed is precisely the same as that in which the city of Pompeii was buried. What may not here lie beneath its drifts! Many columns and worked stones are rolled into the river which runs at the base of these hills; and there are several caves cut with squared openings, only half-buried by the sand.

Though not a stranger to high mountain-passes, I have never experienced such cutting cold nor so strong a wind as in this pass of the Taurus range; neither I nor any of my men could ride, and we were obliged occasionally to lie down until the gusts had ceased: the very rocks of marble seemed cut by it, for they stood in shivered points, through which the wind hissed fiercely. We passed much snow, and were visited by a storm of small pieces of ice, of broken forms and transparent; this was succeeded by beating rain and snow as we descended towards the valley of Alaysoón, where in two hours we arrived thoroughly drenched. However, hearing of some ruins within a few miles, I risked the repetition of the storm, and walked about three miles again up the mountain, through a craggy wilderness, into which I feared the peasant took me only to see some tombs cut in the rocks, as the situation appeared too high and dreary for the living of any age. Tombs we did pass, and then climbed up steep hills which were covered with broken tiles, crockery of terra cotta, lamps, jugs, pieces of glass, etc., but none of sufficient value to be worth picking up. At length I saw many squared stones which had been rolled down the hills, and above me on all the overhanging rocks were the foundations of walls. What was my surprise to find, on ascending, the extensive remains of a superb city, containing seven or eight temples, and three other long buildings, ornamented with cornices and columns, and with rows of pedestals on either side! I know not what these buildings may have been, but from their forming long avenues I imagine they were agoras.

On the side of a higher hill is one of the most beautiful and perfect theatres I ever saw or heard of; the seats, and the greater part of the proscenium remain; the walls of the front have partly fallen, but the splendid cornices and statuary are but little broken. I walked almost round, in the arched lobby, entering as the people did above two thousand years ago. Eight or nine venerable walnut-trees have done some damage, by heaving up the seats. From its peculiar situation I judge that this theatre was entered only on one side, where appeared three or four vomitories together. The whole of the city, with its costly tombs and its inscriptions, both cut in the rocks and on the sarcophagi, is ancient Greek, without a vestige of Roman or Christian character. The helmet, shield, and lance, together with masks and lions' heads, varied the ornaments of the richly-worked Corinthian cornice. I observed in the agoras many of the pedestals were six-sided. The whole town was a pile of superb public buildings, arranged in excellent taste, both for seeing and being seen; the ruins are, for so elevated a spot, extensive, and in their mountainous situation are wildly grand. The theatre faced the south. The town has no trace of walls, but its tombs are to be seen carved in the rocks for miles around, with much architectural ornament. This must, I suppose, be the situation assigned to the ancient Sagalassus; it is now called by the Turks Boodroóm.

My guide kept earnestly begging that I would point out the stones in which he should find gold, thinking that I knew from my books where it was to be met with. The people had spent much time and trouble in cutting pedestals in pieces, imagining from their having inscriptions that they contained treasure. They have in several instances been fortunate, and I saw a split stone, which from its form had probably been a kind of altar; into this they had cut, and, concealed in a hollow in the centre, they had found, they said, much gold money. There are in the village below some traces of foundations, and many squared stones and handsome cornices, and several fluted columns lie about the fields.

I copied the following inscription from a pedestal:

ΑΥΡΗΛΙΟΝΑΝΤΩ
ΝΕΙΝΟΝΣΕΒΑΣ
////ΝΙΗΒΟΥΛΗ
////ΟΔΗΜΟΣ*

In the burial-grounds I saw some Christian columns; and a large handsome trough in the town was also of the same date, having two angels carved in the front. A number of Byzantine coins have also been found in the town. How much it is to be regretted that the introduction of a Divine religion should have unnecessarily put to flight all the divinity of art! The language of Demetrius of Ephesus was prophetic. In architecture and in sculpture the Cross is a brand always attended by deformity in proportion, and total want of simplicity in ornament.

April 1*st*.—We left the valley of Alaysoón in a snow-storm, which had covered the ground nearly a foot deep; and, after mounting a hill towards the south, descended into another valley, in which no snow had fallen, and where the wheat was six inches high, while in the country through which we had passed it had not even been sown. The mountains were also beginning to be clothed with trees, but no bursting leaves yet bespoke a spring in this still elevated region. Another valley succeeded, and the country became far more pic-

* This appears to be of the date of the emperor Aurelius Antoninus.

turesque than any that we had passed through for many weeks. The village of Sádecooe lay on our right. I here first saw the common black crows of Europe; also many red ducks, and a white vulture* with black wing-feathers: my servant shot one of the small black and white birds which we had seen frequently in this mountain region, the white-backed flycatcher.

* Neophron Percnopterus, or Egyptian Vulture.

CHAPTER VII.

PAMPHYLIA.

Arrival at Booják—Visit to the Ruins of a splendid City, probably Selge—Beérmargy—Descent of the Taurus range—Plains of Pamphylia—Adalia—Visit to the Pasha—Botany—Excursion to ancient Cities, probably Perge, Isionda, Pednelissus, Syllium, Side, and Aspendus—Return to Adalia—Domestic manners of a Greek Family—Departure.

After travelling twenty-four miles to the south-east we arrived at the village of Booják. Leaving here my baggage I started with a guide to visit some extensive ruins, which I heard lay about ten miles towards the north-east. The road was highly picturesque, traversing pine-forests, and ascending the whole way, commanded views of various chains of mountains and their cultivated valleys. After passing a rocky plain we entered a wood or wilderness of shrubs, and suddenly came to a cliff of the greatest perpendicular height that I had ever looked over; no description can give an idea of the place. I was at the end of a ridge of mountains of white marble, which terminate abruptly in a deep and rich valley, with villages, of which Dávre appeared the largest, and having only one side accessible, the other three rising perpendicularly, perhaps a thousand feet.

Upon this promontory stood one of the finest cities that probably ever existed, now presenting magnificent wrecks of grandeur. I rode for at least three miles through a part of the city which was one pile of temples, theatres, and buildings, vying with each other in splendour; the elevated site for such a city is quite unaccountable to me. The material of these ruins, like those near Alaysoón, had suffered much from exposure to the elements, being grey with a lichen which has eaten into the marble, and entirely destroyed the surface and inscriptions; but the scale, the simple grandeur, and the uniform beauty of style bespoke its date to be the early Greek. The sculptured cornices frequently contain groups of figures fighting, wearing helmets and body-armour, with shields and long spears; from the ill-proportioned figures and general appearance, they must rank in date with the Ægina marbles now at Munich. The ruins are so thickly strewn that little cultivation is practicable, but in the areas of theatres, cellas of temples, and any space where a plough can be used, the wheat is springing up. The general style of the temples is Corinthian, but not so florid as in less ancient towns. The tombs are scattered for a mile from the town, and are of many kinds, some cut in chambers in the face of the rock, others sarcophagi of the heaviest form; they have had inscriptions, and the ornaments are almost all martial; several seats remain amongst

TOMBS IN PAMPHYLIA.

John Murray London 1839

the tombs. I can scarcely guess the number of temples or columned buildings in the town, but I certainly traced fifty or sixty; and in places where there were no remains above the surface I frequently saw vast arched vaults, similar to those forming the foundations of great public buildings. Although apparently unnecessary for defence, the town has had strong walls, partly built with large stones in the Cyclopean mode. There is no trace of any successors to the earliest occupants. I never conceived so high an idea of the works of the ancients as from my visit to this place, standing as it does in a situation, as it were, above the world.

It is difficult to state the exact situation of the town by reference to the present imperfect mass. A snowy mountain, called by the Turks Dourraz, is due north. Castledar lies west-south-west, Sparta is towards the north-west.

On leaving Boojăk we returned to the road at the other end of the valley, and passed southward through an opening in the mountains into another valley, and afterwards a third, each somewhat forwarder in vegetation than the one preceding it. We were assailed by children, who ran down from the tents in the mountain, bringing bunches of flowers of an unsightly kind, but with so sweet a scent, resembling that of a honeycomb, that they are much esteemed by the Turks: they are a species of the grape, or musk, hyacinth*.

* Muscari moschatum.

At the end of twenty-four miles we arrived at Beérmargy, where we changed horses, having as usual a dinner presented by the postmaster, consisting of soup, pelaf, yohoot and sweets, while the horses were loading, which is a rather tardy operation. From this place to Adalia I found there were four ways; I took one which was circuitous, hearing that it led by some ruins, and a picturesque pass through the mountains. The village which would have been our halting-place was at this season deserted, and the inhabitants were encamped some miles below: being independent with my tent, I determined to take this route and join their camp. Here, as well as upon the highest of the mountains near Sparta, I observed the tortoise pursuing its heavy course across the road; in this district it is of a larger size than those at Troy.

After crossing the valley for perhaps four miles, we suddenly entered a pass between the mountains, which diminished in width until cliffs almost perpendicular inclosed us on either side. The descent became so abrupt that we were compelled to dismount and walk for two hours, during which time we continued rapidly descending an ancient paved road, formed principally of the native marble rock, but which had been perfected with large stones at a very remote age: the deep ruts of chariot-wheels were apparent in many places. The road is much worn by time; and the people of a later age, diverging from the track, have formed a road with stones very inferior both in size and arrangement.

About half an hour before I reached the plain at the foot of this mountain, a view burst upon me through the cliffs, so far exceeding the usual beauty of nature as to seem like the work of magic. I looked down from the rocky steps of the throne of winter upon the rich and verdant plain of summer, with the blue sea in the distance, and on either side, like outstretched arms, ranges of mountains bounding the bay of Pamphylia. This splendid view passed like a dream; for the continual turns in the road, and the increasing richness of the woods and vegetation, soon limited my view to a mere foreground. Nor was this without its interest; on each projecting rock stood an ancient sarcophagus, and the trees half concealed the lids and broken sculpture of innumerable tombs. A colossal recumbent lion without a head, probably having formed the top of some monument, and seats supported by the claws of lions, were amongst the ruins; in one or two places were small remains of Cyclopean walls, perhaps only foundations to perfect the natural rocks, so as to support the tombs above.

Several columns of the Corinthian order were scattered about; but even from these I was unable to ascertain the exact site of the city, which could not however have been far distant from this spot. I should have searched further, had I not anticipated finding the town in the ruins below me, to which I was directed by my guide; but on my arrival I found that these were of little interest, being slightly-built Venetian castles, with their peculiar three-pointed battlements; these are at the entrance to the pass, and are similar to many others found here, which formerly protected each of the entrances to the interior through this range of mountains. As the evening closed in we saw in the horizon a tent under a tree, and by the flickering of lights in the neighbourhood and barking dogs, we knew that we approached an encampment of the Yourooks, who, with the Turcomans, form the pastoral inhabitants of this country.

The larger tent was evidently that of the governor of the village, who with his people moves with the seasons. I rode up, and having asked his protection, pitched my tent in front of his. Cream, bread, water, and fuel were supplied to us; and here, as everywhere else, the greatest attention and hospitality were shown: I was soon surrounded with all I needed, and now, for the first time, am swinging in my hammock.

To describe the next scene I should need the talent of Scott. Looking out from my tent at ten o'clock everything was still and calm. The moon and stars had supplied their cool light, the snow-topped mountains glittered in contrast with the dark blue sky, and the horizon was only broken by the grey shrubs and the tents of the sleeping peasants. Around me lay my five horses tethered, and carefully covered with tattered but gay-coloured clothing; immediately before me was a group of seven Turks in full costume, each having a knife and large ornamented pistols in his belt, sitting round a blazing fire, on which my servant was preparing my supper, discoursing at the same time to his wondering and attentive hearers. They were a most picturesque party. Beyond them was the open, rude, black, goats'-hair tent of the chief, supported by three poles, and built up on each side with loose stones; upon the pole in front were hung his long gun and lance, or pole, and by them stood a Turk as guard. Within, upon carpets and cushions, lay the weather-beaten chief and an attendant; between them was a pan of burning charcoal, the faint light of which shone on the wreathing smoke from their pipes as it curled beneath the black roof of the tent. The scanty service of a Turkish meal glittered on the ground, indicating the finished repast; the contrasted light, the costume, and the calm of the whole scene, were more impressive than any description can represent. Notwithstanding its attractions however, my supper being announced, and the evening air cool, I soon hastened to my warm tent, and slept until four or five o'clock, when a high cold wind from the mountain reminded me of the advantage of more solid walls than those of canvas. I was glad to put on my warm dress, and to be again jogging on horseback. The plain, which from above appeared so rich, I now found to be uncultivated, a little herbage for a few miles round the encampment being the only portion suited even for depasturing the cattle.

I here witnessed the hunting of a stray ox. The man pursuing, mounted on a swift horse, had a long pole with a noose of cord at the end: after a chase of nearly two miles he succeeded in throwing the noose over the head of the breathless beast, which fell panting on the ground; the horse also seemed completely exhausted by the chase.

The bare marble rocks soon appeared on the surface, and for the next thirty miles, extending to Adalia, not an acre of land is cultivated, the whole being bare rock and stone, scarcely concealed by the small shrubs and brushwood. Goats and camels alone find food, and they are seen browsing over the whole distance. About midway on the journey the ground had a hollow sound, and I observed that it was occasionally composed of masses of lime incrusting reeds, sticks, and vegetable matter; at first this appeared to be only in partial lines, the native marble predominating, but the proportion increased until the whole track was of this composition. The vegetation now became varied, luxuriant flowers enlivened the ground, and we had the season restored to us which we left six weeks ago in the west. Rising almost imperceptibly, we were soon on the edge of an abrupt cliff of from two to three hundred feet high, which was entirely formed of the deposit upon, or petrifaction of, vegetable matter, and where the fir and oak flourished luxuriantly. Descending by a zigzag route to our former level, we found ourselves again upon the marble, and passing over a plain. The climate was delightful, but there was no soil to receive its bounties. About fifteen miles before we arrived at Adalia (where I now am) I saw a considerable river on our right hand, which we have not yet passed. The maps are very imperfect as to the rivers and towns here; with regard to roads we cannot expect any accurate information when, as I have said before, the track varies with the state of the weather. In a country where there are no roads there are always many ways; on this account a guide is indispensable, even for a short journey.

April 3rd.—Adalia, which is called by the Turks At*á*lia, I prefer to any Turkish town that I have yet visited; every house has its garden, and consequently the town has the appearance of a wood,—and of what? orange, lemon, fig, vine, and mulberry, all cultivated with the artificial care of a town garden, and now in fresh spring beauty. I see in the bazaar small green almonds; and among the fruit-trees barley is coming into ear: this was the case two months ago at Syra, which shows how greatly climate is influenced by local causes.

My first visit was to the Governor, and greatly to my annoyance he sent my servant (who had as usual presented the firman to ask a lodging) to request me to walk up and take coffee with him, until a house was appointed for me. As I could not avoid the interview, I was compelled to present myself in my travelling-dress, amidst all the servile attendants upon this eastern court, and I alone (in my dirty boots) was admitted to the raised floor. An European chair was placed for me, and I was welcomed with pipe and coffee: the first I ventured to refuse; the latter, fearing to give offence, I reluctantly tasted. The servant, on approaching to take the coffee-cup from me, when at arm's-length, placed over it a beautifully embroidered napkin about six inches square, worked with various colours mixed with gold; this was done to avoid the sight of any dregs that might be left in the cup,—one of the many customs which I have noticed amongst this people indicating excessive delicacy of manners. All who approached the Governor kissed the ground at his feet, and saluted me in the eastern form. I counted the minutes during which I thus sat to be gazed at. But soon a person appeared, to accompany me, and I was conducted to a perfect palace, belonging to a Greek, whose riches far exceeded those of the Pasha, and in which I have possession of a very large room, surrounded with ottomans and cushions placed against the walls. Here luxuries are indulged in to a great extent, though the arts have not kept pace with them; while in our country luxuries tardily follow the advances of art. The painting on the walls of my room is a most ludicrous attempt at landscape and figures.

I had not been long in my apartment before I was waited upon by two messengers from the Pasha, his physician and a friend, who sat nearly two hours talking Italian; they particularly requested that the Pasha might have my card, and that I would call upon him during my stay. I pleaded as an excuse that I had no proper dress; but it would not avail, as the Pasha was, they said, most anxious to pay attention to Europeans: he had begged them to inquire if I had every comfort provided for me, adding, that if I had not, he desired I should come to his palace. In the evening I received a note from the Pasha, written in Italian, requesting an audience, and naming three o'clock (Turk-time—meaning nine o'clock,) the following morning for the interview. I would have sacrificed much to have avoided the ceremony of this visit, but I could not; so I hastily gave a verbal answer, saying that I would send a reply in the morning, thinking it an invitation to a three o'clock dinner.

April 4th.—By eight o'clock in the morning (two o'clock, Turkish time) the Doctor called again, to know if I intended to accept the invitation of the Pasha, and offering from him the use of his kitchen, as he feared I might not like the food of the country. At nine o'clock I went with Demetrius, who acted as my interpreter, and was shown into the private house of the Pasha, who was prepared to receive me. I spent two hours with him in a very interesting manner. He is handsome, and much such a moving spirit as the Sultan. His name is Nedgib Pasha. It fortunately happened that we had many subjects of interest in common, owing to my having travelled at the same time with him through the same line of country, for it was his cavalcade that had required the supply of horses which had inconvenienced me on my journey. He seemed tolerably well acquainted with the points of interest in the country as to antiquities. I spoke of the great hospitality I had received, and expressed my wish that, as the Turks imitated our costume, we should copy their kindness to strangers. This pleased him, and he was evidently as proud of the European character of his own costume and those around him, as he was gratified by the compliment to his country. We then spoke of the natural history of the country, and he told me of the volcanic or burning mountain near Adalia. On my mentioning how much I had been interested by the peculiarities of the mountains, he became all animation, and asked if I understood minerals, and if I thought the country I had seen contained any; my slight geological knowledge served me so well in replying to this inquiry, that the people about him thought me a prophet. I told him that there could be no coal in the country through which I had passed, and that if found anywhere it would be above the marble mountains, perhaps on those towards the north-west, and not in pits as with us. This pleased the Pasha, who gave a nod to one of his attendants, and immediately servants appeared bearing baskets, pans, a candle and stove, and one a lump of coal, which I fortunately recognised as English. The Pasha said that it was so, and that he had brought it with him from Constantinople. In each of the baskets was a piece of slaty stone-coal, which he ordered to be put upon a fire, and also burnt in a candle, that I might examine it; and this he said was found high in the mountains above the marble, and just in the direction which I had suggested. Then a piece of pyrites was shown me as a supposed treasure; I told him that this substance was with us considered almost valueless, although used in some chemical manufactures, but that he would probably find much more and perhaps better coal in the same neighbourhood. Next was handed to me a large metal vase containing some sand of decomposed granite. I picked out the little crystallized quartz, but he directed my attention to the shining particles of mica. I told him whence he had obtained the granite, and what it was, and suggested that the discovery of the coal would be the most valuable; he said they had so much wood that coal would not be required by them, but that he was extremely anxious to find iron or copper, and was sure the country contained both. I said that the metallic veins were so capricious that I could not venture an opinion, but that I hoped his researches might prove as successful as his great undertaking of roads through the country, which I understood he proposed to carry to Constantinople. He then offered me a guard or servants to travel with me, who would procure me more comforts, and offered me introductions to other Pashas; but I was not about to visit the countries they governed. He then insisted upon my using his stable, in which I should find good horses, and asked my servant if it was true that I had all I desired at the house where I was, which was his banker's, adding, "Now do not tell me a lie, for if you have not what you require, I will send dinners and sweets from my own table." On my thanking him, he expressed his hope that I would call upon him again, and, instead of staying two days, would remain a month, assuring me that he would make me comfortable. He rose from his seat and accompanied me towards the door when I came away, which is quite contrary to eastern etiquette, and Demetrius says he never saw it done before by a Pasha.

I withdrew and rambled home, where I had not long arrived before the Doctor was sent to offer to be my cicerone in the town, which I declined; preferring to remain at home all day, resting and writing, and spending some time on a high stage erected at the top of the house, from which there is a splendid view. With my map I can study the whole line of coast of the bay. The town around me is seen inclosed within a double wall; but even here, in the centre, it has almost the appearance of houses in pleasure-grounds rather than of a town; perhaps the greater part is built without the walls. Scarcely a ship rides in the ancient harbour, a few boats occupying a port which has in early ages contained its fleet; the ruined towers still stand in this clearest of water.

A curious effect is produced by strong springs of fresh water rising in the sea at the distance of a few yards from the shore, causing an appearance like that seen on mixing syrup or spirit with water; the sea being so clear that the bursting of the fresh water from among the stones at the bottom, although at a great depth, is distinctly visible. I have already mentioned that the country at the back of Adalia is composed for thirty or forty miles of a mass of incrusted or petrified vegetable matter lying embosomed, as it were, in the side of the high range of marble mountains, which must originally have formed the coast of this country. As the streams, and indeed large rivers, which flow from the mountains enter the country formed of this porous mass, they almost wholly disappear beneath it; a few little streams only are kept on the surface by artificial means, for the purpose of supplying aqueducts and mills, and being carried along the plain fall over the cliffs into the sea. One of these is supposed to have been the ancient Cataractus. The course of the rivers beneath these deposited plains is continued to their termination at a short distance out at sea, where the waters of the rivers rise abundantly all along the coast, sometimes at the distance of a quarter of a mile from the shore. The bottom of the sea beyond this deposit is of marble rock, the foundation of the splendid range of the Taurus.

Friday, April 6th.—I am detained here by the illness of my servant, and am enjoying a rest in this delightful climate. I find the town is small, but clean, and more agreeable as a residence than any that I have before seen in this country. The town stands on a cliff rising sixty or eighty feet above the sea, which has no beach, but breaks against the overhanging rocks; these are apparently formed of, or incrusted by, a stalactitic deposit of lime. I have returned from a walk laden with flowers, and I now inflict upon myself the penalty of ignorance by drawing those with which I am unacquainted; it is a severe one, for their varieties are numerous, many of them being hothouse plants in England*. Among them is a shrub in growth and leaf exactly like the heath, and standing six or eight feet high, but with the flower of the cistus †. A common shrub here is a very pretty tree with a blossom resembling the lemon tree ‡. There is a great variety of the iris, the most common being a luxuriant white one, generally with three very sweet-scented flowers on one stalk; there are also the orchis, and beautiful varieties of the chickweed, and of the garlic, whose silvery flower contrasts elegantly with the green around. The plants found in this country must be indigenous, for none are cultivated. I have not seen gardens, except in this town, during my whole journey; and here they are only for the orange, fig, and vine, which are cultivated more for the shade they afford to the seats beneath them than for their beauty or fruit. The little land which is in cultivation immediately around the town seems at this season to teem with produce. I have seen here two palm-trees, but they were pointed out to me as being uncommon. I have given half a farthing for a sugar-cane which was for sale in the market, with other vegetables grown in the immediate neighbourhood of the town, for the whole cultivation lies within a mile of the

* The Anagallis cœrulea, Gladiolus communis, Pyrethrum, Astragalus, Salvia Horminum, Fumaria capreolata, Muscari comosum, Scilla maritima, Muscari botryoides, and Ornithogalum umbellatum.

† Cistus Fumana.

‡ Styrax officinale, the Gum Storax.

walls; it is most luxuriant, the climate being all that could be wished: but beyond this limit soil is wanting. The sugar-cane is grown here as a vegetable, and is stewed by the Turks in many of their sweet dishes.

In the town of Adalia are numerous fragments of ancient buildings, columns, inscriptions, and statues, which are generally built into the walls of the town with care and some taste. In the court-yard of the house in which I resided there were eighteen wooden pillars supporting the building above, and each of these had for its base an inverted capital of a Corinthian column.

I was much pleased by witnessing the mode of life and domestic happiness of one of the first persons among the Greeks in this country. The master of the family, my host, would rank as a gentleman in any country, and his wife was very ladylike. I saw five sons and two daughters, three men- and four maid-servants, and two slaves, besides one servant provided expressly to attend upon me. It was a strict fast with them, and they expressed their regret that this prevented them from inviting me to join their meals, but I had my dinner from their kitchen at any hour that I wished. The wife, who was very handsome, looked far too young to be the mother of grown-up children. The dresses of Europe would ill bear comparison with their unstudied costume, which was beautiful in its negligence, each dress differing from the others in taste, but all gaily coloured and loose, falling in the natural folds of the drapery. The use of starch or the smoothing-iron is unknown in the country. The display of wealth in the dresses may in description appear ridiculous, but the effect was classical. The cap of the mother was formed of Turkish gold coins, the intrinsic value of which must have been at least £150; it partially covered the forehead and hung down the sides of the face: the coins were arranged as scales of fish or armour, and long chains or a négligé of the same hung from the neck down to the waist with a larger coin in the centre. The children had the same display of rich ornaments; even the one in arms had almost a helmet of gold coins.

The two slaves, who formed part of the establishment, had only arrived the day before, and were not yet appointed to their duties; they were lying about all day basking in the sun. The Doctor during one of his calls asked if I wanted an Arab slave, as there were some very cheap ones in the town for sale, telling me that for £6 or £8 I might have a very handsome fellow. On taking my departure, I found that in my bags had been placed two or three large loaves of excellent household bread, baked expressly for me; and indeed every kind attention was paid me in so delicate a manner that I am distressed to have no opportunity of making any return for such hospitality. The obligation is painful to me; and to the surprise of Demetrius, who says that the Turks are always glad to oblige Europeans, I have persisted in preferring my former mode of rambling, to travelling under an escort from the Pasha. I however accepted the Pasha's firman, called a *Be-u-tee*, a written order for all I may require, and with this we started eastward at about ten o'clock.

It is impossible to find points at a distance from which to see Adalia, as its walls hide it, and these are completely concealed by its rich growth of trees; but the situation of the town is beautiful,—a cliff, whose top is an extensive plain, backed by another cliff at some miles' distance; and this has also its plain of many miles, reaching to the foot of the mountains. These cliffs much diminish the effect of the view of the mountain range from the sea; but in front of the town the bay is bounded by the continued chain of mountains which rise proudly from the sea. I have never seen mountains so beautiful, so poetically beautiful. I remember seeing something of the same effect in those of Carrara from the Spezia road, and again in Greece; and in each case they were, as here, of marble. These mountains have a craggy, broken form, and a grey silvery colour which gives them a delicacy of beauty quite in contrast to the bold grandeur of the granite peaks of Switzerland, or the rich beauty of the sandy rocks of England. The mountains forming the western side of the Gulf of Pamphylia rise from the sea until they are piled up to the height of Mount Climax, whose summit is now capped with snow.

Travelling due east over the plain, I saw nothing remarkable except masses of gravel united by the deposit of lime from the mountain streams, which frequently formed rocks of pudding-stone on each side of the way. There were many wild-fowl of various kinds; the most striking were the ibis, and the black and the white herons with their elegant necks and crests. There were snipes, ducks, and water-fowl in hundreds along our path; we killed some, but are reserving our shot and powder for rarer birds. Leeches are found in such abundance in this neighbourhood, that they are an important article of trade to all parts of Europe, and still more so to America.

The following imperfect inscription I found on a pedestal by the way-side near the spot supposed to have been the site of Laara, about eight miles from Adalia.

ΘΕΜΡΧ
ΣΙΟΥΦ
ΓΡΙΔΟ ΦΙΛΟ
ΗΑΤΡΙ Α
ΝΙΑ
ΟΝΒΟΜΟΙΠΑΙ
ΙΑΠΕΛΕΥΘΕ
ΟΙΤΟΠΑ[illegible]ΙΩ
ΙΚΑΙΕΥΕΗΕ
ΤΗ

Continuing my route for eight miles further, I pitched my tent amidst the ruins of Perge; near me was a small encampment of shepherds, who had brought their cattle to pasture amidst the ruins. The first object that strikes the traveller on arriving here is the extreme beauty of the situation of the ancient town, lying between and upon the sides of two hills, with an extensive valley in front, watered by the river Cestrus and backed by the mountains of the Taurus. An arch, a kind of castle, and the ruins of a temple, bespeak the vicinity of the town about half a mile before arriving at its walls. A few arches and ruins of many scattered tombs lead to an immense and beautiful theatre, the seats of which for the most part remain, rising very steeply one above the other, whence the height is more than in the usual proportion; the width is about 330 feet. Near the theatre is a stadium, or course for races, which is quite perfect, with seats along each side and also forming a circular end. This building is now used as an inclosure for nursing camels. The adjoining town is surrounded by walls and towers, some square and

others round, but the whole purely Greek, there being no trace of any later inhabitants. An enormous building, which can have been nothing but a palace of great extent, forms a conspicuous feature. The Greek shield is often seen introduced as an ornament on the walls, not placed in the centre of the tower nor having a corresponding shield at each corner, but appearing as if hung from the top *. Two or three temples may be traced, but columns are not so abundant as in most of the ruins which I have visited in this country; perhaps they may have been removed. Some cornices and sculpture which remain show the extreme richness of the ornaments.

I observed one very singular feature here which puzzled me. On entering the town I noticed a wall, which at first I thought was Cyclopean, but afterwards found to be of rock or stone, without joints ; on following it, there appeared in places some jointed stone wall, and to my surprise I discovered that this had been an aqueduct, and that the deposit from the water had formed a solid mass or cast, from which the stone walls which had formerly inclosed it had fallen away; in some places these walls remained, but were entirely incrusted in the deposit, which, having filled up the original water-course, extended over its sides, covering the whole structure, and giving the appearance of a solid stone wall. In many water-courses in the town, I found

* In Ezekiel (chap. xxvii. ver. 11.) is the following passage, referring to the colonists of Tyre, from these parts : " They hanged their shields upon thy walls round about; they have made thy beauty perfect."

the arch of masonry inclosing a solid mass of the stone formed by this deposit; and the earthen pipes which were placed upright against the buildings, some of six inches in diameter, were in many instances completely filled up, or had an opening or bore left not larger than a quill; these were probably rendered useless during the existence of the town. The tombs are scattered about for a considerable distance on each side of the city.

It was a beautiful moonlight night, and as I had undertaken to call Demetrius an hour before daylight, that he might find some ducks at their breakfast in a neighbouring stream, I was somewhat restless, and thus rendered conscious that it was a cold night. The howling and barking of the jackals and wolves around my tent lasted until daybreak. At seven o'clock Demetrius returned with his bag of ducks and snipes, and at the same time arrived a present from the neighbouring tents of kymac, milk, eggs, and bread. After my meal I narrowly escaped a tragical adventure. "Every bullet has its billet;" but none was yet billeted on me. As I stood watching the busy scene of striking the tent and packing the horses, I heard the report of a gun, and on looking round saw within two yards of me, and under the same tree, one of my hospitable Turkish neighbours with Demetrius's gun, which had been left hanging on the tree, in his hand, and with alarm strongly depicted on his countenance. All Turks understand the management of their own single-barrelled guns, but this was double-barrelled; and after having carefully let down one lock, he thought he might safely pull the trigger, and he had thus discharged the other barrel. His alarm was natural, and mine would have been as great had I been aware of my danger; the charge entered the ground within half a yard of my feet, where I saw the smoking wadding.

The scenery on leaving this town, and indeed during the whole day, has been beautiful. About two miles on the road we crossed by a ferry the very considerable river Aksoo, the ancient Cestrus, which has cut a deep bed in the rich soil of this valley. For ten miles we travelled east-south-east through a garden of wild shrubs, fruit-trees, and flowers, and then arrived at an ancient city, which I judge from the maps may be Isionda, standing upon, and up the side of, one of the many isolated hills in this singular district. It is entirely of Greek workmanship of a very early date, many of the walls being Cyclopean.

Here is a striking instance of the skill shown by the Greeks in making nature subservient to art. On approaching the city is seen a long line of wall, partly fallen, giving the appearance of strong fortifications having existed; but, on entering, it is found to be the support of a range of seats, forming one side of a long stadium; the opposite seats being cut in the rock, which rises from this theatre, the end of which is circular, as at Perge. The whole side of the rock has been built upon, and it requires close examination to ascertain where the natural rock ends, and the colossal masonry begins. There are many strong walls and towers, and several buildings which may have been either palaces or temples, although but very few columns or ornamented friezes are visible. The summit of the hill, which perhaps may be two miles in circumference, was walled; but I had not time to examine this Acropolis. I was told that the whole surface was strewn with fragments of columns, but that none were standing; the tombs are numerous, and are scattered round the town for a mile in every direction.

In this town occurs the peculiar mode of building the walls with apparently unwieldy stones; but the structure is more simple than it appears to be, consisting alternately of narrow and broad courses, the former being six or eight inches wide, the latter five or six feet, and the whole put together without cement, the joints being admirably squared. On examining the section, I found that the construction was thus:

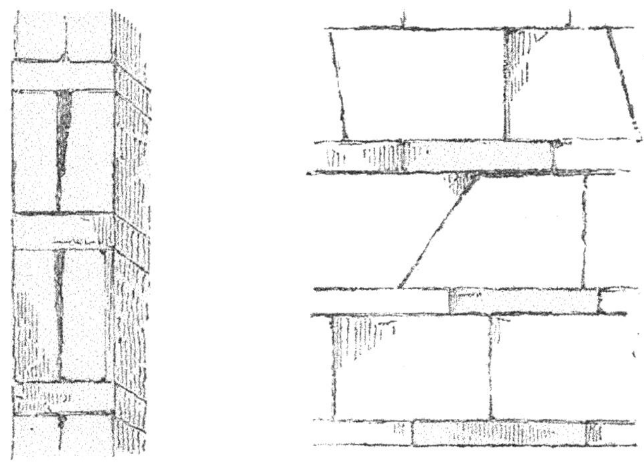

I remember to have seen in the west of England a fruit-wall built upon the same principle, but with bricks,—how different the scale!

Leaving this spot, which deserved more attention, we journeyed south-east for twenty miles over a country capable of producing anything, but with scarcely an acre cultivated. For the greater part of the distance the way was through woods, where the trees grow, die, and fall unheeded. Nature in this beautiful climate has produced a wilderness of the richest trees, shrubs, and climbing plants: I noticed seven or eight different kinds of oak; the delicate-leaved Judas-tree, with its beautiful blossom; the ash and carob; and, more abundant than any, the Siberian crab, with a great variety of the clematis and rose acacia; all intertwined with the vine and fig, so that it was difficult to distinguish the stem which supported the rich cluster. The last year's fruit hung ungathered on most of the trees, or lay decayed beneath them, the whole district being used only for the browsing of camels and goats. The myrtles were prodigious bushes; I measured several which covered a circle forty feet in diameter, the stem being as thick as my body. In no country have I ever seen or heard such multitudes of birds. The nightingales in the evening were almost an annoyance.

April 9th.—This morning at an early hour I mounted the cliff overhanging the modern village of Bolcascooe, where I had slept, to examine the extensive and heavy-looking ruins which broke the horizon when I arrived by moonlight yesterday evening. I found them extending over the whole crown of the hill, and partially down its sides, but their style is of a base age compared with the remains which I have lately seen. The scale is vast, but there is an absence of that most beautiful of all qualities simplicity. Some of the cornices are elaborately rich, and of Greek workmanship; but arch rising above arch, niche above niche, and column supporting column, plainly indicate the influence of the Romans. The remains of an aqueduct several stories high show whence the city derived its water. On the summit of the hill are many ruins of unhewn stone, massed together with cement, the arches being of brick, and the interior walls coated with stucco, which has in some instances been covered with plates of thin marble, and in others painted with red patterns in a rude style.

A kind of stadium forms a leading feature upon this Acropolis, more particularly from its having an immensely high screen or square wall at the end, which has been ornamented in front with a rich projecting marble cornice, a colonnade with a balcony above, and niches, the plaster of which yet retains its colouring of beautiful light blue. The panels of the ceiling in this colonnade still remain, and are ornamented with various devices of dolphins and sea-shells. Having seldom seen any specimen of the ceilings of ancient buildings I copied one of the many still to be seen in this place. There are very few columns remaining;

indeed, so generally were they formed of brick and plaster that I should doubt whether there have been at any age many of marble.

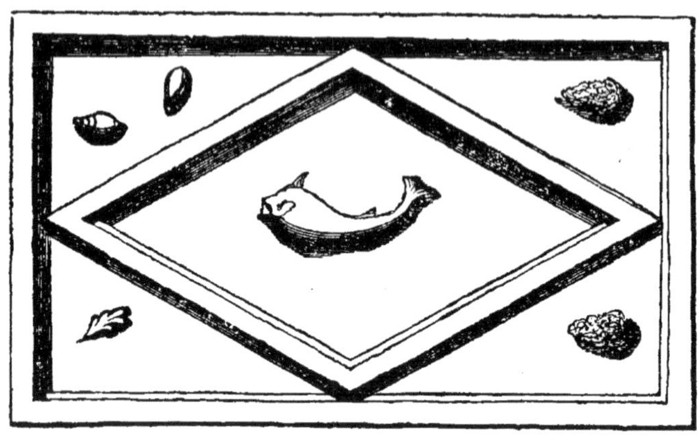

On the east side of the hill is a theatre, highly interesting from being in so excellent a state of preservation; but the architecture, particularly of the exterior, is in the worst taste. It resembles a large factory, from the number of square niches in the walls of its proscenium. Over each of the entrances in the front are long inscriptions, but the sun shone so strongly upon them, and they were so high up, that I could not see to copy them. They are partly concealed by a brick arch, probably an after-thought or addition of the architect. From the form of the letters, although Greek, I judge that the whole town must have been built after the conquest of the nation by the Romans, and after their adoption, not only of the bad taste of their conquerors, but also in part of their letters. I observed the S and V in Roman letters. On the top of the exterior are still entire the stone sockets for holding the poles which supported a screen or covering over the upper seats, as is seen in the Coliseum at Rome. In the lobby are brackets with inscriptions, but the statues which stood upon them have been removed. The remains of the inside of this theatre are far the most perfect of the kind that I have seen; indeed, the whole might be now used for its original purpose. The proscenium is very richly ornamented with niches, and a balcony or portico, all of the most elaborate designs in white marble; the ornaments are heads, masks, dolphins, flowers, and various animals. The eagle, in attitude like the Roman eagle, is several times introduced. The seats remain almost perfect, as well as the lobbies and galleries leading to them. The walls of the proscenium and sides of the theatre have been coloured, and still retain a common red pattern upon the white plaster marked out by black lines in a zigzag form; the niches have remains of a beautiful light blue upon their walls; the masks also retain their colouring. Around the top of the back seats of the theatre is a series of arches, which spring from ornamental circular brick columns, plastered over. The whole of the seats and steps, the floor of the area, together with the side doorways, and the lobbies and apartments to which they lead, are quite perfect. The other buildings in the city are all of the same date and style. In the situation of this town the maps place Pednelissus.

April 9th.—Resuming my travels through a country of the same description, I found in a wood on the side of a rocky hill two towers, and the remains of a third, elegantly built in pure Greek taste, as well as many scattered columns, which probably mark the town of Syllium. The towers, like those of Perge, were in the same style as those seen in Italy built during the middle ages; they have had pediments, and these have had their statues, which generally have been injured or destroyed: but the stones at the corners, and the fragments below, show that they have been placed there.

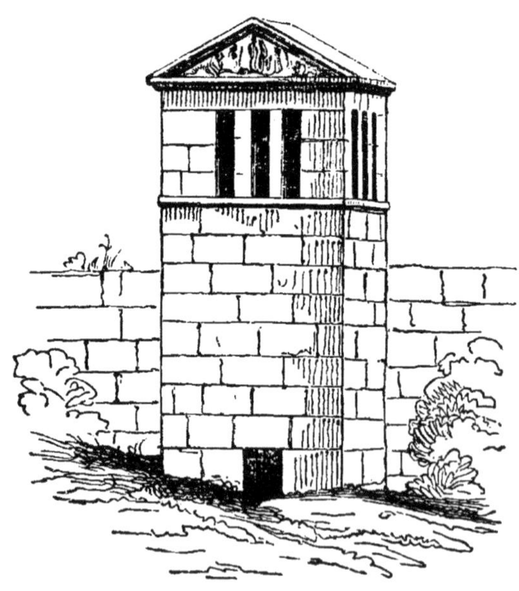

Continuing our route through this rich wilderness, we arrived at Legeláhcooe, which was about an hour's distance from Mánavgat, the post village, on one side, and Side, or Esky-Atália, on the other; the ruins of the latter being my attraction.

I have sent a man off for corn for the horses, and am now sitting in my tent, surrounded by camels, goats, and cows, the care of the inhabitants of a few tents near me; their fires are blazing, and these, with the light of a full moon, and the various rustic noises of the shepherd's pipe, camels' tinkling bells, frogs croaking, nightingales singing in the trees, and owls hooting from the ruins, and now and then a burst of alarm from all the watch-dogs at the approach of jackals or wolves, give a peculiar effect to the scene; while the open sea before and the splendid mountains behind, render the scene as picturesque as it is wildly interesting. In front of the tent Demetrius is engaged in cooking, whilst I am within writing, and enjoying all the independence of this Arab life. My pelaf of kid and a brace of wood-pigeons are brought in with some potatos, which we obtained at Constantinople; and on my finding fault with them as compared with those of England, I am informed that they come from England, the root not being yet grown in this country.

The water-jug universally used in the mountainous district, and which is always presented for me to drink from when sitting on my horse, is of primitive construction, and much resembles in form many specimens which I have seen in ancient terra cotta; it is carved out of the section of a tree or single block of wood.

There is a side pipe, which is used for drinking, and another centre pipe, larger, which, by a reversed incli-

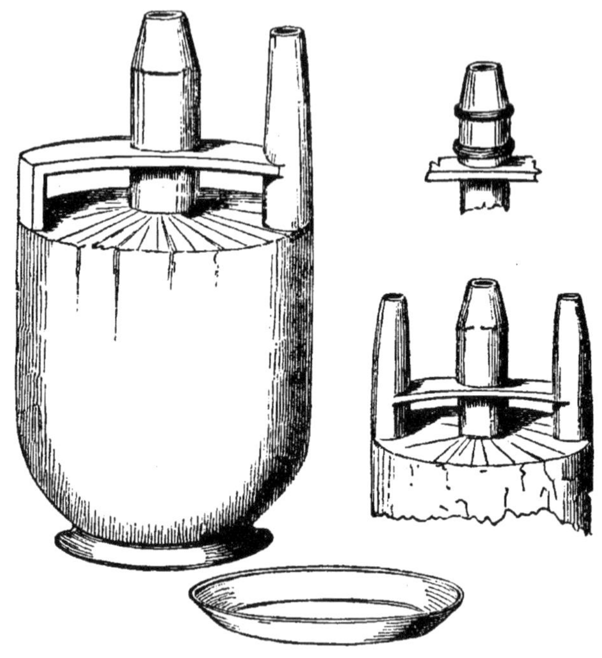

nation of the vessel, is used for pouring out the water more rapidly, the drinking-pipe admitting the air to supply the place of the fluid poured off. The heat of the sun sometimes causing cracks in this wider spout, iron rings are added to repair it; occasionally there is left on the opposite side of the vessel, perhaps for ornament, to match the drinking-pipe, a solid piece of the wood. In these various forms the Etruscan vase may be plainly recognised; which was the original, I venture not to decide. A shallow wooden bowl is often used as a cup, into which a portion of the water is poured; and as this is presented by a Greek female, with the vase in her hand, I can give it no other name than the patera of the ancients.

April 10*th.*—I this morning paid a visit of some hours to the ruins of Side, which were about a mile from the spot where my tent was pitched last night; they are far inferior in scale, date, and age to any I have before seen; the Greek style is scarcely to be traced in any of the ruins, but the Roman is visible in every part; in few buildings, except the theatre, are the stones even hewn, the cement being wholly trusted to for their support. The walls are very slight, and of a period late in Roman history; but few columns or traces of temples remain. I found a piece of a cornice, or tablet, with a small galley carved in a rude style upon it. The theatre has been fine, but is now in ruin, except the seats, which are in tolerable preservation. The whole of the area and lower parts being filled with a wood of trees, it is difficult to judge of the size, but I should think it smaller than three or four which I have seen within the last few weeks. There being no village near, nor any cultivation of the ground in the neighbourhood, the hidden relics and coins will remain for future times to discover. The rambling dwellers in tents could of course give me no information, except that lime was obtained there. I found several kilns, which are supplied from the cornices and capitals of columns, these parts being the whitest and the most easily broken up. The glowing colours in which this town is described in the "Modern Traveller," as quoted from Captain Beaufort's admirable survey, show how essential it is to know upon what standard a description is formed. It would have given Captain Beaufort much pleasure to have gone inland for a few miles, and to have seen theatres and towns in perfect preservation as compared with Side, and of so much finer architecture. From the account which he gives I was led to expect that this would form the climax of the many cities of Asia Minor, but I found its remains among the least interesting.

Returning towards Adalia I have varied the road slightly, but the features of the country continue much the same. The author to whom I have just referred speaks of this coast as being flat, sandy, and dreary; my description of a few miles inland would be remarkably the reverse of this, for I never was in a richer, and at the same time more picturesque country, independently of the interest of its remains. The tourist whose observations are made from his yacht—a common mode of visiting Asia Minor,—can see little. What opinion even of England could be formed from a survey of its coast? What resemblance is there in the bare downs of Brighton to the wooded Warwickshire or the varied beauties of Derbyshire?

On reaching the noble river Eurymedon we fell again into the track by which we had come, crossing the bridge we had before passed. The maps are all so extremely incorrect that I am unable to trace my situation upon them. Having sought in vain for a considerable lake in them, which is laid down as extending from this river to the Cestrus, I have no definite clue by which to discover the ruins of Aspendus. Arrowsmith's map places the modern village of Starus upon the site of Aspendus; but no remains of antiquity are to be heard of in the neighbourhood.

About five miles nearer to Adalia, having crossed the Cestrus, we travelled for nearly ten miles amidst hewn rocks, sometimes apparently forming tombs, but more frequently being the quarries whence building materials have been obtained. This ground must have been in the vicinity of a large city, but not even a squared stone is to be found. Last evening my tent was pitched at what is called *par excellence* "the village," originally standing on the bank of a small lake near the river Kaprisoo; but this lake is now a wilderness of reeds and occupied by water-fowl. Here we shot a woodpecker, and saw a beautiful variety of the jay or roller, of which I have kept a specimen; we also put up a jackal. The village consists of houses, five in number, with walls of wicker-work lined in the inside with mud, and with roofs of reeds. On looking around for a chimney, I saw that the moon was shining through the upper part of the walls, the mud lining only extending about three feet from the ground, though the walls were perhaps five in height; the ground was richly carpeted, and luxurious cushions were placed on either side,—at least this was the case in the hut owned by the Aga, or principal man, in which I might have claimed a lodging;

but I pitched my tent at his door, and made his house my kitchen and servants' hall. Here was the usual assemblage of persons tendering their rural fare. The kymac was somewhat different from that I had before tasted, and was excellent; it had not been allowed time to form a solid scum or crust, but had been broken up and mixed with the sugar of the grape, forming a more agreeable cream than I ever tasted at a London rout.

It is impossible for an equestrian traveller to learn more of the entomology of a country than an extremely superficial knowledge of the varieties of species. There were many butterflies already on the wing which are strangers to northern Europe, and some of the transparent-winged kinds. The insect commonly known in English port-towns by the name of cockroach or black beetle, and said to have been brought from the West Indies, is found here, as is also the bug, which has been considered by us to have come from America in the timber. I see on the trees a great variety of the cimex, and one or two kinds of dragon-fly that I do not know in England. Vermin is certainly not so abundant in the houses of the Turks as in most parts of southern Europe; indeed the people are more cleanly than other nations in similar climates. The chameleon and tortoise are frequently seen basking on the rocks.

The people in the district of this country south of the Taurus are in the peculiar state of having no settled residence, and their manners take their character from this mode of life. I have not seen a village, or even a mosque except in the city of Adalia,—the people all living in tents; and from this circumstance they are less capable of paying the prompt attention to the rites of hospitality which I have met with elsewhere, although they have the same hospitable disposition. Here the firman has lost its power, and I seldom mention it. The only difficulty however that I have had is in obtaining corn for the horses, which generally have to fare like the cattle of the district and eat grass. I have authority to demand corn, but living in their tents, the peasants do not require it, and at this season they have none for their own horses. Barley is the only corn grown for the horses in Asia Minor; I have never seen oats in the country.

April 12th.—When I returned to my hospitable entertainer at Adalia, his family were all going to their church, but they bade me welcome, and I felt myself at home again. The house gave every proof of the goodness of its inhabitants. In a bakehouse were five large tubs of flour, sufficient to furnish bread for a barrack, in process of being made into loaves, which were, according to the custom at this season (Passion-week), to be given away to the poor,—a practice followed in this house to a great extent. Seeing in one of the numerous store-rooms the large stocks of oranges, lemons, dried fruits, seeds, and corn of various kinds, I was half disposed to think my host kept a bazaar; but these were his provident winter stores still unexhausted. Over my door was an ornament formed of palm leaves, which for this week were placed conspicuously in all Greek houses. Some little children dressed up were acting the portion of the life of our Saviour which is commemorated at this season. The Greek Church still dates by the old style; therefore this, as well as all other festivals, is kept by them twelve days later than the date in our calendar.

April 13th.—On returning from a walk of four hours I saw passing my room door ten or twelve visitors, among whom were several priests, and was astonished and afflicted to hear that one of the children of my host, who was well when I left the house, had died in a choking fit, and was actually buried; the persons whom I had noticed were friends come to offer consolation. The family were in such great affliction that I at once ordered my baggage to the boat, and set out on my voyage to Tékrova.

CHAPTER VIII.

LYCIA.

Voyage to Phaselis—Olympus—Phineka Bay—State of the Peasantry—Passage of the Mountains to Antiphellus—Ruins of Patara—City of Xanthus—Inscriptions and curious Sculpture—Tombs—Cottage—Ancient Customs preserved—Explore the Valley of the Xanthus—Ancient City of Tlos—Greek Superstitions—Horses of the country—Mácry, the ancient Telmessus—Curious Tombs cut in the rocks.

April 13*th.*—It is *Friday*; on Friday I attempted to leave England, but in vain, owing to a storm; on Friday I had a wretched voyage on the sea of Marmora; on Friday I packed to leave Constantinople, but was obliged to remain; and now on the same day of the week, at six o'clock in the evening, I am sitting in my boat in the harbour of Adalia waiting for the be-u-tee, or local firman, from the Pasha; it was to meet me on the opposite side of the port, about two hundred yards from the place whence I started, but the boatmen say they dare not go further, and my Friday's voyage is at an end.

Saturday, April 14*th.*—The sun having set, the city gates were closed, and I therefore had to sleep in the guard-room. This morning at three o'clock I was fairly afloat.

The boat is well built, and has the picturesque latteen sails; the crew are four Arabs, speaking a language

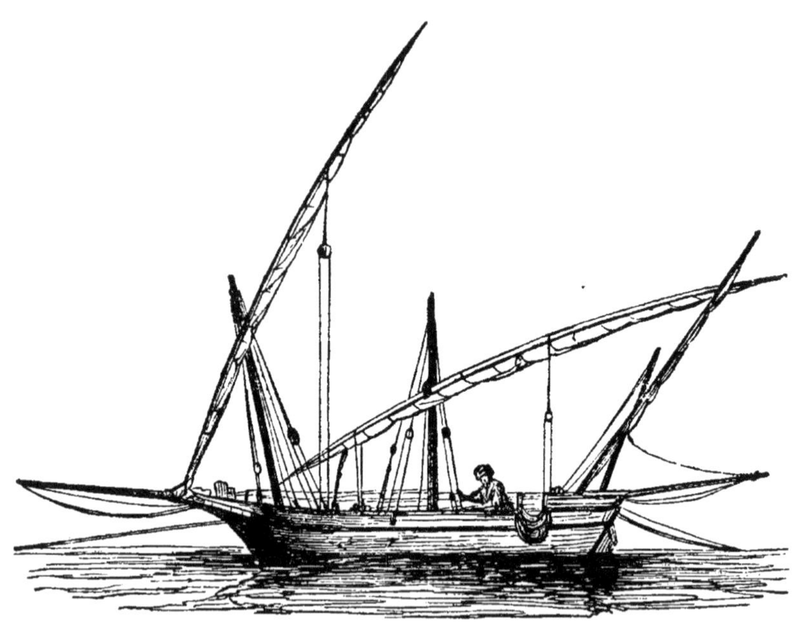

wholly Arabic, which appears made up of r's, a's, and h's, very guttural and peculiar; the name of Hassan reminded me of Eastern tales. As sailors these men are very well in a fair wind, or when once out at sea, but they were arrant cowards.

I never was at sea without forming a resolution in future to travel by land, and still necessity sometimes sends me on the water. My motives for so doing at this time were various; first to avoid, without giving offence, the presents and suite of attendants offered by the kind Pasha; in the next place the Governor represented the track by the mountains as almost impassable with baggage-horses, the usual route when the weather was calm being along the sea-shore; again, I had intended to put in at each point of interest along the coast, and also to save several days in time. These reasons combined made me forget my objection to travelling by sea; but I never become insensible to the monotony of a voyage, as compared with other travel, and continually long for its termination.

In five hours, before eight o'clock in the morning, we were at Tékrova, the ancient Phaselis. I landed, and at once saw the remains of this ancient port. In the same degree in which the ruins of the cities in the interior have raised my conception of the grandeur, both in scale, design, and execution, of the works of the ancients, the vestiges of their ports and harbours diminish my idea of their naval strength or skill. The harbour and town of Phaselis are both extremely well built and interesting, but very small; its theatre, stadium, and temples may all be traced, and its numerous tombs on the hills show how long it must have existed.

The following inscription was over a doorway *.

ΡΧΗΕΡΕΥΣ ΕΡ ΣΤΟΣΔΗ////////ΗΣΕΞΟΥΣΙΑΣ
ΙΟΤΑΥΤΟΑΞΟΡΤΟΙΡΥ//\ΞΟΣΤΟ//ΔΙΗΝΕΙΗΣ
ΤΑΤΗΡΤΑΤΛΟ////

I observed several buildings constructed of highly

* Apparently erected by one of the Emperors.

ornamented materials; this fragment of an inscription exhibits a specimen*.

The harbour is good, and the situation of the place, at the foot of a lofty range of mountains, is highly picturesque. After a ramble of a few hours I returned to my boat, and desired to sail to Déliktash, the ancient Olympus; but the men said they were afraid from the appearance of the sky that there might be wind in the evening, and that they must wait until after midnight for the land breeze, which was the safest. We therefore lay in the harbour the whole day and night, until past two o'clock the following morning; we then ventured to sail to the port of Olympus, which we reached in three hours. This town is upon a still smaller scale. I speak of the traces of the Greek town only, as several of the surrounding hills are covered with the slightly built walls and houses in ruins left by the Venetians.

* An inscription from the people of Phaselis in honour of the Emperor Adrian, grandson of Trajan (?), Proconsul (?).

The form of the Greek letters in many of the inscriptions is not of the very early date, but there are evident traces of the town having existed through many changes. One of its temples has been on a grand scale: I copied the annexed inscription from a pedestal at present standing in its doorway.

ΑΥΤΟΚΡΑΤΟΡΑΚΑΙ
ϹΑΡΑΜΑΡΚΟΝΑΥΡΞ
ΛΙΟΝΑΝΤШΝΕΝΟΝ
ϹΕΒΑϹΤΟΝΑΡΜΕΝ
ΑΚΟΝΜΗΔΙΚΟΝΠΑΡ
ΘΙΚΟΝΓΕΡΜΑΝΙΚΟΝ
ΟΛΥΝΠΗΝШΝΗΒΟΥ
ΛΗΚΑΙΟΔΗΜΟϹ
ΕΓΔШΡΕΑϹΠΛΝ
ΤΑΓΑΘΟΥΔΙϹ*

The following was upon a portion of a stone which had formed the top of a doorway.

ΤΟΗΡΩΟΝ ΦΙΛΟΚΡΑΤΟΥΣ
ΑΥΤΩΝ ΠΕΙΣΙΘΕΑΗΚΑΙ
ΓΞΟΥΣΙΑΝΕΧΕΤΩΣΑΝΑΥ†

* "The Council and the People of the Olympians [commemorate] the autocrat Cæsar, Marcus Aurelius Antoninus, August, Armenian, Median, Parthian, Germanic, * * * * * * in consequence of a * * kind gift * * twice."

† This appears to be a part of an inscription over the doorway of the family mausoleum of Philocrates, with probably a licence for his successors to use the same tomb.

Sailing round the bold rocky promontory and islands to the fine bay of Phineka, we again cast anchor, and I landed on the modern walls of a ruined fort. The objects that first struck me were the number of palm-trees which here grow wild; the leaves are luxuriant, but the trees are not very high. After searching nearly an hour for a trace of human beings, we found an old man and boy, who had hidden themselves from fear. After much explanation of our pacific intentions, the old man gave us the information we required as to the situation of the town, and then made his escape to his tent on the mountain.

Walking for two miles by the side of the river, which wound its way through a swampy meadow, we arrived at a town consisting of two or three houses, described to us as the Custom-house, the Governor's house, and some other official buildings; their erection here being accounted for by the circumstance that this is a navigable river, the only one I have yet seen on the coast of Lycia. Here for the first time I saw symptoms of trade; a few stacks of firewood being prepared to be put into two rowing boats, the whole craft of the place. All this coast is now, as of old, famed for its unctuous woods, and the Turkish name of the district expresses this quality.

Two miles across the little valley, at the foot of the mountains and up their sides, lay the ruins of the ancient Limyra, its theatre, temples, and walls. As the evening drew on I was again in my boat; but the timid sailors were afraid to venture to sea until past midnight, and after sailing for an hour the anchor was again cast in a perfectly land-locked harbour round the headland to the west; and to my surprise and annoyance I was told that, although it was but five o'clock in the morning, we must lie at anchor and wait for the next night's breeze, as there was rain in the clouds, and there might be a change of wind; these expectations were in part realized, and for twelve hours we lay exposed to beating rain and a cold easterly wind.

At the end of a long rainy day, we went on shore in the evening in search of inhabitants, and to endeavour to obtain provisions, for no birds came within our reach from the boat. After following the sound of a flock of goats for two miles through the woods, and in vain seeking the goatherds, who had hidden themselves among the rocks through fear, we at last found some tents; and after much peace-offering, and hanging the gun on a tree at a distance and sitting down to smoke, some boys appeared, and through them we communicated to the women who were in the tents our wish to buy a kid. It required some management to satisfy them that I was not come to carry away the boys for soldiers, or to seize upon the flocks, which until lately the pirates had been accustomed to do without tendering any recompense; at last I threw down some money, to them a large sum, and this was irresistible; it was equal to eighteen pence, and was to be the price of two fine kids. Sitting down to the meal they offered us of honey, bread, and youghoot, we were soon surrounded by a number of wondering children, and I saw the stained finger-nails and broad gold bracelets, or fetters, on the waving arms of the energetic females, who were giving directions through the thorns forming the walls of the tents as to the kids which were to be sacrificed to satisfy our hunger. The people through the whole of this district are in a very wild state; but still the natural, or at all events religiously habitual, character of hospitality is prominent; perhaps fear may be the next leading feature. The greatest favour that you can grant them, and one which if they dare they generally request, is the gift of a little gunpowder; my usual present is two or three charges, which they tie up with great care in the folds of the turban. From this part of the dress I have frequently seen unfolded a little paper of snuff, or perhaps their money, or any valued relic.

Here for the first time I observed that the mountains contained fossil shells, the nummulite being most common; in the rocks were also large masses of long and clear crystals radiating from a centre. The upper parts of the mountains consisted of masses of chips of the same marble as the rocks, and among them many rounded pieces, the whole held strongly together by a matrix of lime. On the shore were the decaying stems of trees much perforated by the teredo, many of its tubes being nearly a foot long.

April 17*th.*—We again put out to sea at three o'clock in the morning, and arrived by eleven at the little port of Kákava, where I determined to change my mode of travelling for one less tedious and affording more amusement. The coast we had passed presented from the sea a barren appearance, and even the outline was monotonous in its grandeur. One peculiar feature in the voyage was the effect of the extremely clear water over the white marble rocks, which here form the bottom of the sea. Upon these rocks I saw the sea-plants standing at a great depth, spread out and motionless, and the whole watery world was thickly inhabited by a great variety of shell-fish; thus was I permitted, as it were, to visit this kingdom of the deep with its crystal atmosphere.

The name Kákava applies to the whole of this district, including several islands; I believe that it signifies Partridge Country, and this bird is here very abundant. I bought of some peasants at this place a hive of excellent honey for about fifteen pence; it weighed nearly six pounds. We encamped in the ruins of one of the churches of the early Christians; and with our clothes, tent, birds' skins and bedding spread in the sun to dry, two fires burning to cook the meat, the boatmen first killing and then cooking our meal, we formed quite a busy group, which excited the attention of the peasantry, who came to share and contribute to our encampment and repast. On the arrival of the horses, for which we had sent to some tents six miles further in the country, I was rejoiced to renew my travels on *terra firma*, and discharged the boatmen, paying for the whole voyage to Mais, for the completion of which I should probably have had to wait many days for favourable winds, although the distance by land is but a ten hours' journey. I had no sooner resumed my land travels than objects of interest appeared: around me were nameless ruins, extending over a mile of coast, and containing numerous cisterns or granaries, ruined buildings, and massy tombs, telling of former extent, and marking their age as about that of the Christian æra. Among the plants found here is a species of clematis, which I noticed as an ornament in architecture peculiar to this neighbourhood; its leaves are elegantly formed, and shine like ivy, and it has thorns*. The vetch seen here is also peculiar†.

On the wild crags of the rocky mountains to the north were many strong, heavy sarcophagi of the ancient inhabitants, which had nevertheless been pillaged; the number of tombs, compared with the size of the ruined towns, would appear quite unaccountable, were it not remembered that they are as imperishable in material as in construction, and that they record not a single generation of the living, but many successive generations of the dead. Ascending for an hour we arrived on a cliff overlooking a beautiful valley of rich cornfields, which appeared as a garden amidst the barren, craggy mountains around. This singular effect was increased by the rocks rising high and perpendicularly

* Smilax aspera.

† Hippocrepis comosa.

TOMBS AT ANTIPHELLUS.

John Murray London 1838

from the valley, which was a perfect level, suggesting to the mind, what in all probability at no very remote period it was, a lake, whose deposit now bears green waving corn. Crossing this valley, in which were the tents whence we obtained our excellent horses, we again continued the ascent of the mountains for two hours, until the evening overtook us, when we pitched our tent as near as we were permitted to those of the timid peasants. Several times we were about to place it, assisted and advised by the owner of the neighbouring tent, when a voice of higher authority from the interior caused us to remove further, to be out of sight of her and her children; a bush or tree was a sufficient barrier, but without some screen the women would have been almost prisoners while we were near.

April 18*th.*—This morning we continued the ascent for two hours, and, after passing some richly wooded ravines, we rapidly descended upon the singularly beautiful but wild and barren neighbourhood of Antiphellus, an active little trading harbour for firewood, containing two or three houses for official persons, and one or two boats to communicate with the important island of Castellorizzo, a few miles from the shore. The ancient town of Antíphellus stood on a finely situated promontory, which still presents a theatre, foundations of temples, and other buildings; but the chief objects of interest in the place are the tombs, which are very numerous; and of the largest kind that I have seen. The rocks for miles round are strewn with their fragments, and many hundreds are still standing apparently unopened; but the greater number have been pillaged during the two thousand years which have elapsed since their construction: they have all Greek inscriptions, but these are generally much destroyed by the damp sea air, which has eaten away the surface of the marble. The cliff overhanging the town is also full of tombs, cut into its face, many being highly ornamented with architectural designs. The form of the sarcophagus found here is peculiar to the district of Lycia. The shape of the lid or top somewhat resembles the pointed Gothic arch. The tombs cut in the rock have some resemblance to the windows of the Elizabethan age, with their stone mullions. It is remarkable that all the tombs cut out of the face of the rock, of which the one represented in the annexed plate is a specimen, are in exact imitation of buildings of wood, the joints representing wedged ties or dovetails, and the overhanging cornices being formed like the ends of beams of round trees, producing a picturesque architectural ornament.

At two o'clock we were again ascending many thousand feet above the very striking coast, forming with its islands, bays, and promontories a perfect map, but differing materially, I am sorry to say, from any map that I have with me, as the following incident will show. When I was at Adalia, taking Arrowsmith's map, which is the best, for my guide, I hired a boat to Meis, the only place of that name mentioned in any of the maps or guide-books, and marked as the port of Mácry,

TOMBS IN LYCIA.

the town I sought; but to my surprise I find that the important island and town now under me are called by all people here—Turks, Greeks, and Arabs—Mais (Europeans call it Castello Rosso, or Castellorizzo); and this Mais, the most important place on the coast, the residence of European consuls, is more than one hundred miles to the south of the only Meis given in the maps. Travelling very slowly up the mountain I was soon again in my tent, in a winterly climate: not a leaf had yet appeared, the corn was but a few inches above the ground, and the almond-trees just bursting into bloom.

April 19*th.*—At five o'clock in the morning the wind almost carried away the tent; but we were the sooner on our way, and for eight hours travelled over the summits of the high mountains. Even here we frequently found massy tombs crowning the pinnacles of rocks, and innumerable chambers for tombs hollowed out of their hard sides, many having beautiful architectural designs cut in the rock, and others with the entrances most ingeniously concealed.

The geological character of the country varied little. The higher region contained more of the masses of conglomerate than that below, in great part composed of rolled stones. During the highest wind that I ever experienced, blowing from the south-east, we contintinned our way, and for many hours were descending rapidly and more steeply than roads could be cut; we walked much of the way, the horses leaping from step to step down the rocks. The cliffs of the deep ravines were now of a softer limestone, affording better nourishment to vegetation; and we were again in a summer climate, although the leaves and branches were stripped off, and even the trees themselves torn up as we passed along by the tremendous gusts of wind. The sea, of which we had a fine view to the north-west, was broken up into waves, and the rocks on the coast were hidden by the clouds of spray. In the afternoon we arrived at the village of Fornas, about six miles from the coast, and nearly on the level of the sea, and hence we walked over the hills to visit the ruins of Patara. About a mile from the acropolis we entered the valley, and, as we descended, the tombs surrounded us on every side. They appear from their form and innumerable inscriptions to be all Greek, but not of a fine age.

ΤΟΗΡΟΟΝΚΑΤΕΣΚΕΥΑΣΕΝ
ΜΑΥΡΙΑΣΩΝΙΑΣΟΝΟΣΔΩΣΙ
ΟΥΔΠΑΤΑΙ ΕΥΣΕΑΥΤΟΚΝΙ
ΤΗΣΥΜΒΙΩΑΥΤΟΥΜΚΙΑΛΥΡ
ΑΠΦΙΩΤΗΚΑΙΠΤΟΛΕΜΩΜΑΝ
ΠΙΤΩΜΗΛΕΝΛΕ Ι ΕΡΟΝΤΕΘΗ
ΝΑΙΗΟΦΕΙΛΕΣΒΙΤΟΙΣΚΑΤΑΧΘΟ
ΝΙΟΙΣΘΕΟΙΣΔΙΚΑΙΑ*

* "M. Aur. Jason, son of Jason Dosias, the citizen of Patara, prepared this mausoleum for himself and his consort, and [their daughter] Aphiote, and [her husband] Polemo, with a view to this, that no other should be deposited there, or he shall owe what is just to the infernal gods."

Proceeding up a valley, apparently formed by a lake, we traced the remains of many small temples in the masses of ruins, though little more than the foundations, or at most the cellas, are standing; from one of these three statues had just been dug out, and sent off to Europe. The following inscription was on the pedestal of one of them.

ΚΟΙΝΤΟΕ · ΛΙΚΙΝΝΙΟΕΕΛΕΥ
ΘΕΡΟΕΡΩΜΑΙ ΕΖΩϹΙΜΟΑΤ
ΤΑΛΟΥΠΑΤΑΡΕΙΤΘΝΠΑΤΕ
ΡΑΜΟΥΚΑΙΛΙΚΙΝΙΠΟΜΕΩ
ϹΙΜΟΝΤΟΝΑΔΕΛΦΟΜΜΘΥ
ΚΑΙΔΙΑΒΟΥΛΙΩΜΗΤΡΙ
ΜΝΗΜ ϹΕΝΕΚΕΝ*

A triple arch leads hence to the city, and the brackets upon it for busts or statues have Greek inscriptions; it is not in pure taste. Several ruins of large Christian churches are here seen in massy piles of stones, the materials of former temples. The theatre is, as usual, excavated from the hill sheltering it from the sea; but the quantity of sand brought down by the river Xanthus, and by the almost continual eddies of wind occasioned by the high mountains of the Cragus range, have formed banks of sand along the coast, which is drifted over the walls of the theatre, so that the area

* "Quintus Licinnius, a Roman citizen; to Zosimus, son of Attalus, of Patara (my father, and the father of Licinnius; Zosimus my brother); and to Diabulius my mother, for the sake of remembrance."

of it is more than half filled up, and the whole, with many other ruins, will soon be entirely buried and left for future ages to disinter. The harbour is now rich with the vegetation of shrubs, and many fine clusters of palm-trees.

The city has been extensive, but the buildings are for the most part constructed of fragments of earlier ages, when symmetry of form was better understood; no building of the early Greek age remains entire. The river Xanthus lies to the north of the city, with the once splendid bay, which is now a desert of moving sand, only marked by the silvery course of the river winding its way to the sea. Colonel Leake and other writers having mentioned that the valley of the Xanthus has not been explored by Europeans, and that cities may probably be traced near its course, I have determined to seek a route to Mácry up this valley, instead of by sea or across the range of Cragus.

April 20th.—On starting this morning from Fornas we for the first time had to take asses for our baggage, and these were procured with difficulty. For eight miles to the north-east we first skirted, and then crossed, a perfectly flat plain, without a stone upon it, no doubt formerly a bay of the sea; the accumulated sand has rendered it partially fit for cultivation, although the greater portion is still a morass; on the drier part pasturage is afforded for numerous herds of cattle. I saw thousands of snipes, whose numbers we diminished for our larder; and these being of a

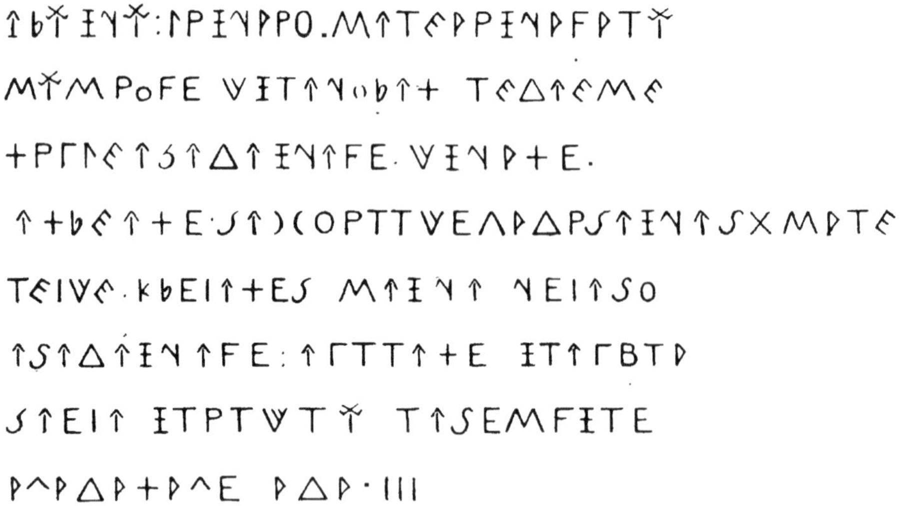

↑bϮ ΞΝϮ : ΓΡΞΝΡΡΟ . Μ↑ΤϾΡΡΞΝΡFΡΤϮ

ΜϮΜ ΡoFΕ ΨΞΤ↑ΝobΤ+ ΤϾΔ↑ϾΜϾ

+ΡΓΓϾ↑ƧΤΔ↑ ΞΝ↑FΕ · ΨΞΝ Ρ+Ε ·

↑+bϾ↑+Ε · Ƨ↑)(ΟΡΤΤΨΕΛΡΔΡƧ↑ΞΝ↑ƧΧΜΡΤϾ

ΤϾΙΨϾ · ΚbΕΙ↑+ΕƧ Μ↑ΞΝ↑ ΝΕΙ↑Ƨo

↑Ƨ↑Δ↑ΞΝ ↑FΕ : ↑ΓΤΤ↑+Ε ΞΤ↑ΓΒΤΡ

Ƨ↑ΕΙ↑ ΞΤΡΤΨΤϮ Τ↑ƧΕΜFΞΤΕ

Ρ^ΡΔΡ+Ρ^Ε ΡΔΡ · ΙΙΙ

On Rock Tomb at Xanthus.

↑ΒϮΞΝϮ : ΓΟΞΝΡFΨ : Μ↑Ν↑ΓΡΞΝFΡΤϮ

Ρ+)Κ)Ι(ΡΔΕ : ΛϾΙϾΒΕΔ↑+ . ΤΕΔ↑ΕΜϾΙƧ↑ :

+ΧΓΡΨΜ↑+ : Τo+↑Ƨ · Ƨ↑ΕΙ↑ΞΤΡΤΡΟϮ ΜΕΞΤϾ

ΡΛΡΔ↑+ΡΛΕ · ΡΔΡ Ο– . Ƨ↑ΙϮΤΡΕ · ΞΤΡΤΡ

ΡΟΡ ΙΙΙ–Ƨ↑ΓΕΙ↑ΤϮ+ ΡΙΙΕΞΤΡΨ · Λ

ΡΔϾ ↑+Β . Ƨ↑ΜΞΝ↑Ϯ↑ϾΔ↑+↑

↑Ƨ↑ΔϮΞΝ↑FΕ)Ƨ↑ΓΕΙΤϮ : ϮΤΡΕ : ΞΤΡΤϮΓΡΞ

ΡΤΛΡ+Ε :

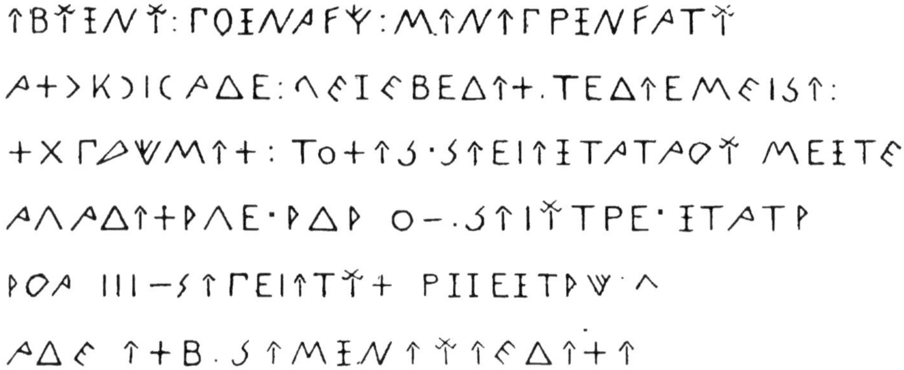

On Sarcophagus Tomb at Xanthus.

John Murray, London, 1839.

different kind to the common one in England, I have added one to my collection of skins. It was noon before we had found the Governor of the tents which form the frontier village of Kooník, when taking the riding horses, we started to see the ruins of the city of Xanthus, which lay at about two miles' distance, upon or overhanging the river of that name. The other horses were to wait our return. We had no sooner entered the place of tombs, than objects of such high interest to the antiquarian, sculptor, and artist appeared, that I determined to send for the baggage, and pitch my tent here for the night.

April 19th.—It is now noon, and I regret that I have not had time, and do not possess sufficient talent, to examine completely the objects here, which alone afford inducement to the man of taste to visit this country, even from distant England. The remains appear to be all of the same date, and that a very early one. The walls are many of them Cyclopean. The language of the innumerable and very perfect inscriptions is like the Phœnician or Etruscan, and the beautiful tombs in the rocks, on the side of the entrance of one of which is the following inscription, are also of a very early date.

Note to annexed Plate of Inscriptions.

Very learned and ingenious papers have been read upon these Lycian inscriptions, before the Royal Society of Literature in February, and before the Philological Society of London in April, 1839, by James Yates, Esq., M.A., F.R.S., &c.

↑BϮꟾИϮ : V O
PV : MϮИ ↑ΓP
ꟾИPFPT Ϯ : M↑
Δ↑ : ↑ΓꟾNϮME
↑+BE : +XΓPV
ИP : ꓘ↑IPTΛ E

The annexed plate shows the character of the tombs; they are wholly cut into, or formed by cutting away, the rock, leaving the tombs standing like works of sculpture.

In the ruins there are many parallelisms to the Persepolitan, as may be seen in this entrance of a tomb.

Drawn by Charles Fellows — Lithographed and P[illegible]

ROCK TOMBS AT XANTHUS

The elegant designs evince the talent of the Greeks, and the highly poetical subjects of the bas-reliefs, the temples, friezes, and tombs, some of them blending in one figure the forms of many, probably to describe its attributes, are also of Greek character. The ruins are wholly of temples, tombs, triumphal arches, walls, and a theatre. The site is extremely romantic, upon beautiful hills; some crowned with rocks, others rising perpendicularly from the river, which is seen winding its way down from the woody uplands, while beyond in the extreme distance are the snowy mountains in which it rises. On the west the view is bounded by the picturesquely formed but bare range of Mount Cragus, and on the east by the mountain chain extending to Patara. A rich plain, with its meandering river, carries the eye to the horizon of the sea towards the south-west.

The city has not the appearance of having been very large, but its remains show that it was highly ornamented, particularly the tombs, two of which I have put in my sketch-book somewhat in detail, as well as some other sculptures. I did not find any well-formed Greek letters; in an inscription over a gateway, and on one or two architectural stones, the Greek alphabet was used, but not the pure letters. There is no trace of the Roman or the Christian age, and yet there are points, such as the costume in the bas-relief, the attitude and appearance of groups of figures, that reminded me of the times of the Crusades and of the Romans.

I have attempted a sketch of the most beautiful of the tombs, and I add the description by pen to make my drawing more intelligible. It is a sarcophagus, entirely of white marble, standing on the side of a hill rich with wild shrubs,—the distant mountains, of the silvery grey peculiar to marble rocks, forming the background. Being finely worked, the polish has greatly assisted in its preservation from the effect of the atmosphere. The roof is somewhat grey, and the fractures of the lower parts are tinged with the shade of red which white marble assumes after long exposure to the weather, and in places with yellow blended with brown. On the top, or hog's-mane, is a hunting scene; some figures are running, others are on horseback galloping, with spears in their hands and mantles blown by the wind, chasing the stag and wild boar, which has turned to attack the pursuer; the whole of the figures, although in a small frieze, are well formed and finished. On each of the sloping sides of the roof are two stones projecting about a foot, as found on all these tombs, but which upon this are carved into lions' heads crouching on their paws; upon one side of the roof is a group in which a warrior, carrying a shield, is in the act of stepping into his chariot, which is of the early simple form, with wheels of four spokes only, and is driven by a man leaning forward, with his arms stretched out holding the reins and a whip or goad: four beautifully formed horses, prancing in various attitudes, are drawing the car. The chariot and

horses appear sculptured on the other side of the roof, differing only in the attitudes of the figures. In the upper panels at the ends or gables are traces of small carved figures. On the side of the tomb shown in the annexed sketch, under two lines of the peculiar characters of this town, (perhaps Lycian,) is a group of figures, which I will describe, beginning from the left-hand. A finely-formed figure in a simple robe, his hands folded before him, and with a head of bushy hair, stands, as if in attendance behind the chair or clawed seat of the principal figure, who, clothed in rich folded drapery, with short hair, sits in the attitude of a judge, with one arm somewhat raised; before him stand four figures: the first is mutilated, but appears similar to the second, who has long bushy hair, confined round the head, and looking like a wig; his attitude is that of a counsellor pleading for the others; the loose robe falls gracefully from one shoulder, and is thrown over, so as almost to conceal one arm; two other figures, differing only in having the hair shorter and the arms hanging down, stand apparently waiting the decision of the judge, and complete the well-formed group. At the end, on a larger scale, are two figures of warriors, clothed only with girdles of armour round their loins, and petticoats reaching nearly down to their knees, resembling the figures of the ancient Britons. The background on the same stone contains a long, but, from mutilation, partially illegible inscription, which I did not attempt to copy.

On the opposite end of the tomb are two other figures of the same size; one, clothed in a loose robe, stands in a commanding attitude fronting the spectator, with an arm raised over the head of a naked figure also standing. Were this marble found elsewhere, the group might be taken to represent the baptism of our Saviour, but the character of the figures does not support this idea, although the attitudes would be precisely correct for the ceremony.

On the other side, under a single line of inscription, is an animated battle-scene; men on horses are fighting with others on foot; all have helmets, and

those on foot have shields; some fight naked, others with a loose shirt or blouse descending below the thighs, and confined by a belt round the waist. The horse of the principal figure is ornamented with a plume, and the rider has a kind of armour to protect his legs. The groups upon the two sides are three feet six inches high, by nine feet in length. I have

rawn by Charles Fellows

ithographed and Printed by C. Hullman

FROM THEATRE AT XANTHUS.

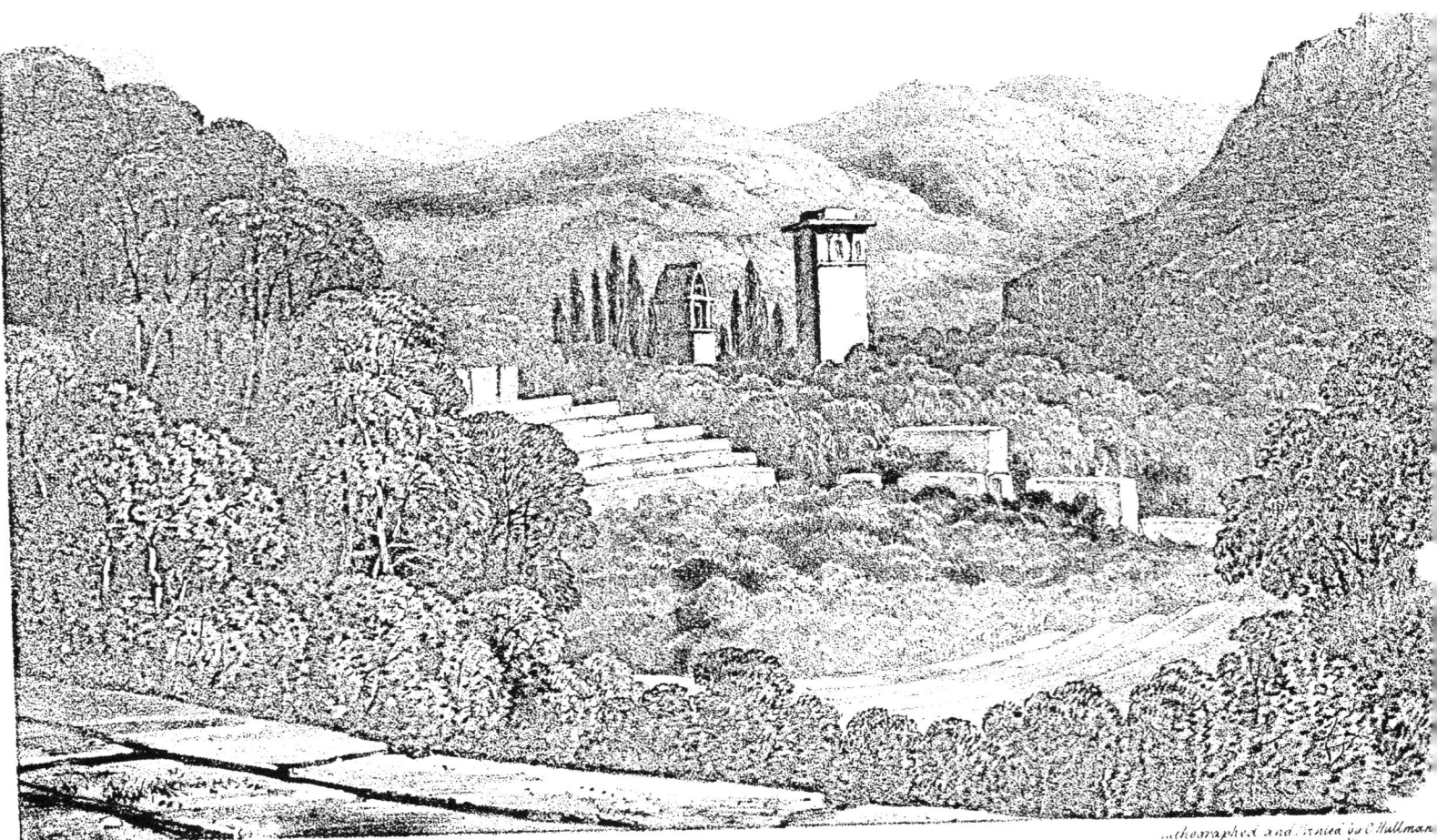

not described the architectural form, leaving that to be gathered from the sketch.

The *hog's-mane* does not at either end extend to the full length of the roof; and at each extremity of it is a

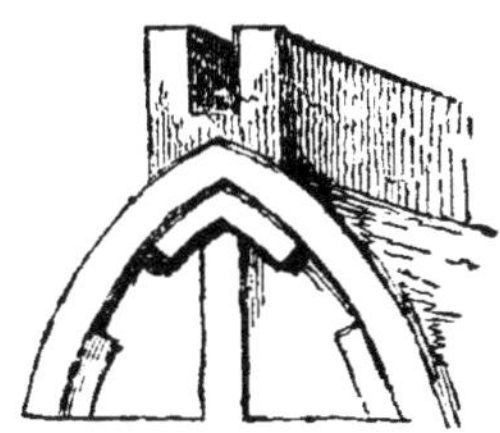

niche for attaching another stone. It is probable that there may have been at each end, when the tomb was perfect, some ornament, perhaps a helmet, or figure of an animal corresponding in character with the other subjects. It is not surprising that so beautiful a tomb should have been broken open in all parts; but as each chamber is now exposed, I trust that it may not receive further injury.

Upon another tomb, or high square pedestal, near the theatre at Xanthus, are some curious bas-reliefs, which, to assist the imperfect representation given by my drawing, I will describe. On the north and south sides are four figures of similar design; the head is that of a female with the Greek cap and hair, the breast is exposed, and the body, which terminates with the trunk, has wings and a tail like a pigeon's; from under the wings comes a bird's claw, clasping the legs of a child which is carried in the bosom of the figure: the child appears to have wings wrapt over its body, or this may perhaps be folded drapery. The figures are all flying from the centre of each group and upwards. In the middle of the south side, seated on an elegant Greek chair, is a small figure wearing a loose robe, with a long stick resting on his shoulder and two balls or fruit in his hands. A female figure draped, but much mutilated, is presenting a pigeon held by its wings. In the middle of the north side is an old man, with a peculiarly pointed beard, seated on a stool, under which is a pig; he also has loose drapery, and a stick resting against his shoulder and held in his hand: before him is the figure of a warrior delivering up his armour; in one hand he holds the helmet, in the other a mantle. On the east side an old man is seated in a chair like the one on the north side; he has one hand raised, holding what appears to be a small bird towards his face, and before him a child is presenting a cock; behind the child is a male figure and a dog tied with a string; behind the chair of the old man are two figures, one holding an apple downwards in his hand, the other raising one towards his mouth. On the west side a dignified female, having a Greek tiara on her head and loose mameluke sleeves, is seated on a cushioned arm-chair, one arm resting on it, and the other raised with the hand open towards a cow suckling its calf, which are on a small scale, and placed half way up this compartment; below this representation of the

John Murray, London

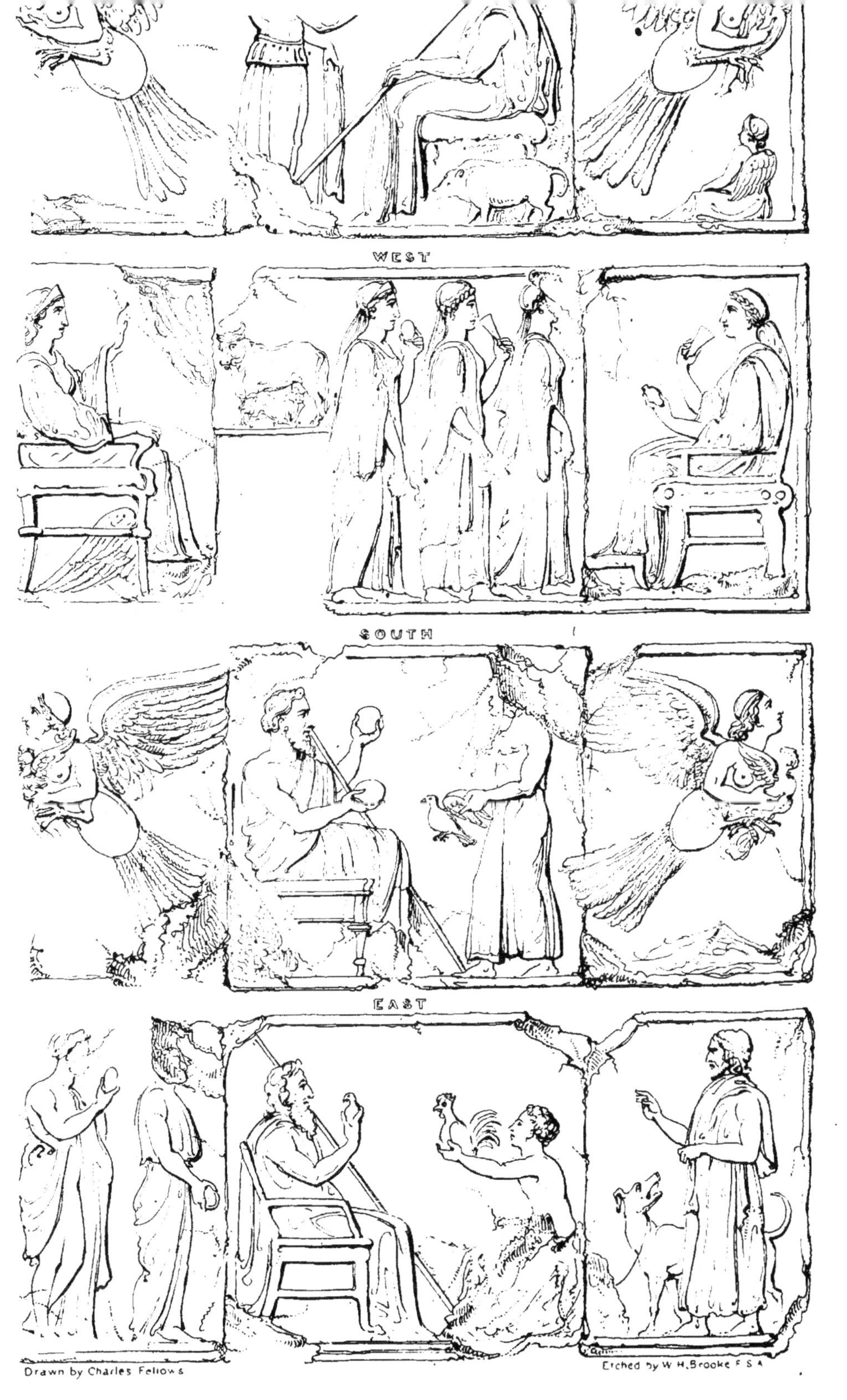

Drawn by Charles Fellows

Etched by W. H. Brooke F.S.A.

SCULPTURE ON TOMB AT XANTHUS.

cow and calf was probably the door into the tomb, which has been destroyed, leaving a squared hole; under the chair of the female are apparently the wings of a large bird. In the centre, three figures, similarly dressed, are standing or walking, each with one hand down holding fruit, and the other lifting a cup or patera towards the mouth. Before them sits a female on a handsome cushioned arm-chair, with a footstool; her hair is plaited round her head, and in one hand she has a patera, in the other a glass or cup held to the mouth. I cannot explain the design of the groups on any of the four sides, of which the centres scarcely seem to form parts, although each side is in a single bordered compartment. The figures, which are about three feet high, are well executed in white marble. The compartments, about nine feet in length, form the top of the tomb, and are raised nearly twenty feet from the ground upon a square pedestal of grey stone, and roofed with two flat stones of a similar material. There is no inscription on this tomb.

Close by this is another similar tomb, of the same dimensions, entirely covered with the singular characters used in this city. In the walls of the acropolis a great number of beautifully wrought marbles are built in as materials, without any regard to their elegant Greek sculpture. Lions, warriors, chariots, and horses are to be traced in many fragments, and birds, like our game-cocks or pheasants, fighting. On the site of a temple of rather small dimensions lay a pretty frieze, about ten or twelve feet long and one in width, representing a series of small dancing figures with flying drapery; not less than fifteen of these were remaining. This temple, standing upon the brow of a hill, and six or seven others which may still be traced along the same cliff, must have produced an exquisitely beautiful effect.

A sketch of the cottage occupied by the peasantry in this part of the country, will show that scale alone is wanting to make it the temple of the former inhabitants; the tombs cut in the rocks in successive ages are also precisely similar in architectural design.

In the houses of the Greeks only is wine to be met with, and by them it is taken far too freely. In their mode of manufacturing it another trace of antiquity is recognised. They add a flavour of turpentine, obtained from the fir-apple; this was also the custom with the ancient Greeks, and the fir-apple is found in all bacchanalian emblems surmounting the vine-wreathed thyrsus or staff of the god.

The only wheat grown in Asia Minor is bearded, and this is the peculiar kind represented in the figures of Ceres and upon ancient coins.

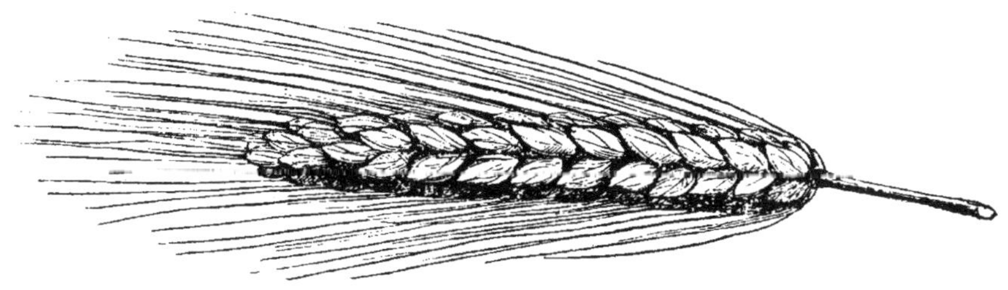

April 20*th. Demelheér.*—We have had a most beautiful ride of fifteen miles from Xanthus, crossing the river, which is of considerable size, at a ford a mile and a half below the ancient city, where its yellow turbid waters cover double the width of its usual deep bed; then turning up the valley we traced its course the whole way, scarcely diverging a mile from it, sometimes ascending hills, wooded with well-grown trees, from which were seen the many picturesque windings of the river. The valley is the most beautiful that I have seen in Asia Minor. I cannot conceive a more picturesque point than the spot where I have pitched my tent tonight, on the edge of a precipice commanding a view of the whole valley, with fine rising pasture land around, and backed by wooded mountains towards Mácry. The soil here is light, but affords good pasture for sheep; and in the valley cultivation is more attended to than in any country that I have seen for many weeks.

The people seem well off, but their life in tents gives them an independence of manners and character not very pleasing to a traveller. They are exceedingly careless about money; having enough to eat, they wish for nothing more. Both man and beast are in a most wild state. We are now at one of their encampments, and though we ordered the horses to be ready at six o'clock this morning, at seven the men had not gone for them, and there was so much difficulty in catching them, that they did not appear until one o'clock in the afternoon. They were good horses, but had no shoes, and were not accustomed to bridle or saddle; nor was the man who brought them more familiar with these equipments, for he tied my stirrups together under the horse with the girths, and did not dare to encounter the intricacy of a common bridle, but asked my guide which way upwards to put it on. The Turks have not the least ingenuity; they never apply any instrument to a double purpose, and if they see any contrivance which is new to them, they exclaim, "Allah! Allah!" even about the merest trifles.

April 21*st.*—We rode eight miles to the village of Cousk, which consists of the house and establishment of the governor of this district; and here an hour was wasted in obtaining a teskary, or local order for horses. At the next village, Doovér, we again forded the river, and gradually rising from the valley for about five miles, arrived at two or three mills, turned by the copious streams which descend from the mountains behind the ancient city, the ruins of which had attracted me to this place. It is called in the maps Pinara, but from the inscriptions I discovered it to be Tlos.

Leaving our baggage we rode up the mountain for two or three miles. A few tombs bespoke the approach to the ancient city; but its splendid and appropriate situation would alone point it out as the site of a Greek city. The remains now standing are very extensive, consisting of extremely massive buildings, suited only for palaces; the design appears to be Roman, but not the mode of building nor the inscriptions: the original city must have been demolished in very early times, and the finely-wrought fragments are now seen built into the strong walls, which have fortified the town raised upon its ruins. The theatre of the ancient city was large, and the most highly and expensively finished that I have seen; the seats not only are of marble, as has been the case in most that I have seen, but the marble is highly wrought, and has been polished, and each seat has an overhanging cornice, often supported by lions' paws. The cornices of wreaths, masks, and other designs are records of a luxurious city. There are also ruins of several other extensive buildings with columns, but their positions are not so good, and they may probably be of the date of the later town. The most striking feature in the place is the perfect honeycomb formed in the sides of the acropolis by excavated tombs, which are cut out of the rock with architectural ornaments, in the form of temples, etc., some showing considerable taste. The sketch which I have taken will convey an idea of this peculiar collection of tombs better than a written description. There were many other portions of the neighbouring rocks as much excavated as these.

Neither at Patara nor here is there the least trace of inscriptions similar to those at Xanthus; but there are several in the Greek language, which may assist in deciding the date of the place.

ΦΛΑΥΙΑΣΦΙΡΜΗΣΥΙΟΝΔΟΜΙ
ΤΙΟΥΑΠΟΜΕΙΝΑΡΙΟΥΤΟΥ
ΔΙΚΙΟΔΟΤΟΥ
ΤΛΩΕΩΝΗΒΟΥΛΗΚΑΙΗΓΕΡΟΥ
ΣΙΑΚΑΙΟΔΗΜΟΣ*

* "The Council, the Senate, and the People of the Tloeans * * [commemorate] * * [the husband?] of Flavia Firma, and son of the judge Domitius Apominarius."

Charles Fellows

C. Hullmandel

TOMBS IN THE ROCK OF ACROPOLIS AT TLOS.

ΙΟΥΛΙΑΝΤΕΡΤΥΛΛΑΝ
ΓΥΝΑΙΚΑΙΟΥΛΙΟΥΜΑΡΕΙ
ΝΟΥΤΟΥΔΙΚΑΙΟΔΟΤΟΥ
ΤΛΩΕΩΝΗΒΟΥΛΗΚΑΙΗΓΕ
ΡΟΥΣΙΑ
ΚΑΙΟΔΗΜΟΣ*

ΟΛΙΕ
ΤΛΩΕΩΝΤΟΙ
ΔΗΜΟΙΝ'ΤΙΟΝ
ΕΥΝΓΕΝΗΕΠΙ
ΤΗΔΙΗΝΕΚΕΙ
ΟΜΟΝΟΙΑ†

///ΘΗΕΠΙΤΟΥΛΑΜΠΡοΚΑΙΘΑΥΜ' ΗΓΕΜ
ΦΛ'ΚΛΕΠΟΥΔ' ΜΑΡΚΕΙΑΝΟΥ‡

On a handsome sarcophagus is the following inscription.

ΜΕΙΔΙΣΑΡΠΗΔΟΝΟΣ
ΣΕΝΕΙΔΑΡΜΑΛΝΔΡΟΕΙ
//ΥCΠΙΤΗΜΗΤΡΙ
//ΑΙΤΕΙΜΑΡΧΟΣΚΑΙ
ΣΑΡΠΗΔΩΝΟΙΦΕΡΕΚΛΙ

* "The Council, the Senate, and the People of the Tloeans [commemorate] Julia Tertulla, wife of the judge Julius Marinutus."

† " * * * to the People of the Tloeans, * * * with a view to permanent concord."

‡ "Erected in the time of the famous and wonderful general, Flavius Cassius Marcianus."

ΟΥΣΕΠΙΤΗΕΑΤΩΝΜΑ
ΜΗΦΙΛΟΣΤΟΡΠΑΣ
ΕΝΕΚΑ*

In this part of the country I have seen, to my surprise, many women with uncovered faces; they are of a peculiar and fine-looking race, the Chingunees, and appear to have none of the shyness so general among the Turkish women. Today some girls of this tribe sat down by us and sang very prettily; these singing-girls in appearance and occupation resemble the gipsies of Europe; their music has something of the character of the Tyrolean mountain airs, but softened by the Eastern language, and would be very pretty were it not for a nasal twang, which perhaps may belong only to the rural musicians. The men are itinerant tinkers: among the Greeks, both here and in Greece, they are employed as blacksmiths, a trade which is avoided by the Greeks from religious scruples. This is one of the many superstitions traditional in the Greek church, and which are perpetuated by the priests, themselves the least informed among the people. I was told by one of them as a reason for this observance, that a blacksmith made the nails used at the crucifixion, and that, having made more than were required, he and his craft were cursed. He also informed me that the mo-

* "Midi [son or daughter] of Sarpedon * * * * to a [sweet] mother: Timarchus and Sarpedon, the sons of Pherecles, to their grandmother, from love and affection."

tive for hanging up in their churches the eggs of the ostrich, which with other large eggs are constantly to be seen suspended from the roof by a long string, was that this egg is an emblem of faith; and he was surprised that I was not aware that the ostrich, after laying its egg, retires to a distance and looks at it, until by the heat of its eye the egg is hatched; this undoubted fact so strongly shows the faith of the bird, that its egg is considered a fit emblem of their religion.

The mode of burial among the Greeks also furnishes another instance of their credulity. The outward marks of respect are scarcely visible in their burial-grounds, little more being left to mark the place of interment than a row of stones, indicating the oblong form of the grave; but a pipe or chimney, generally formed of wood or earthenware, rises a few inches above the ground, and communicates with the corpse beneath; and down this tube libations are poured by the friends of the deceased to the attendant spirit of the dead. The same practice prevailed among the ancient Greeks, and is to be traced in many of their tombs. The custom of hiring women to mourn with cries and howlings, is also retained by the modern Greeks at their funerals.

April 22nd.—We were detained until half-past two o'clock today waiting for horses, which were to have been ready at six o'clock in the morning; they, like the people, are wild, and live a happy and independent life. The chase after the horses occupied the whole day, about fifty being pursued over the open plain until four were taken; three were mares entrapped by catching the foals: they were led captive by tying unfolded turbans round their necks, for none of the peasants possessed a halter.

The breeding of horses seems to be carried on to a great extent here, there being herds of many hundreds in the valley. The only kind of horse in this country is that of which such spirited representations are to be seen in the ancient marbles; there is much of the Arabian about the head; the chest is large in proportion to the fine bone of the legs, and the ears are small, as in the antique. I have not seen the hogged mane, which was so common in the early ages. Shoes are not used, and I doubt whether the horses of the ancient Greeks were shod at all; no trace of shoes is to be found on any antique statue. The ox of this district also is precisely the same as that in ancient statues, and there is no other breed in the country: the cow is by no means common, the milk of the sheep, goats, and buffalos being that generally used.

We started from Doovér with four horses, whose feet had never worn a shoe, nor their mouths felt the bit, and which therefore required much tutoring. The foals trotted by our side the whole distance to Mácry, about twenty-two miles. The pace of the horses, taught by the Turks, is a singular kind of run, between an amble and a canter; it is at the rate of six miles an hour, and so easy that you cannot rise in the stirrup. Being unaccustomed to this motion, I took the trouble to teach my horse the more natural pace of trotting, which I preferred for long travelling. As we gradually wound through the range of the Cragus, which bounds Mácry on the south, the country assumed the forest character, and the view as we descended to the bay was very rich. We did not reach Mácry till ten o'clock at night; and though the wind was cold, at intervals of perhaps five or ten minutes a stream of hot air blew past us, which in the dark I attributed to lime-kilns burning near the wayside, though there was no smell of the fuel; but I hear that there are none in the neighbourhood, and that this wind is peculiar to the place.

April 23rd.—Today, until eleven o'clock, there was a moderate wind from the sea, which lies to the westward, but since that time gusts have come down from the mountains towards the east, so violent that branches have been blown off the trees, and the water of the shallow bay has been raised in waves and spray in a contrary direction to the general current of the wind. The mountains to the north are obscured at times by clouds of mist, but no rain falls; and I believe that this collection of vapour may probably be the effect of the contrary eddies and local stagnation of the air occasioned by the peculiar formation of the hills, the currents of cold air rushing down from the snowy mountains replacing the heated air of the valley. I must mention, as perhaps connected with this peculiarity, that the village of Kiacooe, six miles south, where the governor of this district lives and whence post-horses are usually obtained, is suffering so much from the plague that it is now placed under quarantine, and consequently I have to hire horses elsewhere, and at a high rate. The people say that this weather is considered very unhealthy. No such place as Meis is known here, although appearing an important town in the maps, and mentioned in the "Modern Traveller" as the port of Mácry.

The town, or rather the little port or scala, is inhabited principally by Greeks, and consists of about fifty houses, or magazines, where much trade is carried on in acorns, gall-nuts, and firewood. This is the site of the ancient Telmessus, of which there are but few remains. The theatre, of extremely plain architecture, is very large, and in tolerable preservation, with the exception of the proscenium. A number of caves, partly built and partly cut in the rock, extend along the coast, and appear to have been dungeons or guard-rooms for a fortified town; many foundations and walls remain, but it is difficult to trace the plans of the buildings.

The chief objects of interest are the tombs, which are of several kinds and dates*, some appearing from

* The Soros or Sarcophagus tombs at Telmessus, which are considered more modern than those excavated in the rock, Professor Porson decides, from an inscription in Dr. Clark's Travels, to be of a date

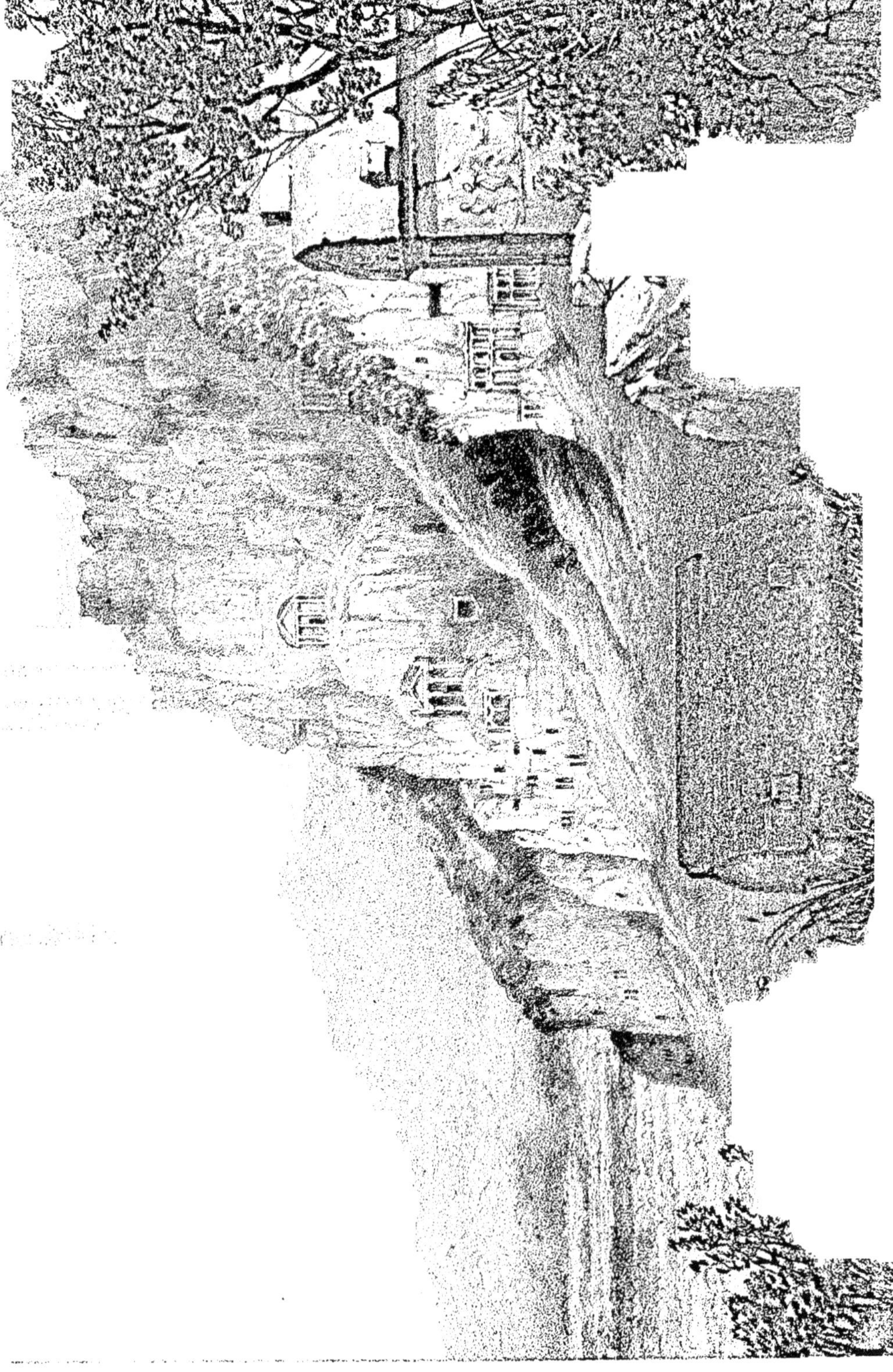

the style to be of as late a period as the Romans; those standing on the hills and near the town have been much shaken by the earthquakes so frequently felt here. The most beautiful specimens are those cut out of the live rock which has been excavated, leaving what in appearance are finely built temples. A singular consequence of this mode of *building* is seen in a column broken at the base, but remaining suspended by the capital. The tombs are in most cases approached by steps, and the columns of the portico stand out perhaps six feet from the entrance to the cella; the imitation of a door is carved in panels, with ornaments and nails finely finished. The entrance has originally been effected by sliding sideways a panel of the false door; but this tedious process has not suited the despoilers of these tombs, who have entered by breaking open one of the panels. The interiors vary but little; they are roughly worked, and are about nine feet by twelve, and six feet in height; on the three sides are the seats, or more probably benches, upon which the coffin or urns have been placed, three feet six inches in height. Some tombs are larger, affording accommodation for the mourners within them. The outward architecture varies so much that I can do no more than refer to the accompanying sketches, which will assist in making my memoranda intelligible.

"evidently older than the 100th Olympiad," making the date probably before 377 B.C.

On the panel of one is an inscription, but rendered nearly illegible by the filtering of the water through the rocks above, which has deposited so much stalactitic matter, as to bear down with it even the portion of the solid rock forming the projecting ornaments.

METO MNHMIE
TNTΩYΠ XONTIΛNE
TOIΣ ONOΣ
OYEIΣ ΠΓHIK
MNHE N
TOMN E*

* This seems to be monumental.

CHAPTER IX.

CARIA.

Route by Dollomón, Koógez, Hoóla—Variation of Season—Moóla—Gipsies—Stratoniceia—its Ruins and Inscriptions—Mylasa—Primitive mode of felling timber—Labranda—Kizzlejik and Báffy to Miletus—its Ruins—Inhospitality of the Peasantry—afterwards explained.

April 24th.—After a delightful ride of above forty miles, I am in my tent at Dollomón. The route for the first six miles was over plains, but we soon entered a most beautiful series of wooded mountains, with bold cliffs rising above finely grown trees. At intervals we came upon narrow valleys of rich pasture, with crystal streams winding towards the sea, which frequently opened upon us to the left, but so intersected by promontories and islands as to present the appearance of lakes. No part of Asia Minor that I have seen is so picturesque as the whole of this district, throughout which the hills are well wooded from their tops to the sea.

These hills are of a schisty limestone, much coloured by a red ochry deposit from the water, which filters through it. Vegetation is here far more luxuriant, but I have noticed few new species of plants; there are some curious varieties of the cyclamen, candytuft, and wild lavender. The lilac and white cistus grow four or five feet high, and are very full of bloom, as is also the wild sage. The heath is almost a tree, being ten feet high, with a stem as thick as my arm. I see a great number of plants with a white leaf, like flannel, which grows as luxuriantly as the acanthus, but none are yet in bloom*. On all the mountains in this district the scarlet lichen clothes the rocks.

My collection of birds has received an addition to-day in the bee-eater, of which we have shot several specimens; its plumage is beautiful. The bees make their nests upon the turpentine firs, which cover the hills, and from which they gather much honey; and these birds follow them in flocks, flying very quickly, making a loud clear chirp while on the wing, like starlings, but more sonorous, and generally settling upon the fir-trees. Hitherto the magpies have been in such numbers as to annoy us; I have counted thirty or forty together. The common jay gradually succeeded them; and now the most frequent bird, which is scarcely ever out of hearing, is the beautiful blue jay or roller, amusing us constantly by making somersets in the air like the tumbler pigeon. I have seen the common brown partridge today for the first time.

April 25th.—We are now at Koógez, twenty-five

* Salvia æthiopis.

miles further to the north-west, and on the way towards Moóla. I am perfectly lost in the maps, which have no resemblance to the country either in form, rivers, or names of places. On leaving Dollomón, after crossing one very large and another small river, we ascended a considerable mountain, and by two o'clock looked down upon a splendid lake, or rather bay, for the water is brackish, a neck twelve miles in length connecting it with the sea; it is six or eight miles across, and a number of small streams run into it, but no river of any name. I observed up these streams, at perhaps six or eight miles' distance from the brackish water, the sea-crab, apparently enjoying the fresh clear water of the stream.

All the governors in this district are the remnant of the old Derebbes, whose power but a few years ago threatened that of the Sultan; they were then continually at war with one another. The sudden destruction of the Janissaries, and since then the equally certain but more gradual extermination of the independent families of the Derebbes, have secured the quiet state of the country, and perhaps the stability of the government. At my halting-place last night, as well as here, the governor's palace or establishment formed the whole village; in it the post was conducted, and in fact there was no other house in the place. The father of the governor here was a Derebbe of great power and importance; his house, which has now half of its quadrangle in ruins, would have accommodated many hundred dependents, and adjoining was another ruin of a large barrack. Ten ships of war, subject to his command, then floated in the lake, and all the country around was dependent upon him, and served him through fear. The power of the family is now extinguished, and I am lodged in one of the half-ruined apartments of the palace. The governor is very civil, but throughout this southern part of the country I find the firman is looked upon in quite a different light from what it is where the Sultan's new policy is more rapidly working its way. But some progress has been made here; for a few years ago my lodging would have been a prison, or the hold of a lawless brigand or pirate. All these families know that the Sultan is watching them, and only waiting for some breach of the law on their part, or other pretext, to deprive them entirely of power; and this knowledge has completely cowed these haughty chiefs.

On a small island near the shore of this lake or bay are five or six cottages of Greeks, and a ruin of an early Christian church. The cross represented on the

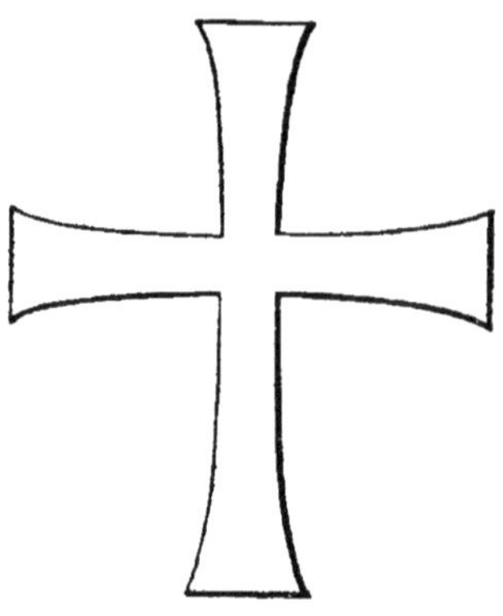

early Christian buildings is always of the form here represented, which is very similar to the one shown at Ravenna as a relic of that æra. The Greeks have here their little place of worship. In this colony I observed a marked peculiarity, namely a litter of pigs, the only specimen of this animal that I have seen; probably they are the only ones in Asia Minor, for the Turks object to the animal, alive or dead, as unclean.

April 26th.—Five mares, each with its foal, were brought at seven o'clock to carry us to Hoóla, forty miles distant. They had been fetched eight or ten miles from the tents of their owners, the Chingunees or gipsies, who here are the principal inhabitants of the mountains. We halted at one of their tents as we passed to arrange our baggage; and the women, who were unveiled, displayed a strength as great as, and an activity far greater than, would be found in the tents of the Turks. During our short pause a number of women and their children assembled round us. What a study for a Rembrandt or a Murillo in the singular but extreme beauty of some of the group! There was a mother with her child, perhaps five years old, dark as a negro, but of a far healthier and richer colour, almost veiled by its wild hair, which had never been cut, and perhaps never combed; its neck was hung with beads, coins, and various chains; its very few clothes hung loosely, leaving the arms and legs bare. The mother was young and of a peculiar beauty; with much elegance and softness, yet with the dignity of a

Meg Merrilies; she had somewhat of the Græco-Egyptian style of face, the features being rather long. Her hair, which was formed into a band round her head and partly plaited, flowed with a long handkerchief down her back. Her clothes were loose and few; the breast was open, and the legs bare from the knee; the arms also were exposed. With this appearance even of poverty in the dress, there was at the same time a considerable display of wealth; on one of her wrists I saw three broad gold bracelets, or bands of plain gold, about three quarters of an inch wide, and on her neck other gold ornaments. A bunch of fresh flowers was stuck into the hair, a very common ornament among the people throughout Turkey; it is placed so carelessly, and still with so much taste both as to position and selection of colours, that a stranger cannot but be struck with it; and this is done without the aid of a glass, for there can scarcely be one in the whole country: I have seen none in the houses of either rich or poor, both Greeks and Turks having religious scruples against their use. I observe my guides frequently picking up flowers, and sticking them carelessly into the folds of the turban, generally with the blossom hanging downwards.

From some goatherds in the neighbourhood I obtained two musical instruments, a long flute and a kind of guitar, used by the inhabitants. They had themselves made them, and played several airs upon them, one of which I recognised as the same I had heard played on a flute of a similar kind during the dancing of the Dervises at Constantinople*.

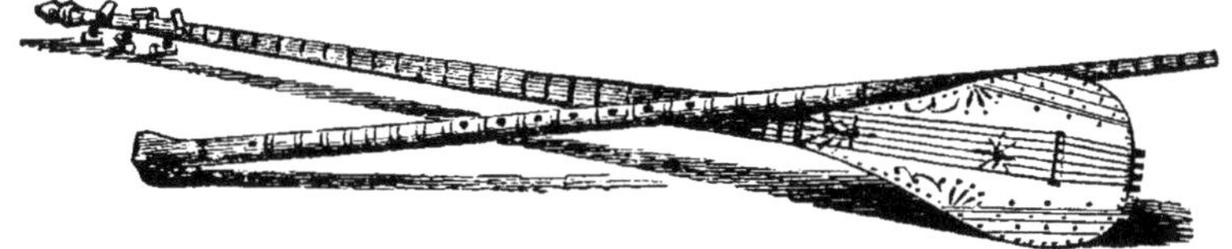

The country is still most richly wooded: another species of the plane is common here, far inferior to the one of which I have before spoken; it grows upright and very high, and does not throw off the bark, which is rough; it has a leaf with five points like a star, which when touched emits a strong smell†. The trees here form a complete wilderness of rich thicket,—a happy land for the birds, which have miles of impervious woods, where they dwell in multitudes: the vines are matted over the tops of the highest trees, and covered with fruit, not a bunch of which will be

* The same instruments, the present mode of playing upon them, and even the usual attitude whilst playing, are exactly represented in the following figures, copied from an Egyptian papyrus at the British Museum.

† Liquidambar imberbis.

gathered except by the birds. I passed along a thicket of this kind for nearly twenty miles yesterday, in which nightingales and thrushes were singing most delightfully; and in the evening the nightingales hymn my vespers, regardless of the light in my tent, until the fatigue of travelling bids me sleep.

Hoóla lies in the mountains, and is the first place that I have passed since leaving Adalia deserving the name of a village. Its elevation has carried me back a month in vegetation; here however the trees are in bloom, and generally green. For the first time I see rye cultivated; oats are unknown in the country. The distance from Koógez to Hoóla is about forty miles, and twelve miles further is Moóla, which lies still higher in the mountains. These are again becoming bare, and of marble, and the twelve miles have carried the season back almost to winter, the walnuts, figs, and fruit-trees scarcely showing a leaf. The map distance is perhaps not more than four miles, yet the climate is that of another country.

April 27th.—Moóla is a town of considerable size, and stands at the south-eastern end of its valley. Thence I travelled north-west for twenty-four miles to the post-village called Aerni-cooe (or Stable-village), and the next morning continued the same line for eight miles to Esky Hissá, the ancient Stratoniceia. This valley is varied by hill and dale, and has its mountain, river, and meadows; indeed it contains within its range so extensive and varied a country, that it would be easy to imagine oneself in a far distant region; I have fancied myself at home, for at this elevation (about four thousand feet) the season and the products of the soil are precisely those of England, the trees just in leaf, the flowers coming out, and no plant to be seen that is not known in our country.

The ancient town of Stratoniceia has extended over a considerable space, and, judging from the remains, must have been formed of magnificent buildings. Five or six temples may still be traced, and it has its theatre in the hill on the west of the town. Many of its walls are built of the ruins of former structures, which appear to have been all of white marble. One immense cella of a temple still stands in the centre of the town; its walls are of the large stones used by the early Greeks; and at each corner is a sculptured shield, with a sword or spear across the back of it, as seen so frequently in Pamphylia. A handsome cornice still runs round a part of the walls. The stones within the portico are covered with inscriptions; I copied one, which from its position, and the form of the beautifully cut letters, must have been among the earliest.

ΝΗΜΟΣΥΝΟΝΑΝ ΗΣΟΙΝ ΛΑ
ΑΥΡΟΝΜΕΤΡΗΣΑΣΜΟΝΣ ΑΓΜΑΤΙ Λ
˥ΕΜΟΝΤΕΚΑΤΕΡΟΝΜΗΝ/ ΠΕΜΒΟΛΟΥΣ ΛΑ
ΝΑΑΝΤΙΣΕΤΥΧΕΤΗΣΑΠΑΙΔΕΥΤΟΥΤΥΧΗΣ ΛΑ
ΠΑΡΗΣΙΑΝΟΜΟΙΑΝΟΥΚΕΧΟΝΒΡΟΤΩΙΣ ΚΗ
ΠΑΡΗΙΟΡΕΙΤΑΙΚΑΙΟΝΑΡΙΟΝΜΗΣΑΣΤΑΔΕ ΛΑ

ΤΩΣΕΓΡΑΨΑΤΟΙΣΦΙΛΟΙΣΙΧΡΗΣΙΜΟΝ Λ
ΣΥΝΟΙΠΡΟΝΟΙΑΑΟΙΠΟΝΕΙΣΤΟΔΕΥΤΕΡΟΝ ΛΑ
ΣΥΠΕΡΙΝΟΗΤΟΝΗΔΚΝΑΓΓΕΙΛΑΙΣΤΙΧΟΝ ΛΑ
ΥΠΕΡΤΑΤΟΙΣΓΑΡΗΜΩΝΕΥΧΗΝΗΡΗΚΛΙΔΙΙ Λ
ΡΕΜΒΗΝΟΔΩΠΕΡΑΣΑΣΤΗΝΕΤΗΣΙΑΝΧΑΡΙΜ ΛΛ
ΕΥΔΑΙΜΟΝΗΣΑΣΔΕΛΤΟΝΛΝΔΤΙΘΩΘΕ
ΑΦΕ*

The walls of the cella on the outside were literally covered with inscriptions, which might all be deciphered by devoting time to them. Many parts of columns still stand in their original positions, and also two or three fine arches and doorways, indicating the magnificence of the former buildings. The following are fragments of well-cut inscriptions.

ΙΒΕΡΙ◁

ΚΕΝΤ

ΩΚΑΝΕΙΣ

The next has been over a doorway.

ΙΟΕΥΣΕΒΕΙΚΑΙΤΗΠΑ
ΚΤΟΝΣΙΣΜΟΝΑΝΕ†

* This inscription seems to record the fulfilment of a vow to Jupiter and Juno.

† This appears to have commemorated an escape from an earthquake.

The present village is scattered over a wide space, and is formed of, and within, the ancient ruins.

The road hence to Mellássa, the ancient Mylasa, is varied by many small hills, from which it descends steeply to a plain, with the town standing at the end of it. Along the whole line of road I observed much ironstone, and some almost pure iron-ore: the small hills were all of the micaceous schist which I have before endeavoured to describe; it varied much in colour, being sometimes as white and shining as silver, and forming a sand like Calais sand, but glittering with mica; at other times being almost jet black, then red, blue, green, or yellow. The broad veins of marble were highly crystallized in many places, and almost transparent, resembling the agate rocks of the central country; the slaty schist was shivered into splinters a foot long, and in some places into flakes as thin as paper, the whole indicating the effects of great heat. The country was entirely covered with a forest of fir-trees; the mode of felling which is so singularly primitive, that the American Indian alone could do it in a more simple manner. The bark is cut for two or three feet, and the trunk wounded with the long knife of the people; afterwards for a season the turpentine bleeds from these cuttings, and they then set fire to it, thus consuming the trunk to the depth of about an inch: the tree is then again chipped, and the fire applied to the renewed discharge of inflammable sap. Some years are thus employed in felling a large tree, which at last falls, borne down by a heavy gust of wind. After the tree is down, the slow habits of the people are still shown in their further operations. The small branches alone are cut off for firewood; the trunk is then chipped or grooved on the upper side, so as to catch the rain-water, to promote the decay of the wood; and in this state the tree lies, sometimes across a path,—which is turned in consequence for several years,—until, falling to pieces, the parts are carried away on the camels and asses employed in the trade of furnishing firewood to the villages and sea-ports. The timber, although extremely straight and good of the kind, is used for no other purpose than fuel, and in every neighbourhood many hundred trees are undergoing the process above described. The smaller trees, laid in lines around the cultivated grounds, are used as fences, the branches soon harbouring luxuriant vegetation, forming a thicket, through which the cattle seldom break.

The water-jars of this western part of Asia Minor are made of red clay, and are in form precisely like the terra-cotta vases of the ancient Greeks. These jars, which stand but insecurely, are seen tied to the trunks of trees by the wayside, and kept constantly filled for the use of the traveller. This extremely grateful supply of water, in parts of the country remote from natural springs or aqueducts, is a religious care for the ablutions before prayer. There are very frequently endowments for the maintenance of this devotional observance. Upon fountains supplied by small aqueducts are frequently Turkish inscriptions relating the motive and occasion of such bequests to the stranger and traveller. The replenishing of these jars is usually the care of the women, who may be seen carrying them upon their backs, slung by cords in the manner represented in this sketch.

On descending to the plain of Mylasa towards the south-west, the mountains, or rather elevated valleys, assume a singular appearance, presenting a long table-land, ending abruptly in a bold cliff. This portion of land is backed by high mountains, and from its form I conceive that it is of the same character, and has the same origin, as the volcanic country in the interior.

An imposing fortification stands upon one of these cliffs, erected during the time of Soley Bey.

On entering Mellássa I was amused by a gravestone in a Turkish burial-ground, formed of a robed female statue of white marble, stuck head and shoulders downwards into the ground: the projecting feet had been broken off, but the folds of the drapery showed that the statue must have been of good Greek workmanship. In the town I also saw a beautiful body of a child, about a foot or eighteen inches long, with one arm over its breast, built into the wall of a house; the head and legs had been broken off. I wished to purchase it, and was told that the occupier of the house would willingly part with it for a trifling sum, but that he could not because he was a rich man. On inquiring into the reason of this, I learned that the stones of the country are the right of the governor, as lord of the manor; and that if he heard of a rich tenant selling one, he would assert that the stone contained gold, and levy a tax or fine upon him of some thousand piastres. This arbitrary power proceeds doubtless from a very bad system, but in its operation is not without its advantages. The law of the Koran, by which the country is governed, is known to all, and its comprehensive declaration, "Thou shalt not steal," is easily understood. If any man obeys the law, he is secure, even from the caprice of a Sultan; but if once he breaks it, the offender has placed himself at the mercy of a governor, whose sole object in purchasing his district is gain.

Drawn by Charles Fellows

Lithographed and Printed by C Hullmandel

TEMPLE AT LABRANDA.

The offender is therefore fined according to his power of paying; his life or liberty would be no gain to the governor, and thus his gold is his only ransom; the effect of this system is that a rich man very rarely breaks the law. I have often heard that to be rich in Turkey was dangerous, and I now see the meaning of the expression.

Every house, wall, or fence is formed of the stones of the old town, which must have contained very highly ornamented buildings. There remain standing some walls and many foundations, a beautiful Corinthian arched gateway, and a single fluted column; the latter stands conspicuously in the upper part of the present town, which is a place of considerable importance.

April 30th.—Yesterday I travelled thirty-two miles; today I have only completed twenty-four, bringing me to this village, Báffy, near the southern end of the lake of the same name. About eight miles on my journey today I saw the ruins of Labranda, near the modern village of Iakly. The only conspicuous building of the place is a beautiful temple of the Corinthian order, but I think not of the finest age: its situation is by no means good, which is rarely the case with the temples of the early Greeks: it stands in a recess in the hills, and is consequently not seen without approaching close to it. There are twelve fluted columns, and four not fluted, but apparently prepared for this ornamental finish. Other columns lying on the ground are reeded, and yet are evidently for the same temple. From several features about it I should fancy that the temple had never been completed. The symmetry of the fluted columns is much disturbed by a kind of panel or tablet, not let in, but left uncut, projecting above the fluting. On each tablet is an inscription. I copied

two from those on the columns at the back or west end, which were the easiest of access. The contents of the two are in effect the same.

ΜΕΝΕΚΡΑΤΗΣΜΕ
ΝΕΚΡΑΤΟΥΣΘΑΡΧΙΑ
ΤΡΟϹΤΗϹΠΟΛϹΙΙϹϹΤ
ΦΑΝΗΦΟΡϢΝΤΟΝΚΙΟ
ΝΑΕΥΝϹΝΕΙΡΗΚΑΙΚΕ
ΦΑΛΗΠΡΟΝΟΗϹΑΜΕ
ΝΗϹΤΗϹΟΥΓΑΤΡΟΕ
ΑΥΤΟΥΤΡΥΦΑΙΝΗϹΤϹ
ΚΑΙΑΥΤΗΣΣΤΕΦΑΝΗΦΟ
ΡΟΥΚΑΙΓΥΜΝΑΕΙΑΡΧϢ*

* *Translation.*

"Menecrates, son of Menecrates, the chief physician of the city,

On a small hill to the north-west there are several foundations of other buildings, apparently walls, but of very limited extent.

At half an hour's distance is the picturesque village of Kizzlejik. The country here is extremely beautiful, and is again becoming ornamented by the trees and shrubs of a warmer climate; and among them the Italian stone-fir, which I think I have not seen since leaving the Troad.

The little village of Báffy lies among hills richly wooded, and inclosed between two ranges of mountains. Its distance from the neighbouring lake, which is shut out from the sight, is about two miles. At the southern end of the lake are the ruins of a considerable town; but as a day would have been occupied in visiting it, I was satisfied with the distant view across the water. Walls inclosed it, and an island in front was covered with buildings. In the Useful Knowledge map the place is marked as Heracleia, and Myrus is placed higher up the Mæander; but from the information I received I should rather give this town, and the lake also, the name of Myrus.

A series of wooded hills, and an impervious thicket, with not even a goat to browse upon it, extended along the side of a lake for twenty miles to Palláttia, the ancient Miletus. The lake, which is brackish, is con-

wearing a wreath, provided this column with its base and capital in memory of his daughter Tryphænete, herself also wearing a wreath, and being a director of the Gymnasium."

nected with the Mæander by a river celebrated for its fish, about two miles long. A little colony of Greeks, who had their fishing establishment on this spot, gave me much information as to the state of the plague in this part of the country: they were themselves in quarantine, and kept away from us, but presented two fine fish of a kind which I did not know, and a loaf of bread. I insisted upon making a return in money, and at last a bowl of water was handed to receive my small coins. Unfortunately at all the post-villages the plague was raging severely, which not only greatly increased my trouble in obtaining horses, but quadrupled my expenses. The system of each village isolating itself by local quarantine is now generally adopted even by the Turks, although they do it in a careless way. In this part of the country we found some exclusively Greek villages,—for here the villages of Greeks and Turks are very frequently distinct,—the appearance of neatness at once bespeaking the former nation, and the presence of a pig, and the absence of the stork, giving further proof that no Turk lives in the place.

Miletus was probably once on a headland or island in a bay or lake, for its hills rise out of the perfectly dead flat of the valley of the Mæander, which at this point is about ten miles across, and runs up towards the north for five miles, and then eastward as far as Denezleé. Of its upper part I intend to see more. The land here is almost wholly pasture or swamp; and the river, which is deep but not broad, by its winding course shows the origin of our term for that peculiarity; it *meanders* as much as the river at Stirling. Its waters bring down a large quantity of mud and sand, and this deposit going on for ages doubtless accounts for the nature of the soil of the immense plain, which has not a rock or stone larger than a rounded pebble, except the fragments of some columns or ancient buildings.

At Miletus are the remains of an enormous theatre. An aqueduct may be traced, and the site of several temples; its other remains are only walls, apparently of Roman or Christian date, and many of its broken columns are evidently Christian. There are the ruins of a Christian church, formed out of a Greek temple, of the Corinthian order, whose fine arched vaults have supported the structure of each age, of which the ancient Greek has proved the most durable. Here I pitched my tent: before me stood a fine mosque, built of the ruins of Christian churches; but its doom was also sealed; the stork alone occupied its ruined walls.

The modern village contains but a few huts, the unhealthy situation and inactivity of the people having reduced their numbers to less than fifty. I was recommended by them (for they would not point out which was their Aga,) to remove to a little distance, as they had very recently had illness among them. No mark of hospitality was shown to me, and on applying to hire horses I was shunned by all. The authority of the firman was useless, for they would not point out the chief to whom I might present it: the temptation of money was also of no avail, as they said they did not want it, and their horses were at pasture in the plain: others led me to suppose they would bring horses; but all failed, and I was unable to proceed. The children were not checked for calling us Ghiaours, and we were laughed at by the people,—a situation by no means soothing to the temper of either an Englishman or a Greek. My servant Demetrius swore at the whole nation of Turks, and upbraided me by asking where was the great hospitality for which I praised this people. Not being disposed, in consequence of one instance to the contrary, to condemn all the nation, I said that there must be some cause for our being so neglected here.

Some peasants passing through to the next village, Sansoón, were prevailed upon as a favour (for they were not influenced by money) to carry the baggage; and a lad, partly by our intimidation and partly by his own poverty, was led to take the bold step of supplying us with two riding horses, which we agreed should go with us for a fixed sum to Chánly, the second village on our route; the others were going there also, but they would only agree to carry the baggage half way, and this as a favour. We no sooner got out of the village, than sociable chat commenced, and the mystery of our ill usage was solved. Last year four Europeans,—it is to be feared English,—the Captain, two Milordos, and another person, paid a visit to the ruins from their vessel; they hired horses to return to the sea, a distance of about ten miles. On the way Milordos struck one of the Turks; a quarrel ensued, and a lad was severely beaten, and left they say half dead. The Turks upon this put down their load, leaving the party half way upon the road, to get as they could to their vessel, but offered no violent retaliation. On their return the whole village swore to have no intercourse with Europeans in future; and in order to do this without breaking the law, they would not point out their chief, to whom, or of whom, alone an application or complaint can be made. The lad who accompanied us was of a neighbouring village, but was cautioned by the people of Palláttia that we did not intend to pay him, and that he was sure to be well beaten by us. We could not remove from his mind the fear of this, and as we found plenty of horses at the Greek village of Sansoón, at his earnest request we released him from his bargain of accompanying us further, and he, to his great joy and surprise, returned home without a beating, and with money in his pocket. This incident, I think, shows how much forbearance and philosophy there is in the conduct of these people.

CHAPTER X.

SOUTH OF LYDIA.

Priene—Sansoón—Thunder-storm—Natural History—Chánly—Scala Nuova—Ephesus—its Remains—Idín, the ancient Tralles—A Market-day—Valley of the Mæander.

May 1*st*.—The Greek village of Sansoón is prettily placed, house above house, upon the rocky slopes of the mountain, and commands a splendid view of the valley and lake which we had passed. An horizon of beautiful mountains, rising behind richly-wooded hills, gives bounds to the plains below.

Within a mile of Sansoón towards the sea, and upon a bolder and more precipitous rock, stood the ancient Priene. The admirable choice of situation for these two towns shows that the taste of their ancestors is inherited by the modern Greeks. The Turkish village of Sansoón, which lies in the valley a mile below, is now for the most part in ruins, and at this season is wholly deserted by its inhabitants for their tents in the hills. The villagers of the Greek Sansoón soon came within their legal quarantine distance to learn our wants, and on my return from a walk I found my servant gossiping with thirty or forty wondering and intelligent hearers who stood around him. These inhabitants were all employed in spinning, winding, or working in some way; and their industry seemed, from the appearance of the houses and everything around, to have met with its reward. The implements for spin-

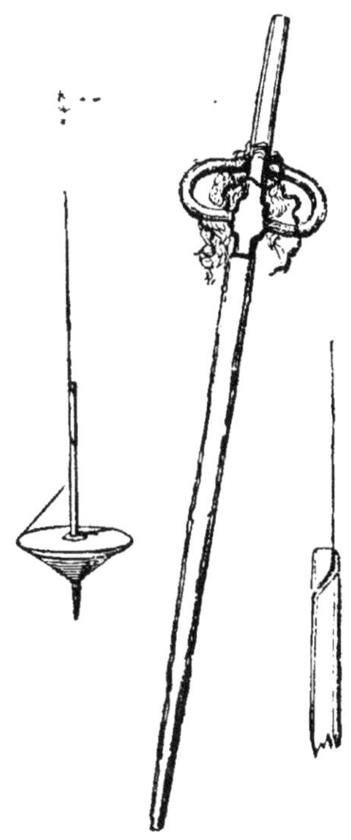

ning and the mode of using them are precisely those seen in the vases and sculptures of the ancient Greeks. I observed the same mode throughout the country, the store of wool being sometimes placed within the capacious sash or shawl, instead of on the distaff. The men are often employed in spinning the goat's hair and coarse wool for the making of the tents. We made our purchases of bread, fowls, wine, and eggs, and the basin of water received the small return for our stores, and horses were brought to us in the morning.

I was not able to examine closely the ruins of Priene, but saw many old walls covering an extensive slope of a hill, out of which, as if built by art, spring perpendicularly the rocks on whose top was the aeropolis: a few walls also remain, and the cliff has been perfected in its face by the walls of the early Greeks, who worked well in concert with nature. A theatre behind is, as usual, cut out of the face of the hill.

In my tent at Miletus I experienced an awful night of successive storms of thunder. My tent appeared to be the target at which every weapon of the elements was aimed. The setting sun left us oppressed by a sultry heat; soon afterwards a gust of wind made the cords quiver and the canvas belly before the howling blast; the rain followed in torrents, loudly hissing as it fell, and scarcely turned from its downward course by the power of the wind; the tent was lit up by the successive flashes of lightning, and the peals of thunder, had they not been softened by the long echos as they rolled into the distance along the ranges of mountains on either side, would have awakened even Demetrius; but he lay fast asleep. I called to him; but the noise of the falling rain on the tent had rendered his ears deaf to feebler sounds, and he slept on. Fine, calm, clear moonlight succeeded, and every dripping leaf multiplied the stars; but it was not in stillness; for the clouds, which had been borne beyond our horizon, were still pealing in their distant progress, leaving the mountains vibrating their notes. After slackening the braced cords of the tent, I lay down to sleep, but was again awakened by a repetition of the storm. The lightning, which seemed to linger on the canvas, showed me by my watch hanging at a distance that it was three o'clock. While dozing I was startled by seeing amidst the flashes a light and smoke within the tent, and, calling with all my strength to awake Demetrius, found that he had just been roused by the storm and had struck a light, and that it was his brimstone match which I had mistaken for a thunderbolt. To converse was impossible, and listening to the twice-told tale of the storm I soon again fell asleep, leaving Demetrius, who acts the Turk only too well, sitting with his pipe listening to the thunder, which lasted till near eight o'clock in the morning. The only traces of the tempest which I then observed were the noisy cries of myriads of gulls and sea-birds hovering about, probably in search of the animal wrecks left by the storm.

May 2nd.—The ride of fifteen miles to Chánly, (probably the ancient Neapolis,) standing not far beyond the promontory of Trogilium, is for half the distance up the steepest track I ever rode over. From the summit of this main range, of which Trogilium forms the termination, (although Samos is geologically a continuation of it,) is seen on either side a perfect and beautiful map,—the only good map of this country,—on the one side extending to the mountains forming the Dorian Gulf, and on the other to those of Chios and Smyrna. The road now descended, but not so precipitously, and my time was fully employed in admiring the great variety and beauty of the trees and other features of the natural history of the spot. There is an oak here that I have not before seen, or at any rate not in so luxuriant growth; it affords excellent timber, although not a very lofty tree; the leaf is eight or ten inches long, and cut almost into ribbons like the fern*. The dazzling colours of the bloom of the pomegranate makes one regret that it should ever fade into so insipid a fruit. A tree very common here, having the leaf and growth of an ash, but of a dark colour, is now covered with fruit nearly ripe, blue and about the size of currants, but growing in erect bunches like that of the laurustinus; it is called chicurea†. Another has a leaf in shape between the willow and the peach, but more like the former, the back of the leaf being white: it bears a small yellow flower from the stem, which scents the air more strongly than any blossom I am acquainted with, more powerfully sweet than the orange blossom of Sicily; the fruit is reddish and like a small date; it is called gegefer‡. The trees are

* Quercus Cerris.

† Pistacia Terebinthus.

‡ Elæagnus angustifolia.

neglected here by man alone, the birds and insects enjoying them undisturbed. I have seen several woodpeckers and a small nut-boring bird, the nuthatch.

The entomologist would here find a wide field for study. I thought England in my younger days a rich and beautiful one, but here the insects, like man, assume a far more gay costume. There are many gaily-coloured species of the blossom-eating tribe of soft-winged beetles,—some in form like the diamond-beetle, though not so brilliant. A large species of the Gryllus tribe seems to ape the birds, flying on every side from tree to tree, and chirping with a shrill note. The butterflies are becoming very numerous, and each day shows some new variety; the beautiful *Panorpa coa*, with its long balancing wings, tempted me to its destruction.

The mulberry-trees which were under cultivation around the village of Chánly bespoke its Greek inhabitants. There is another village bearing the same name, but wholly of Turks, about four miles distant, whose inhabitants are now fast falling before the plague. Chánly was in quarantine; but knowing that we did not come from an infected place, the people were not very strict, and furnished us with horses, with which we proceeded along the bay, to a spot a few miles beyond Scala Nuova, where we pitched our tent. At this town many victims were daily carried off by the plague, and this prevented my being able to procure post-horses. On approaching the city I skirted its walls, and here, as with most Turkish towns, the favourable impression is perhaps highest before entering. Scala Nuova, in situation and outward appearance, is particularly beautiful; being built upon the side of a hill, every house is visible. The town is walled, and has a handsome aqueduct. Its little harbour, which was tenantless, is formed and defended by a curious neck of land and an island; on the latter is a tower for its defence, and the whole city has the appearance of a fortification. It ranks among the largest of the towns in the country, but at present is cut off even from any commerce by the plague.

My next move was a three hours' ride to Ephesus, a place so familiar to the mind that one cannot but feel disappointed at not seeing realised all the ideas associated with it. The vicinity of Ephesus to the coast, as well as to Smyrna, has enabled many travellers to visit this celebrated city, and the memory of the past may perhaps have led them to indulge too freely their imagination whilst contemplating the few silent walls which remain.

Of the site of the theatre, the scene of the tumult raised by Demetrius, there can be no doubt, its ruins being a wreck of immense grandeur. I think it must have been larger than the one at Miletus, and that exceeds any I have elsewhere seen in scale, although not in ornament. Its form alone can now be spoken of, for every seat is removed, and the proscenium is a hill of ruins. I was here reminded that the names used in this country remain still unchanged; for as I sat on a broken portion of a seat under the shade of the wild fennel, which grows here ten or twelve feet high, and to which spot I had been called to see a sleeping snake, my thoughts still running upon Demetrius's tumult, *my* Demetrius rushed in through the vomitory of the theatre, preceded by a tumult of frightened birds, to pick up an owl which he had destined for my collection.

A splendid circus or stadium remains tolerably entire, and one of those gigantic and nameless piles of buildings seen alike at Pergamus and Troy, here and at Tralles; by some they are called gymnasia, by others temples, and again, with I think more reason, palaces. They all came with the Roman conquest, and, as I have said at Pergamus, no one but a Roman emperor could have conceived such structures. In Italy they have parallels in Adrian's Villa near Tivoli, and perhaps in the pile upon the Palatine. Many other walls remain to show the extent of the buildings of the city, but no inscription or ornament is to be found, cities having been built out of this quarry of worked marble. The ruins of the adjoining town, which arose about four hundred years ago, are entirely composed of materials from Ephesus, and these old castle and mosque walls have become in their turn our quarry for relics of antiquity. The few huts within these last-named ruins, which are perhaps a mile and a half from Ephesus, still retain the name of the parent city, Asa-

T 2

look,—a Turkish word, which is associated with the same idea as Ephesus, and meaning the City of the Moon. The ancient wall, carried on the ridge of the mountain to the south of the city, is a fine specimen of very early Greek architecture; it has only the horizontal line of joints regular, the others being irregular as in the Cyclopean: the doorways are also of the early Græco-Egyptian, as seen at Assos.

We travelled nearly fifty miles in a south-easterly direction, through frequent storms of rain, to Idin or Goozel Hissá, the ancient Tralles, where we arrived on Friday the 5th of May. Of the old town there remains only enough to show that it occupied the elevation which overlooks the present city. Upon this are still standing the foundations of walls, and the ruins of one of those palaces which I have before mentioned, and whose fine arches are conspicuous for many miles around. This building has evidently been repaired many times, the stones of the upper part containing inverted inscriptions and ornaments. Within the arches, which have been plastered, remain some paintings, with the same design on each, and, within painted wreaths, inscriptions now quite illegible. If these works were coeval with the building, assuredly painting did not flourish in the same age as architecture. This elevated ground has been laid open in many places, which are worked as quarries for the modern town; the troughs and cisterns now in use have all been pedestals, capitals of columns, or tombs.

The modern town, which is of considerable extent, has the appearance of a village, from the number of trees growing among the houses. Bazaars form the streets, which, as usual, are completely shaded from the sun; but here trees supply the place of the mats which are used for the purpose in most towns. The market-day occurred while I was here. I have in England been at fairs and races, and have witnessed the commemoration days in Paris, and the masquerades and carnivals in Catania and Naples; but all fall short, in gay variety and general beauty of costume, of this Turkish market. The foliage of the plants and trees growing in the streets formed a pleasant relief to the dazzling whiteness of the veils, and the splendid colours of the embroidered trowsers, of the multitudes of women attending the market; light blue worked with silver was very commonly seen in the dresses of the peasants, and every turban had its bunch of roses or other flowers. The noise of voices was louder than is usual in scenes of the kind; for the passing of camels and loaded asses through the crowd called forth continually the warning voice of the driver. The women had their children tied on their backs, and these, with the gay colour of their dresses and their heads ornamented with coins, contributed their part to the general picturesque effect.

For about forty-five miles up the valley, the country varied little in either its geological or botanical features. The hills on the northern side, which rise at times many hundred feet, are formed of gravel and sand, slightly held together by partial drippings through lime, which have produced a cement; this peculiarity has caused the caverns, which are seen in numbers, and are said to extend far into the hills. The strata of this formation are for the most part perfectly horizontal, and appear to have been left by an earlier bed of the river. These hills, worn and broken down by time, are now standing cut into sections, and sloping in every variety of conical shape to the valley. The Mæander winds on the other side of the plain, about six or eight miles from the road.

In the evening of Sunday, the 6th of May, I pitched my tent at Goojták, a town built like Idin upon the slope of the range of hills. On the other side of the valley I had a distant view of the ruins of the ancient Antiocheia, hanging over the river Mosynus, and commanding the entrance of its valley. On the banks of the Mosynus, higher up the valley, are also the ruins of the city of Aphrodisius.

During the whole day we have had fruit-trees on either side; and, indeed, this is the orchard of Asia Minor, whence the boasted figs and raisins of Smyrna are chiefly obtained. Among the flowers there was no species to add to my list except the hollyhock.

CHAPTER XI.

PART OF THE WEST OF PHRYGIA.

Caroura—Valley of the Lycus—Laodiceia—Remains—Hierapolis—its Ruins—Curious Hot-springs—Vultures.

May 8th.—FROM Goojàk the valley of the Mæander somewhat changes its character, having a more sandy and poorer soil, without trees, and with few pastures and little cultivation. The hills are formed of the sand from the rocks of micaceous schist, which glitters on the arid and stony level plain. The river now approaches the northern side of the valley, and its course is marked by the verdure of the neighbouring swamps; the stream is deep and rapid,. contained in high banks, or sunk in its own channel; its water is of a red colour, and its size is about that of the Moselle.

At a house at which I stopped I saw a slice of a fish which is frequently taken in this river; it is without scales, round in form, and nearly a foot in thickness. I am told that it is generally taken weighing as much as one hundred, and sometimes one hundred and fifty pounds (fifty okes). It has a large mouth, of the common form, and unlike that of the sturgeon. Does the conger eel ever attain this size? This part of the river must, allowing for its windings, be two hundred miles from the sea, and the water of course is always fresh.

The sandy hills became now more and more varied in colour, being by turns red, perfectly white, and brown; as we advanced, they receded, and the plain stretched into a comparatively open country. Crossing the valley, we left Ghera, the ancient Caroura, on the right, and after a long ride arrived at Caracooe, which stands at the foot of the hills on the southern side. These furnish a plentiful supply of water for irrigating the land, which in consequence is generally under cultivation, although a very light sandy soil.

A ride of sixteen miles up the valley of the Lycus brought us to Laodiceia, now called Esky-Hissá. A place of the same name (which means Old Castle) stood on the hills to our left, half way from Idin; it is called in the map Sultan, and its site is indicated by a burial-ground by the road-side, filled with old wrought stones. The way to Laodiceia was over perfectly barren sand-hills, with no trace of vegetation; the views were limited by the series of rounded hills, and there was nothing to vary the dreary ride but a flock of bustards, upon which we came suddenly; we had no ball, and our shot only tickled them. As we advanced towards the ruins of the ancient city which stand upon these sterile hills, we saw hovering over a ravine before us three or four eagles, and on coming to the spot we disturbed a grand assemblage of them. I counted nearly a hundred, of which eight or ten were large and black, the others the smaller white eagle, or rather vulture, one of which we shot. Among the tombs of the now deserted city we saw the object which had attracted this winged party,—the bones of a camel picked nearly clean; the guests, who were now watching us from the hills around, only waited our departure to renew the feast: they seemed to be the only living creatures that ever visit the spot, except the cutters of gravestones, who have quarries of white marble wherever the remains of a temple are to be found.

All the buildings of this city are constructed of an extremely coarse conglomerate or petrified mass, and the cornices and ornamental parts alone are of marble or other fine stone. I saw many remains of thin slabs of marble for lining or covering the walls, still partially retaining the cement which attached them. This town is said to have been destroyed or injured several times by earthquakes; but the hills on which it stands do not show any signs of volcanic changes; indeed the alluvial strata throughout the whole of these hills are so horizontal and undisturbed that they can scarcely afford any subject of interest to the geologist, although combined with rock, and bearing cities upon them which are among the earliest in history. The change which is taking place, by their being washed down into the valley, is rapid only when viewed by a geologist. There is no trace of any volcanic matter in the stones carried down by the streams, which are all either of white marble or micaceous schist brought from the high mountains which peer over these hills on either side of the broad valley.

At the entrance to the old city stand the massy remains of a bridge, of which the uncemented stones have been shaken apart in a most singular manner, to be accounted for only by attributing it to an earthquake. A paved road leads to a triple-arched entrance to the city; but in the immense space which was occupied by it, and is now covered with its ruins, I could satisfactorily distinguish only a few of the ancient buildings. There are two theatres cut from the side of the hill, of which the seats still remain tolerably perfect, the proscenia being heaps of ruins. The one facing the east has been extremely handsome, with seats all of marble, supported by lions' paws. Many of the seats had initials cut rudely upon them, and in different Greek characters, probably marking the seats as individual property. Several temples may be traced by their foundations; but the principal remains are the vast silent walls, which must have been built about the time of the Romans and Christians, although their purpose is involved in much doubt: for churches they are inapplicable, and in the places in which I have before noticed them such remains would be improbable. There is little trace of the architecture and ornament of churches; and but few tombs are to be seen which appear by their carvings to be of Christian date.

Up the valley towards the south-east stands Mount Cadmus, and I heard that at its foot, about twelve miles from Laodiceia, there were considerable ruins, probably of the ancient city of Colossæ. Descending rapidly into the flat and swampy valley of the Lycus, we crossed in a diagonal line to the city of Hierapolis, six or seven miles from Laodiceia. My attention had been attracted at twenty miles' distance by the singular appearance of its hill, upon which there appeared to be perfectly white streams poured down its sides; and this peculiarity may have been the attraction which first led to the city being built there. The waters, which rise in copious streams from several deep springs among the ruins, and are also to be found in small rivulets for twenty miles around, are tepid, and to appearance perfectly pure; indeed I never saw more transparent water, although I perceived at a depth of perhaps twenty feet a dark green hue visible between the surface and the white marble of the columns and Corinthian ornaments which lay at the bottom. Gas continually rises in bubbles, emitting the noxious smell of hydrogen. This pure and warm water is no sooner exposed to the air, than it rapidly deposits a pearly white substance upon the channel through which it flows, and on every blade of grass in its course; and thus, after filling its bed, it flows over, leaving a substance which I can only compare to the brain-coral, a kind of crust or feeble crystallization; again it is flooded by a fresh stream, and again is formed another perfectly white coat. The streams of water, thus leaving a deposit by which they are choked up, and over which they again flow, have raised the whole surface of the ground fifteen or twenty feet, forming masses of this shelly stone in ridges which impede the paths, as well as conceal and render it difficult to trace out the foundations of buildings. The deposit has the appearance of a salt, but it is tasteless, and to the touch is like the shell of the cuttle-fish. These streams have flowed on for ages, and the hills are coated over with their deposit of a filmy, semitransparent appearance, looking like half-melted snow suddenly frozen.

The town stands upon the high cliff, over which these streams fall in cascades, commanding a fine view of the valley, and has many of the picturesque advantages which would be sought in a modern watering-place; the mountains rise up at the back, and wooded ravines offer shade for summer rambles. The ruins are crowded and extensive; and here again are some remains unaccountable from their immense proportions: in this place they might be taken to have been baths, but I still incline to the idea that they were palaces. The theatre has been richly ornamented, and many of the cornices so much as to impair their simplicity and beauty; these, together with most of the groups of figures, bear the traces of an age more devoted to luxury than pure taste. The inscriptions found here have been copied by others. The stone used in building is the conglomerate of the neighbourhood.

A singular effect is seen upon the square pillars of a colonnade standing on each side of a court-yard of the palace; they are formed of chips of marble of all sizes, held together by a matrix of reddish stone, similar to what we call scagliola. Time or an earthquake has warped them, and they now stand in curves, bulging out in various directions, without any fracture. A kind of tomb is found here which I have not observed elsewhere, a distinct temple or house, probably a place of mourning for the friends of the deceased interred beneath. These tombs are numerous on each side of the town. Buildings such as these may have been referred to when, in the time of our Saviour, persons are spoken of as dwelling among the tombs.

Descending from the ruins we proceeded across the plain towards the valley of the Mæander; and after we had ridden about twelve miles, night coming on, we pitched our tent.

I have mentioned that we killed a vulture this morning at Laodiceia. It was shot at about nine o'clock, and at the time was washing itself in a stream after its hearty meal upon the dead camel. It was wounded in the head and neck, and dropped immediately; but upon taking it up, its talons closed on the hand of my servant, making him cry out with pain. He placed it on the ground, and I stood with my whole weight upon its back, pressing the breast-bone against the rock, when its eye gradually closed, its hold relaxed, and to all appearance life became extinct. It was then packed up in my leather hood, and strapped behind the saddle. The day was oppressively hot, for we trod upon our shadows as we rode across the plain. Until this evening (at eleven o'clock) the vulture remained tightly bound behind the saddle. My servant, on unpacking, threw the bundle containing it into the tent, while he prepared boiling water for cleaning and skinning it. Intending to examine this noble bird more carefully, I untied the package, and what was my surprise to see it raise its head and fixed its keen eye upon me! I immediately placed my feet upon its back, holding by the top of the tent, and leaning all my weight upon it; but with a desperate struggle it spread out its wings, which reached across the tent, and by beating them attempted to throw me off. My shouts soon brought Demetrius, who at length killed it by blows upon the head with the butt end of his gun. My ignorance of the extreme tenacity of life of this bird must exculpate me from the charge of cruelty.

CHAPTER XII.

LYDIA.

Aneghoól—Philadelphia—Opium-gathering—Sardis—its Remains—Cavalcades of Travellers—Camels—Cassabá—Return to Smyrna—Retrospect—The People—Climate—Scenery.

Yesterday, May the 8th, we crossed at a scarcely fordable place the river Lycus, which brings down a white milky water, apparently from a limy country. We now had to cross the Mæander near the ruins of the ancient Tripolis, and gradually ascended a valley or ravine, leaving the post-town of Bulladán on the left. After passing a picturesque series of hills and deep rocky beds of small rivers, we entered the valley formed by the Cagamus, in which stands Philadelphia.

We slept at Aneghoól, distant from Hierapolis about fifty miles, and this morning proceeded sixteen miles further to Philadelphia. The soil in the valley is extremely poor, but by irrigation crops of barley are obtained.

A new feature has appeared in the landscape; the fields of opium are all in bloom, forming a very beautiful object; but these flowers are not so gay as our garden poppies. They are all luxuriant plants of the single poppy, three feet high, their colours being white, lilac, and purple, in nearly equal proportions. The business of collecting the opium has just commenced. The green seed-pod is wounded or scratched with a delicate point, when the milky sap exudes; this is afterwards collected by scraping, and a purifying process is all that is then required to produce the opium fit for the market. The work is chiefly done by women, a delicate hand being required throughout the process; and as the whole harvest may be destroyed by a shower, the crop is a precarious one. The entire produce is monopolized by the Government at a fixed price, and the sale of opium is not allowed in any part of the country.

Of the ancient city of Philadelphia but little remains; its walls are still standing, inclosing several hills, upon the sides of which stood the town, but they are fallen into ruins. They are built of unhewn stone, massed and cemented together with fragments of old buildings; some immense remains of buildings, huge square stone pillars, supporting brick arches, are also standing, and are called the ruins of the Christian church. All the remains which have been pointed out to me as ruins of Christian churches appear to have been vast temples, perhaps erected by imperial command, and dedicated to nominal Christianity, but showing, in the niches and brackets for statues and architectural ornaments, traces of heathen superstition.

Descending the valley, which widened as it joined that of the Hermus, after a ride of thirty-six miles we arrived at Sart, the ancient Sardis, the last of the Seven Churches that I had yet to see. Its situation is very beautiful, but the country over which it looks is now almost deserted, and the valley is become a swamp. Its little rivers of clear water, after turning a mill or two, serve only to flood instead of draining and beautifying the country. On the principal of these streams, the Pactolus, at the distance of a mile from the city, stand the remains of a colossal temple, the proportions of which resemble those of Agrigentum; but it is very doubtful if this was ever completed, for though two columns of the Ionic order remain standing, and the ruins of four others, these are the only parts left to record the vastness of such a fallen temple; the columns also are prepared for fluting, but have never been cut; and the ornaments of the capitals differ from each other, and appear not wholly finished. Do these unfinished fragments indicate the period when Pagan art expired before Christianity? The remains of this city vary much in date; the early part, containing a theatre, stadium and temples, may be readily traced, but the masses of wall composing the rest of the city speak with certainty only of its extent; one, the largest, of these piles of buildings must have been a palace, consisting of distinct, long rooms with circular ends. The earth which has fallen from the crumbling hills above has buried great part of the buildings of the city.

Two or three small bridges, from their architecture, appear to be of an early date.

Among the ruins is seen the beautiful arum, or snake plant, as this species is here called, from the appearance of its stem: it grows to an enormous size; there is one near the spot where I am now standing eight feet high. No description or even painting can represent the exceedingly velvet-like richness of the crimson or damson colour of the calyx and petal; it is one of the most splendid of plants. The scent is far from agreeable, filling the air with the smell of rats. While standing perfectly still, sketching this plant, I have been amused by watching the tortoises basking by the water-side; seven or eight little ones have been playing upon the back of their mother, crawling up and down, and fighting for the most elevated part of her shell; but upon my making the slightest movement, they scampered down the bank and dived into their secure retreat.

Opposite to the town, and at the distance of three or four miles across the valley and river, are the curious mounds of earth which are said to be the tombs of the kings of Lydia, and near them is the lake of Gygæus. These mounds are in great numbers the whole length of this valley, and many are of stratified earth, whence it must be very doubtful if they be tumuli. I have taken drawings of several of them.

Twenty-eight miles further down the same valley is the modern town of Cassabá, which lies on the regular caravan route between the interior of the country and Smyrna. On overtaking the long cavalcades of a governor or wealthy person, which generally consist of thirty or forty fine horses richly caparisoned, my servant always rode forward to ask permission to be allowed to pass; this being granted, I proceeded, receiving as I passed a most kind but dignified salutation of welcome as a stranger.

It is amusing to see this moving establishment of luxuries,—one horse loaded with long pipe-cases, another with carpets and rugs; and the wife or children follow in an equipage, which I must describe by a sketch.

The animal, which is commonly a mule, is led: it carries two panniers, in which are the passengers, inclosed in a tent of white calico, fringed and ornamented with red, upon poles fixed to the panniers; there are small eye-holes behind and in front, which I observed were much used; a light ladder, used for mounting and dismounting, is suspended from one of the poles. These conveyances give a peculiar effect to the cavalcade, which is in keeping with the costume of the multitude of servants in attendance.

Strings of camels are continually passing, each comprising about forty-five, and headed by a man upon an ass who leads the first, the others being mostly connected by slight cords. It is a beautiful sight to see the perfect training and docility of these animals. The caravans, as the weather is becoming warmer, are beginning to travel by night, generally halting at about ten or eleven o'clock in the morning. The care of the camels seems to be very much left to the children. I have just watched a string of them stopping on an open plain: a child twitched the cord suspended from the head of the first; a loud gurgling growl indicated the pleasure of the camel as it awkwardly knelt down, and the child, who could just reach its back, unlinked the hooks which suspended from either side the bales of cotton; another child came with a bowl of water and sponge, and was welcomed by a louder roar of pleasure as it washed the mouth and nostrils of the animal. This grateful office ended, the liberated camel wandered off to the thicket, to browse during the day; and this was done to each of the forty-five, which all unbidden had knelt down precisely as the one I have described, forming a circle which continued marked during the day by the bales of goods lying at regular distances. On a given signal in the afternoon, at about three o'clock, every camel resumed its own place, and knelt between its bales, which were again attached, and the caravan proceeded on its tardy course. I am not surprised at finding the strong attachment of these animals to the children; for I have often seen three or four of them, when young, lying with their heads inside a tent in the midst of the sleeping children, while their long bodies remained outside.

From Cassab*á* a ride of forty-eight miles through a beautifully varied and picturesque country brought us again to Smyrna, called by the Turks Ismeér, on the evening of Saturday, the 12th of May.

SMYRNA, *Sunday morning, May* 13*th.*—I quite enjoy to be again sitting on a chair, with a table before me, and shall spend this day of rest in thinking over the interest and pleasure of the past three months. My first feeling on making the retrospect cannot but be gratitude that I have escaped even the slightest accident, on a journey of three thousand miles, through a country little travelled, and in which there are neither carriages nor roads.

How soon is a new habit acquired! I have just been observing a party of Europeans on their way to church; the men tightly swathed in their clothes, the ladies with their stiffened silk, bound down in plaits, huge bonnets, artificial flowers placed erect, and discordant colours, seemed to me deformities compared with the natural, easy and graceful costume to which three months' intimacy has attached me.

How different are now my feelings towards the Turks, from those uncharitable prejudices with which I looked upon them on my first arrival at this place! To their manners, habits, and character, equally as to their costume, I am become not only reconciled, but sincerely attached; for I have found truth, honesty and kindness, the most estimable and amiable qualities, in a people among whom I so little looked for them.

The pervading character of this people is their entire devotion to their religion. It forms the civil as well as moral law; and instead of being interrupted by worldly business and interests, is indissolubly associated with the occupations of every hour of the day, and every action of the life. Prayer is with them universal, and peculiar to no place,—sought equally in the field and chamber as in the mosque. Every one pursues his own devotions, independently of a priesthood, (which here does not exist,) with perfect simplicity and without ostentation. The character, habits, customs, manners, health, and whole life of the people appear formed by their religion. I have not read the Koran, and my judgement of the religion is therefore formed from its professors, who appear indeed to be not *mere* professors. That the religion regulates all civil relations and duties, I have been constantly made aware by the replies to my questions, why this thing, or that thing was done; the invariable answer being, that their religion commanded it. The law and the religion, being one, are taught together to the children from their infancy; and on any breach of the duties thus inculcated, the Sultan's power to punish is absolute, and its exercise sure.

The feature in the character of the people which first presents itself to the stranger and sojourner among them, is hospitality. They are indeed given to hospitality. It was proffered to me by all ranks,—from the Pasha to the peasant in his tent among the mountains,—and was tendered as a thing of course, without the idea of any return being made. No question was asked; distinction of nation or religion, of rich and poor, was not thought of; but "feed the stranger" was the universal law.

Their honesty next strikes the traveller. It was my constant habit to leave on the outside of my tent the saddles, bridles, cooking apparatus, and everything not required within, where I and my servant slept without the least fear of losing anything, although persons were passing by and gratifying their curiosity by examining my property. I never lost even a piece of string. On noticing this to my servant, a Greek, he *excused* the honesty of the Turks by saying that their religion did not allow them to steal. There is sufficient temptation to offend, in the dresses commonly worn by the women and children, richly embroidered with the current gold coin of the country; but the law, "Thou shalt not steal," seems to receive from them implicit and universal obedience.

Truth, the twin sister of honesty, is equally conspicuous in them; and here again the Greek apologizes for them,—"The Mahometan dares not lie; his religion forbids it."

The national custom, which makes it the privilege of the son to do the offices of an attendant to his father, instils into the character of the people the duty of honouring parents. In every relation and circumstance in which I saw them, in their families and among strangers, love and kindness to one another seemed to prevail: sincerity banishes suspicion, and honesty and candour beget openness in all their dealings.

In obedience to their religion, which, like the Jewish law, forbids taking interest for money, they abstain from carrying on many lucrative trades connected with the lending of money. Hence other nations, generally the Armenians, act as their bankers.

From their religious devotion they derive a submission to the Divine Will so entire, that it has drawn upon them the misrepresentation of being Fatalists. To prevent evil they are as earnest as others: I have seen them using all their efforts to extinguish fires; and have often been solicited by them for medicine, and they eagerly receive advice to check illness: but if the fire cannot be arrested, they submit, and say, "God is great!" and if the malady terminate in death, though of a child or parent, the nervous eye alone shows the working of the heart, and the body is committed to the grave with the submissive reflection, "God is great and merciful!"

The permission given by the Mahometan law to polygamy is one of the serious charges brought against the moral character of its professors. But though the law allows several wives, it is a liberty of which the people seldom take advantage. I have seen in thousands of instances the Turk in his tent, with his one wife, appearing as constant in his attachment to her as a peasant of a Christian country. It is in the palaces of the rich and great alone that, in the midst of luxury and state, many wives are assembled.

Before I visited this people I fancied their character was cruel; but so far from finding proofs of this, I have noticed that their treatment of the brute creation, as well as of one another, is peculiarly the reverse. Instruments of punishment for beasts of burden are scarcely known. Their only influence over the camel is obtained by kindness and rewards, and its obedience is most complete. The absence of fear in all birds and beasts is very striking to an European, and is alone sufficient to exculpate the Turks from this charge.

To the abstinence of this people from wine, the peculiar law of Mahomet, is perhaps to be attributed very much of their moral as well as physical health. The stream of intemperance, which would undermine the pure principles of conduct above adverted to, is thus totally arrested. The physical result of this law is strikingly manifest in the absence of cripples, and the general exemption of the Turks from illness; toothache being almost the only ill, to which they are often subject. One of the moral benefits of temperance may be traced in the exemption of the people from abject poverty. I have seen no beggars except the blind, and few persons looking very poor. The people's wants, which are few, are generally well supplied; and in every tent there is a meal for the stranger, whatever be his condition. I have never seen a Turk under the influence of opium; and I believe that the use of this stimulant is confined to the licentious inhabitants of the capital.

Does not Christian Europe stand rebuked before these faithful followers of the false Prophet? Were we as devoted to our religion as the Mahometans are to theirs, what a heaven upon earth would our lands be! The superstitions, and the total want of morality in the professors of the Greek Church, may well deter the Turks from seeking to change their faith. The disciples of the Greek Church frequently become followers of the Prophet when it will forward their commercial or political success; but there is scarcely ever an instance of the conversion of a Turk to what is called Christianity. At Constantinople I attended the Church of England service, which was admirably performed by an English Missionary. The clergyman's family, and one Armenian, with myself, formed the whole congregation.

My intimacy with the character of the Turks, which had led me to think so highly of their moral excellence, has not given me the same favourable impression of the development of their mental powers. Their refinement is of the manners and affections; there is little cultivation or activity of mind among them. Their personal cleanliness, the richness and taste of their costume, and the natural delicacy of all their customs are very remarkable. In society they are always perfectly at their ease; and among the peasantry I noticed none of the sheepishness so often exhibited by rustics in the presence of superiors.

Their modes of expression are very figurative. When their conversation was translated to me by my interpreter, I could have fancied myself listening to the "Arabian Nights," the language was so poetic, and so often enriched with proverbs and peculiar forms of expression. I will instance one, of which I noticed the frequent use, and which is very characteristic of this people. On parting with a Turk, to whom by several days' companionship and exchange of kindness I had become attached, the wish which I should express at parting would be, that we might meet again; he would say, "Mountains *never* meet, but men *may*!" I do not regret not having studied the language, for I experienced no inconvenience in conversing through my dragoman. The literal translation of an interpreter, familiar with the expressions of the country and the forms of etiquette of the people, is, I think, the best mode of attaining a ready intercourse with them. The Mahometan never speaks a foreign language, and therefore does not expect that a stranger should do so.

Having noted my observations on the manners and character of the people, it now only remains for me to put down the remarks which present themselves to my memory, on the climate of the country and the features of the scenery of its several districts.

As I selected the coolest season for my tour, any remarks that I make on the climate must in part be derived from other sources than my personal experience. Nor can they at once apply to the whole of the country, as the various elevations present winter and ripening summer within one day's journey.

If a line be drawn upon the map to include the elevated table-land of the interior, and the field of burnt or volcanic production, it will precisely trace the boundarics of the ancient Phrygia on the north, the west, and the south; following even the singular forms in which it projects into the districts of Caria, Lycia, and Pamphylia. This circumstance leads me to imagine that the name of Phrygia may have been connected with the climate and nature of the soil. The cold from the great elevation is so severe, that no plants are to be seen but such as are found in the Highlands of Scotland, where they suffer less from severity of climate than here. The summer in this high land must be of very short duration, for the corn was not sown in April, and is frequently gathered amid the snow in October.

On descending from this elevated country, every diversity of climate is met with, till the traveller reaches the productive valleys of the rivers and the warmer lands on the coast. But at the present season (the month of May), at Sardis, Cassab*á*, and here (Smyrna), the women still retain their fur-lined jackets, and the merchants their fur cloaks. During the summer the heat becomes intense as the morning advances, but before noon a land breeze is drawn down from the cold mountain country, which brings a refreshing coolness, with the shade of clouds, and not unfrequently flying showers. In the early part of the evening the heat again becomes oppressive: the dews are very heavy.

To the intense cold of the winter it must be attributed, that neither the aloe nor the cactus, nor any succulent plant, is to be seen in the country; the frosts would destroy them. The orange- and lemon-trees are with difficulty preserved in the sheltered valleys; the olive seldom flourishes in a similar situation; and they are all far inferior in growth to those of Sicily, Calabria, or Greece. The country is supplied with oranges and many other fruits from the island of Crete. The extremes of the seasons are further shown by the migration in the animal kingdom, which takes place to a great degree.

The remarks contained in this Journal upon the geological character of each district may have given some idea of its superficial appearance, but I will attempt a general sketch of the country for the lover of the picturesque. The scenery of Lydia and Mysia is varied and beautiful, its hills being well wooded, with splendid forest-trees. In the forms of the mountains there is more of beauty than grandeur; and the peculiar feature is the great contrast or division between the hills and valleys; the latter being so level as to appear formed by lakes. In Bithynia the scenery is of a bolder character; its fine mountain range of Olympus giving to it a resemblance to Switzerland; its valleys are also rich, with luxuriant woods. The flat-topped hills and immense table-lands of Phrygia, from their great elevation, often swampy and seldom bearing a tree, present more of the wild and dreary than of the picturesque. Pisidia, including the Taurus range, again partakes with Bithynia of the Alpine character, but the woods in this district are not so finely grown. The extreme beauty of Pamphylia is derived more from distant effects than near views. The marble mountains which form the distant horizon shoot their jagged peaks of silvery rock, or capped with snow, against the clear sky, while their bases are washed by the blue ocean which they inclose in their wide-stretched arms. Lycia is more mountainous, and resembles, but far exceeds in the boldness of its cliffs and the richness of its vegetation, the scenery of Parnassus. Its valleys, and particularly that of the Xanthus, are of peculiar beauty. Caria abounds in scenery of the most picturesque kind, its coast being broken into bold headlands, whose ranges, continued into the sea, rise in rocky islands. The south-east of Lydia is less beautiful, and much resembles Sicily or Calabria; but on approaching Smyrna this district has valleys equal to those near Salerno or Naples. The artist visiting Asia Minor would be richly rewarded.

SUPPLEMENTARY CHAPTER.

REMARKS FOR THE GUIDANCE OF TRAVELLERS.

Hoping that some of my friends may be induced to visit this interesting country, I shall give a few hints as to the machinery of travelling, which may be found of use to them. A tent is the first requisite, the old cities and places of the greatest interest being frequently distant from the modern towns or khans; and a good tent makes the traveller quite independent of the state of health of the town, which I found a very important advantage. It is desirable that the tent should be of a waterproof material. I found great use in an oil-cloth hammock, which was occasionally slung from pole to pole, but always of service to spread under my mattress when the ground was wet. A carpet may be procured in the country, but a mattress must be taken; also a canteen, containing the usual requisites for cooking and for making tea, and a lantern. Arrow-root is the most portable and convenient material for the traveller's store; it may be prepared in five minutes, and a basin of this will stay the appetite until the dinner can be prepared, which,—what with pitching the tent, lighting the fire (often with green-wood), and the process of cooking, must be frequently delayed an hour or two after the traveller halts. Rice is necessary, and tea a great treasure.

I have always found the convenience of carrying a gimblet among my travelling stores; it is a substitute for nail, hook, and hammer: inserted into the wall it forms a peg by which my clothes are frequently kept from the dirty or damp floor, or to which I can hang my glass, watch, or thermometer. The traveller will of course be prepared with every requisite for the tailor, and will take a few simple medicines.

For œconomy in travelling it is well to take only five or six horses; if this number be exceeded, another guide is required, and the pay to the ostlers is increased. The traveller who wishes to pay liberally and be well attended by the post, must calculate that five horses will cost him, with these extra payments, as much as seven; and this sum will cover all expenses on the road to guides, ostlers, etc., amounting to seven piastres per hour, or about four miles. On the ordinary lines of road he may travel three hours in two, being six miles an hour; this saves time, but the expense is the same. However proficient the European traveller may be in the Turkish language, I should recommend his taking a servant who can act as dragoman, as he will be thus enabled far better to understand and fall into the manners and customs of the people.

The most acceptable presents to the inhabitants are not such as are of the greatest intrinsic value, but articles of use which it is difficult for them to procure. The traveller will do well to supply himself with copper caps for the people in authority who have had percussion guns given to them, but which are rendered useless from the want of these, and also gunpowder for the peasantry: by all classes a sheet of writing-paper is much valued; leads for patent pencil-cases are very acceptable; and a common box-compass will furnish much pleasure, occasionally directing the Mahometan to the point for his prayers. I have been often asked in a delicate manner by the Greeks if I possessed a picture of our queen or reigning sovereign; a common print of this kind would be highly prized.

The traveller sleeping in a room without glazed windows, in a tent, or on the floor, will find the bed which I will attempt to describe a great treasure. For the plan of this bed I was many years ago indebted to my friend Mr. Godfrey Levinge, and have ever since by its use been rendered independent of all the insect world. The gnats, flies, beetles, etc., never agreeable even if harmless, are constantly attracted by the light of the candles or the warmth of the mattress; and this simple contrivance I have found the only plan for preventing their intrusion. Thus insuring an undisturbed night, I have cared little for their attacks by day. The whole apparatus may be compressed into a hat-case. A pair of calico sheets (No. 1.), six feet long, sewed together at the bottom and on both sides, are continued with muslin of the same form and size sewed to them at their open end (No. 2.), and this

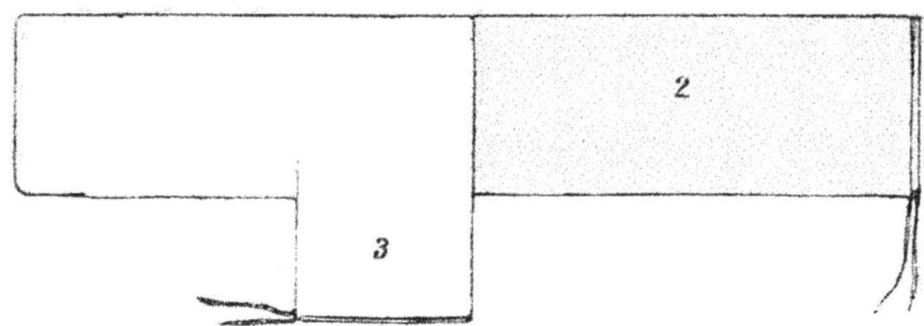

muslin is drawn tightly together at the end with a tape; within this knot are three or four loose tapes

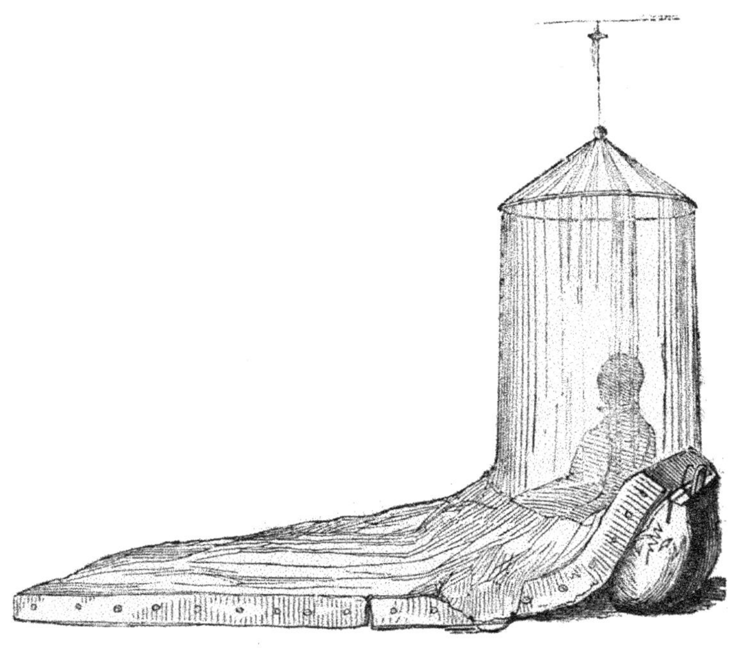

about eighteen inches long, with nooses at their ends, through which, from within, a cane is threaded so as to form a circle, extending the muslin as a canopy, which in this form is suspended.

These canes must be in three pieces, three feet long, each fitting into the other with a socket or ferrule. The entrance to the bed is by a neck (No. 3.), from the lico, with a string to draw it tightly together when you are within: it is desirable that the traveller should enter this bed as he would a shower-bath, and having his night-shirt within. When the end formed of muslin is suspended, the bed forms an airy canopy in which the occupant may stand up and dress in privacy, no one being able to see him from without, while he can observe all around. I have often, when annoyed by insects, sat to read and write within this shelter in the evening, with a candle placed near me. To prevent accident from tearing the apparatus, I have found that the best mode of entering was to keep the opening on the middle of the mattress, and, standing in it, to draw the bag-entrance over my head. The foregoing sketch will, I think, supply the place of any further description.

Before concluding these hints to travellers, I should mention that the tourist in Asia Minor would do well to reverse my route, commencing with the southern country, and proceeding northwards as the warm season approaches.

It may also be useful to know, that on leaving this country by way of Syra, a quarantine of three weeks has to be performed at that port, which will enable the traveller to proceed to Athens or any part of Greece. Another quarantine of fourteen days is required before landing from that State in any other part of Europe. The duration of the term in each country varies, however, according to the state of health in the eastern cities. This double quarantine may be avoided by proceeding at once to Malta, where one long imprisonment will enable the traveller to enter freely any European port.

APPENDIX.

Since the completion of the printing of this Journal, the Author has been favoured with the following valuable Notes by his friend Mr. James Yates.

"49, Upper Bedford Place, London,
May 7th, 1839.

"My dear Sir,—In perusing your Volume I find that you have adopted the translations I proposed for the various inscriptions. I add a few remarks, which you may, if you please, use in an Appendix. I observe also in your printed Journal before me, several points highly interesting as connected with the illustration of Greek and Oriental antiquities; and I venture to send you a few detached observations on them, which may form a second Appendix.

I am, dear Sir,
Most truly yours,
James Yates."

APPENDIX A.

Nos. I—III.*—Page 27.

From Soma, between Thyatira and Pergamus.

No. I.

Ονησιμος ὁ πατηρ

* The numbers refer to the order of the Inscriptions.

και Χρυσαιεις ἡ μητηρ
Πολυχρονιῳ τῳ γλυκυ-
τατῳ τεκνῳ μνειας χα-
ριν εποιησαν, και ἑ-
αυτοις.

The ornamental form of the letters in this beautiful and perfect tablet is very remarkable.

No. II. may perhaps be read thus:

Θευδας και Μενα(λκας), i. e. Theudas and Menalcas.

Theudas was a contraction for Theodorus.

No. III. seems to contain the words *μνειας χαριν*, "for the sake of remembrance."

No. IV.—Page 28.

Near Soma.

Πομπηιος επο(ιησε)
τῳ ιδιῳ (τεκνῳ)
εκ των ιδιων αυτου
(μν)ειας χαριν.

No. V.—Page 30.

Near Pergamus.

εν ανδ
ρο σατραπευοντο-
ς επι Πιτταμιος Ισ-
αγορου, Κρατευας ε-
δωκεν Αριστομεν-
ει π
εποικισαι προς τῳ
φυτῳ τῳ επι Κρατευ-
ᾳ φυτευθεντι· ὁ δε πε-

ριβολος εστιν της ἑ-
ης σπορου κυπρων ἱκ-
ατον ἑβδομηκοντα·
και οικοπεδα και κιλ
φορος δε του κηπο(υ)
χρουσους ἑκαστο(υ)
ενιαυτου.

The following translation may perhaps convey the sense.

"* * * * *when Isagoras was satrap* [or governor] *over Pittamis, Crateuas gave to Aristomenes this* * * * * *to build upon it during the existence of any tree planted in the time of Crateuas* (*the hedge of* 170 *cypresses was planted by him*), *both houses and* * * *. *But the produce of the garden is golden* [or highly valuable] *every year*."

Remarks.

When Isagoras was satrap.] According to Passow (*Handwörterbuch*), "Satrap" was a general term for a governor.

Pittamis.] We find from Stephanus Byzantinus and others that there was a sea-port not far from Pergamus, called *Pitane*, or *Pitanæ*. Probably the name was further varied, and one of its forms may have been *Pittamis*. Steph. Byzantinus gives the female gentile name Pitanitis, which would be regularly formed from *Pitanis*.

During the existence of any tree planted in the time of Crateuas.] For want of a better explanation I have supposed this grant to have been like a building-lease for lives. The duration of a tree may have served for a term, as well as the life of a man or a child. But I know of no ancient authority in support of this conjecture.

The hedge.] An interesting fact is here proved, viz. the use of the cypress for hedges in ancient times; and the circumstance seems here to be mentioned in a parenthesis, because, on the foregoing supposition, the lease would not expire till all these cypresses were dead.

No. VI.—Page 31.

Near Pergamus.

This inscription is so complete, having been copied by Mr. Fellows in the manner described at p. 27, that it is unnecessary to express it in the common Greek characters. The letters between brackets are supplied, as they are destroyed in the original marble.

Remarks on the Translation.

In the Treasurership of Demetrius.] The *οικονομος*, i. e. the Treasurer, or Steward, of a Greek city, was also called Ταμιας, as is the case with Demetrius in this inscription. This office was one of high rank and dignity, probably equal in dignity with that of Archon. Josephus (Ant. Jud. lib. xi.) mentions together the *οικονομοι* and *αρχοντες* of cities, as if equal in importance. See Schleusner, Lex. N. T. v. Οικονομος. Belsham's Translation, etc. of Paul's Epistles, on Rom. xvi. 23. Demetrius may have been so called from being dedicated to Ceres (Δημητηρ), whose worship, as we learn from this inscription, was established in the city of which Demetrius was Treasurer.

Relations by marriage.] The word *γαμβρειωτης* is not now found in any author; we can only form a conjecture respecting its meaning.

Should then rise from the lamentation and go forth.] Εξανιστασθαι, "to rise, or stand up from," is used here in a very specific sense, which I do not find explained in any Lexicon. It is illustrated by the language in Gen. xxiii. 3., speaking of the ceremonies observed by Abraham in honour of his deceased wife Sarah, "And Abraham *stood up* from before his dead;" in the LXX. *καὶ ἀνέστη Ἀβραὰμ ἀπὸ τοῦ νεκροῦ αὐτοῦ.* This denotes the termination of the process described in the preceding verse, *κόψασθαι Σάῤῥαν καὶ πενθῆσαι.* In the case of Abraham, we perceive that after "standing up," the next thing was to bury the dead; and accordingly in the inscription before us, εξανιστασθαι is followed by εκπορευεσθαι: that is, the "standing up," or the termination of the dirges, howlings, and beatings of the breast in the house of the deceased, is followed by the "going out," or the procession accompanying the corpse to the tomb, or to the funeral pile. Here we find mention of the mourning women only, because the preceding portion of the law decides that they were to continue till the fifth month, whereas the mourning men and boys were to leave in the fourth month.

Pouqueville, in his Travels in the Morea, etc., gives the following account of what was done during his residence in Greece; and no doubt these modern observances are very similar to the πενθος or κηδεια mentioned in the inscription.

"A codja-bachi of the town died in our vicinity, and public prayers were ordered for the repose of his soul. It was not sufficient that his wife and children, with rent garments, proceeded to his grave, striking their face and bosom; but, as he was a man of power, the honour of his family required that the pomp of religion should be displayed in respect to his manes, and the most famous criers were put in requisition to attend his funeral. These criers were women, who soon arrived with a joyful countenance, in the hope of receiving a salary proportionate to the importance of their functions. They began by drinking off some bumpers of wine, and ascertaining the price they were to receive. They then inquired the name, qualities, and good actions of the codja-bachi, of which his valet informed them, taking care to enlarge upon each circumstance. They now placed themselves round the coffin, and began to groan and murmur. Afterwards they cried in faint accents, but gradually raised the voice till it had attained a high pitch. The substance of their lamentation was as follows: 'Oh! what a fine brave man! His ancestors were noble and illustrious. His father and grandfather were codja-bachis, and he was one himself. He might have become a prince; and who knows but he might have restored the empire? He prayed like a saint; and never failed to burn incense before the image on holidays. Let us weep over him.' And then their cries recommenced. These lamentations continued for a length of time, and were repeated to every person who came to see the corpse. After the interment, at which the criers also attend, the whole family return to partake of a repast, when they eat and drink, and their grief is at an end."

The trains appointed in the law as a matter of necessity.] For this sense of *αἱ εξοδοι*, meaning the train of attendants which might accompany the body to the funeral pile, see the word in Valpy's edition of Stephani Thesaurus. I have supposed *επαναγκον* (which I do not find in the Lexicons,) to mean the same as *επαναγκες*.

Those men and women who do not obey.] After these words the following have by some accident been omitted:

"and that it should be forbidden to such women, as being profane, to sacrifice to any of the gods for ten years;".

Ceres Thesmophoros ...... Artemis Lochia.] I have not found direct testimony to the existence of temples of these goddesses at Pergamus. But the worship of Artemis, or Diana, was established almost universally in Asia Minor, and was of the highest antiquity; and the coins of this part of Asia Minor show that the worship of Ceres also was very general.

The date of this inscription may perhaps be about 300 B.C.

Nos. VII—XII.—Pages 48—50.

From Assos.

No. VII.

+ Λουκιανου

Ανγοερκαδ(ο)υ
Μακεδονος
και Κανεικης,
περι ῳ και δι-
α(ι)τᾳ εν τοις
αρχειοις απο-
κειται.

I offer the following attempt at a translation:

"The tomb of Angoercadus
the Macedonian,

+ The tomb of Lucian. and Canice;
about whom and
his mode of life
an account is pre-
served in the archives."

It appears probable that this tomb first received the remains of the Macedonian, and afterwards of Lucianus, whose name is placed apart on the left hand. The cross prefixed to it probably denoted that he was a Christian. The same name, Lucianus, appears in No. XII., also from Assos, and with a cross in like manner prefixed.

No. VIII.

ὁ ἱερευς του σεβαστου θ-
εου Καισαρος, ὁ δε αυ
ν Ασιαρχος ὁ Κοιντος δο
ος και πατριος βασιλευ.

Translation.—" The priest of the august god Cæsar, and the * * * Asiarch Quintus," etc.

Asiarch.] The term is well explained in the following note on Acts xix. 31. by the Commissioners for the Education of the Poor in Ireland (*Scripture Lessons, New Testament, No.* 2.) :

" Asiarchs were officers who presided at the religious rites. They were selected from among the more wealthy citizens; and, although they held the office only for a year, they continued in courtesy to enjoy the title."

No. IX.

* * * * * * * * *
* * * *και ἱερευς του Διος τ* * *
(Κ)*αισαρι Σεβαστῳ και τῳ* Δ * *

No. X.

Επι Σεξτου Απι * * *
*υ ανθυπ
(ατο)υ κα
* * * *
*νος της πολ
* * * *
ταθεισης.

No. XI.

Εκ της προσοδου των αγρ(ων απελιπε νεις επισκευ-)
ην της πολεως Κλεοστρα(τος, υἱος πολεως, φυσει δε
Α)πελλικωντος επε

No. XII.

\+ Επιμελ(ε)ια
Ελλαδιου
* * * * * * πο-
λιτευο *
(ε)κ του * * * Αυιου Λουκ(ι)ανου.

i. e. By the care of Elladius
* * * *
from the * * * of Avius Lucianus.

Portions of the inscriptions numbered VIII., IX., and XI. were copied by Dr. Hunt in 1801, and are published in Walpole's Memoirs, p. 128. I have inserted in parentheses the parts of No. XI. which are supplied by Hunt's copy, and add a translation of the inscription thus far restored: "Cleostratus, a son of the city, but by nature a son of Apellicon, left for the adorning of the city from the income of his fields," &c.

No. XIII.—Page 60.

From Alexandria Troas.

I have been enabled to give the translation at the bottom of page 60, by comparing this inscription with one published by Spon in his *Miscellanea Eruditæ Antiquitatis*, pp. 173, 174. He saw at Alexandria Troas three pedestals having the same inscription, except that the numerals at the bottom were VII., VIII., IX., respectively. He has published that with the numeral VII.*, and the next in order is evidently that brought by Mr. Fellows. In this the name of the man to whose honour the statue on the pedestal was erected, and the word FLAMINI, denoting his office, must be supposed to have stood at the beginning, and to have been lost. The following part of the inscription, copied by Mr. Fellows, may be thus restored.

DIVI.AVG.COL.CL.APRENS.
ET.COL.IVL.PHILIPPENSI
EORVNDEM.ET.PRINCIPI.ET
COL.IVL.PARIANA.ET.TRIBVNI
MILIT.COH.XXXII.VOLVNTAR.
TRIB.MILIT.LEG.XIII.GEM.
PRAEF.EQVIT.ALAE.I.
SCVBVLORVM.
VIII.
VIC.

Apri, also called Apros, was a city of Thrace, and was erected into a colony by Claudius. Philippi, the well-known city of Macedonia, became a Roman colony when the Romans obtained possession of that country. Parium was a city in the Troad.

* We find it also in Pococke's *Inscriptiones Antiquæ*, p. 41. But he did not know whence it came.

No. XIV.—Page 112.

From Nicæa.

The year 6316, which is the date of this inscription, would correspond, according to the Byzantine computation, to A.D. 808. (Ideler, *Handbuch der Chronologie*, ii. p. 460.) The Michael of the inscription may, therefore, have been Michael I., who reigned about that time. Pococke has published this inscription in his *Inscriptiones Antiquæ*.

No. XV.—Page 113.

From Nicæa.

Ονησιμον
Ονησιμου τον αγαθον, εραν(α)
(ταμ)ιευσαντα, και γυμνασιαρχη-
σαντα ενδοξως, και ἑστιασαν-
τα το συνεδριον μεγαλοπρεπως και
* * * * * * * *
* * * * * * * *
(τ)ην μεγιστην αρχην επαρχοντων
Αριστταινετιανου Αμμιανου
και Παυλεινιανου Τρυφωνος,
(γ)ραμματευοντος Αυρ. Συμφορου
Καικοῦνος δια βιου Αυρ. Στεφανου.

Remarks.

Instead of εραvα ταμιευσαντα, it has been proposed to read γραμματευσαντα, " who discharged the office of scribe."

The inscription contains the following contractions, which may be compared with those in No. XVII.

MN for μν .

ΝΕ — νε
ΝΜΕ — νμε
ΜΕ — με
ΗΝ — ην
ΤΕ — τε

The expression *δια βιου* ought perhaps to be translated "for life," or "during his life." See Travels in various Countries of the East, edited by Walpole, pp. 551, 552.

No. XVI.—Pages 113, 114.

From Nicæa.

Χειλιαρχον λεγ. ιδ. γ ιδ γεμιν.
Χελιαρχον λεγ. ιε. επιτ(ρο-
π)ον Σεβ. επαρχειας Γαλλιας
(Α)κυιτανικης επι κε νσον,
επιτρ. επαρχειας Μυσιας
(τη)ς κατω, επιτρ. επαρχειας
ακης, επιτρ. δουκ. επεαρ-
(χει)ας Δαλματιας και Ιστρι-
(α)ς, επιτρ. δουκηναριον
Αλεξανδρειας, του ιδιου
λογου
+ Λουκηνος Αρχελαος τον
οὐ φιλον. αι.

Remarks.

This inscription is published by Von Hammer, *Umblick auf einer Reise nach Brussa,* pp. 187, 188. He says it was high up in the wall by the Land-gate, where the water flows into the city.

He shows from Tacitus the great valour and celebrity of the

14th Legion in the reign of Otho, and that under Nero the 15th repulsed the Persians.

The name of the person celebrated must have been at the head of the inscription.

I translate **ΤΟΥ ΙΔΙΟΥ ΛΟΓΟΥ** "at his own cost," supposing it equivalent to PECVNIA SVA in Latin inscriptions.

"The Lower Mysia" is evidently the same as *the Lesser Mysia*, which was near the coast and low, "the Greater Mysia" being for the most part lofty and mountainous.

A Ducenary Steward (*Procurator Cæsaris Ducenarius*) was one of the highest rank, receiving a salary of two hundred sesterces.

Orellius shows that the 14th Legion was called Gemina. (*Inscriptionum Lat. Selectarum Collectio*, No. 922.)

No. XVII.—Page 116.

From Nicæa.

Remarks.

We find the first part of this inscription in Pococke's *Inscriptiones Antiquæ*, p. 28, as well as in the work of Von Hammer.

M. Aur. Claudius became Emperor A.D. 268; was second time Consul, and may be supposed to have become thereby "second time Proconsul" of Bithynia, A.D. 269; and died A.D. 270. This seems to fix the exact date of the inscription. Claudiopolis in Bithynia was no doubt named from the same Emperor. The other individual mentioned in the inscription is styled Ὑπατικος, Consular, a title denoting that he had been Consul. In the Fasti Consulares we find that A.D. 268 the Consuls were "Paternus and Marianus." Probably "Marianus" ought to be Macrinus.

The splendid orator.] I doubt whether this translation is correct, but can suggest none better.

On the titles "Proconsul" and "second time Proconsul," as applied to Roman Emperors, see Orellii Inscrip. Lat. Select., No. 19, where Nerva is styled Proconsul.

This inscription contains the following contractions; compare No. XV.

PI	for	ρι
Ҏ	—	τρ
ΜΕ	—	με

No. XVIII.—Page 127.

North of Cotyæium.

Αγαθη τυχη. Θεοις, θειοις, και δ(ι)-
καιοις, Ἡροφιλ(ος) * * *
παρα ευχην * * * *
Ασιλας και Ασκληπας,
οἱ Ασκληπα * *
Κουρναετηνοι * *

From the last word it appears probable that the place where this inscription was found, was anciently called Curnaëtos.

No. XIX.—Page 142.

From Æzani.

Αουιδιος Κουιντος Αιζανειτων Αρχουσι, Βουλῃ, (και) Δημῳ χαιρειν. Αμφισβητησις περι χωρας ἱερας ανατεθεισης παλαι τῳ Δια τρειβομενη πολλων ετων, τῃ πρόνοιᾳ του μεγιστου Αυτοκρατορος τελους ετυχε· επει γαρ επεστειλα αυτῳ δηλῶν το πραγμα ὁλον, ηρομηντε ὁτι χρη ποιεῖν, δυο τα μαλιστα την διαφοραν ὑμῖν κεινοῦντα, και το δυσεργες και δυσευρετον του πραγματος παρεχομενα μει(ω) αστῳ φιλανθρωπῳ, το δικαιον ακολου-

θως τῃ περι τας κρισεις επιμελειᾳ τ(ην) πολυχ(ρ)ονιον ὑμων μαχην και ὑποψι-
αν προς αλληλους παυσε(ι)ν (εφη,?) ὡς εκ της επιστ(ολ)ης ἡν επεμψεν προς με
(αισ?)θησεσθε, ἡς το αντιγραφον ὑμῖν πεπομφα, (και απε)στειλα Δεεσπεπῳ τῳ επι-
τροπῳ του Σεβαστου, ὁπως γεωμετρας επιτηδ(εις εκλ)εξαμενος εκεινοις
προσχρησηται την χωραν διαμετρων κακ ὑμ ειν γενησεται
καὶ εκ των ἱερων του Καισαρος γραμματ(ων δ)εδηλωκα ὁτι οδειτε-
λειν ὑπερ ἑκαστου κληρου κατα την φασ ησανη
μερας λαβητε την επιστολην εκαε
χωρας τελεσεηναμη παλιν τινες
βραδειον απολαυσαι την πολιν τη
γενωνται. αρκει γαρ αυτοις το μεχρι
φαδεκαι της προς ἑσπερον επιστο
μο εγραφεν (και?) ερρωσθαι ὑμας ευχ(εται).

Remarks.

The latter part of this inscription is too imperfect to be translated. It probably contained exhortations to amity, with some further directions respecting the measuring and allotment of the territory. It appears also to refer to a copy of the Emperor's letter, inscribed to the westward on the same temple, and perhaps one of the Latin inscriptions noticed by Mr. Fellows. (See p. 141.) The inscription contains internal evidence that the temple was erected to Jupiter (*τῳ Διϊ*): we might expect to find the temple of the principal divinity of the city in its acropolis; and from the evidence of coins (*referred to in Holstenii Annot. in Steph. Byz., v.* Αιζανοι,) we learn that Jupiter was the principal divinity of the Æzanitæ. We may also conclude that the emperor mentioned in the inscription was Hadrian, both as the known patron of this city, and on account of his especial interest in temples dedicated to Jupiter. The concluding sentence of the inscription was probably added by the stone-cutter, and may have run thus: "* * * * * * * * wrote this inscription, and prays that you may enjoy health."

No. XX.—Page 144.

From Æzani.

Ὁ αρχων των Πανελληνων και ἱερευς θεου Ἁδριανου Πανελληνιου
και αγωνοθετης των μεγαλων Πανελληνιων Κ * Ιασων, και οἱ
Πανελληνες, τοις επι της Ασιας Ἑλλησι, χαιρειν.
Μ. Ουλπιον Απουληι(ο)ν Ευρυκλεα τον Αιζανειτην φθαν(ο)μεν ηδη και ε(ξ)
ἑτερων γραμματων μαρτυριας της παρ᾽ ἡμων ανεγνωκοτες, (?) επεσταλκο-
τες ὑμῖντε αυτοις ὑπερ αυτου, και τῃ πατριδι, και τῳ μεγιστῳ Αυτο-
κρατορι· δικαιον δε ηγησαμεθα, και του κρατιστου * Ιασονος παραλαβον-
τος την α(ρ)χην, μαρτυρησαι αυτῳ τα αυτα επιεικειᾳ τε και αιδοι πασῃ
κεχρημενῳ περι την πολιτειαν των συνπανελληνων, και το αξιωμα
το ὑπ * * χον αυτῳ ανωθε και απογενους επιμαλλον προαγομενοι
δι᾽ ὡν και πραττων διατετελεκε παρα παντα τον (?) * * * * *
χρονον.

Ερρωσθαι ὑμας ευχομαι.

Remarks.

The Panhellenes appear to have been a college or company of Greeks from all parts, who, besides the general advantages supposed to arise from their association, had annual processions, accompanied by sacrifices and athletic games. Jason, their Archon (i. e. President, or Grand Master), is styled "Priest of the god Hadrian Panhellenius." In this title of Hadrian there is an obvious reference to that of Jupiter Panhellenius, who at an earlier æra was worshiped in Ægina. Dr. D. E. Clarke found at Megara an inscription, perhaps designed for a statue of Hadrian, and raised to him by the Hadrianidæ (who were probably a fraternity of his worshipers, similar to the Panhellenes), calling him Ολυμπιον, Πυθιον, Πανελληνιον, τον ἑαυτων κτιστην και νομοθετην και τροφεα.

One of the Arundel marbles (No. 47. pp. 55, 56. of the Oxford edition, 12mo,) mentions twice "the singers or minstrels of the god Hadrian," Ὑμνῳδοι του θεου Ἁδριανου.

An inscription published by Spon (*Miscell.*, p. 364.) shows, that the festival of the Panhellenia was celebrated at Athens.

Dio Cassius says (lib. 69. p. 1164. *ed. Reimari*), "Hadrian completed the Ὀλύμπιον at Athens, in which his own image is set up (ἐν ᾧ καὶ αὐτὸς ἵδρυται). * * * * He left directions to the Greeks to construct his own chapel (σηκὸν), which is called τὸ Πανελλήνιον; and he appointed games (ἀγῶνα) in reference to it, and gave to the Athenians much wealth, and an annual supply of corn, and the whole of Cephalenia." So Spartian says (c. 13. referring to Hadrian's second visit to Athens), "Opera, quæ apud Athenienses cœperat, dedicavit: ut Jovis Olympii ædem et aram sibi: eodemque modo per Asiam iter faciens templa sui nominis consecravit." It seems not improbable that the worship of Hadrian was associated with that of Jupiter in the temple on the acropolis of Æzani.

Nos. XXI—XXIII.—Page 147.

From Æzani.

Lucianus appears to have been a common name in Asia Minor; probably also Marsyas. The worship of Diana was extremely prevalent there.

No. XXIV.—Page 148.

From Æzani.

Κουαρ(τ)-
ος και Σα-
τουρνεινος
Ονησᾳ αδελφῳ
μνημης χα-
ριν.

No. XXV.—Page 164.

From Sparta in Pisidia.

Ὑπερ μνημης και αναπαυσεως Παυλου Επικ(α?)διου. Ανεκτισεν τον ναον των αρχανγελων.

This inscription appears evidently Christian, and perhaps, even as such, not very ancient. The Greek Υ has the form of the Latin V. Paul Lucas observes, that the Christians were particularly numerous, and had four churches at Sparta. *Voyage dans la Grèce, l'Asie Mineure*, &c., tom. i. ch. 34. p. 248.

No. XXVI.—Page 169.

From Sagalassus.

Αυρηλιον Αντω-
νεινον Σεβασ-
(το)ν ἡ Βουλη
(και) ὁ Δημος.

i. e. "The Council and the People [commemorate] the August Emperor Aurelius Antoninus."

This inscription was no doubt intended for a statue of that emperor. His name occurs also on the coins of Sagalassus. (*Holstenii Annot. in Steph. Byz.*, *v.* Σαγαλασσος.)

The remains of this once splendid and populous city were first visited in modern times by Paul Lucas, who saw with astonishment the assemblage of beautiful buildings, little injured by time, and rising like a magical creation in the desert. See his *Voyage dans la Grèce*, &c. l.c., and his *Third* "Voyage," tome i. Also Mannert, *Geographie der Griechen und Römer*, B. 2. p. 174.

No. XXVI*.—Page 190.

Between Adalia and Perge.

In this inscription I can make out only a few words; e.g. *φιλοπατρι, τον βωμον* (the pedestal?) *απελευθερῳ, και ευεργετῃ.* It probably recorded the name and merits of the individual whose statue surmounted the pedestal.

Nos. XXVII., XXVIII.—Pages 211, 212.

From Phaselis.

No. XXVII.

The first line may be read thus:

(A)ρχιερευς, (σ)εβ(α)στος, δη(μαρχικ)ης εξουσιας,

i. e. "Chief Priest, august, of tribunitial authority."

No. XXVIII.

The inscription on this cornice may be restored as follows:

Νερουας υἱωνῳ Τραι(αν)ῳ (Ἁδριανῳ)
(αν)θυπατῳ τῳ πατρι πατ(ριδος)
(οἱ) Φασηλ(ιται)

i. e. "The citizens of Phaselis to Trajanus Hadrianus, grandson of Nerva, Proconsul, Father of his country."

In Spon's *Voyage*, (tom. i. p. 380.) we have an inscription from Heracleia in Caria, in which the Emperor Hadrian is called "Trajanus Hadrianus, son of Trajan, grandson of the god Nerva." As Trajan was adopted by Nerva, so Hadrian was adopted by Trajan (*a Trajano pro filio habitus, Ælii Spart. Hadrianus*). This shows why Hadrian is both called Trajan, and represented as the grandson of Nerva. Ælius Spartianus also mentions, that he received the title of "Father of his country."

Nos. XXIX., XXX.—Page 213.

From Olympus.

The pedestal from which the inscription No. XXIX. is taken was no doubt surmounted by a statue of the Emperor and philosopher Marcus Aurelius Antoninus. Mannert (*Geographie*, B. 2. p. 135.) seems to think it doubtful whether the city existed so late as the reign of this Emperor. The inscription before us settles the question: it shows that Olympus was still a considerable place.

The form of the Omega is well deserving of notice, **W** for **Ω**; it shows a transition to the small or cursive form, *ω*. It occurs again in the inscription from Labranda, p. 262.

No. XXX. may be read thus:

Το ἡρωον Φιλοκρατους
αυτων Πεισιθεᾳ και
εξουσιαν εχετωσαν αυ.

Nos. XXXI., XXXII.—Pages 222, 223.

From Patara.

No. XXXI.

Το ἡρωον κατεσκευασεν
Μ. *Αυρ*. Ιασων, Ιασονος Δωσι-

ου, ὁ Πατα(ρ)ευς, ἑαυτῳ και
*τῃ συμβιῳ αυτου * * * * * * **
Απφιωτῃ, και Πτολεμων αν(ηρ ε-)
πι τῳ μηδενα ἑτερον τεθη-
ναι, η οφειλησει τοις καταχθο-
νιοις θεοις δικαια.

The form Y for Y in the word *συμβιῳ* is peculiar. It approaches in form to some of the Lycian letters.

No. XXXII.

Κοιντος Λικιννιος, ελευ-
θερος Ῥωμαι(ο)ς, Ζωσιμῳ Ατ
ταλου, Παταρει, τον πατε-
ρα μου και Λικιννιου (?) *Ζω-*
σιμον τον αδελφον μου,
και Διαβουλιῳ μητρι,
μνημ(η)ς ἑνεκεν.

Nos. XXXIII—XXXVII.—Pages 238—240.

From Tlos.

No. XXXIII.

Φλαυιας Φιρμης υἱον Δομι-
τιου Απομειναριου του
δικ(α)ιοδοτου
Τλωεων ἡ Βουλη, και ἡ Γερου-
σια, και ὁ Δημος.

In the translation I have supposed *υἱον* to govern *Δομιτιου* as its genitive; but, considering the imperfect state of the inscription, and that the Lycians were in the habit of calling themselves after the mother, and not after the father (*Herod.* i. 173.), it is very possible that we ought to translate the first line thus: " Son of Flavia Firma."

In No. XXXVII. the Lycian name "Sarpedon," with which the Iliad has made us so familiar, occurs twice. "Meidi" is perhaps the same with a name, apparently "Mada," which occurs in one of Mr. Fellows's Lycian inscriptions.

No. XXXVIII.—Page 246.

From Telmessus.

We may trace the word *μνημης*, and perhaps supply in the last line *το μνημειον.*

Nos. XXXIX—XLI.—Pages 255, 256.

From Stratoniceia.

No. XXXIX. is written in trimeter iambics. The letters **KH**, **Λ**, **ΛΑ**, placed after each line, were probably intended to express the number of letters in the line, viz. 28, 30, and 31.

No. XLI. may perhaps be read thus:

** * ευσεβει και τη πα(τριδι*
σωθεις ε)κ των σεισμων ανε(θηκε).

No. XLII.—Page 262.

From Labranda.

Μενεκρατης Με-
νεκρατους, ὁ αρχια-
τρος της πολεως στ(ε)-
φανηφορων, τον κιο-
να συν σπειρη και κε-
φαλη προνοησε μ(ν)η-
μης της θυγατρος

αυτου Τρυφαινετης,
και αυτης στεφανηφο-
ρου και γυμνασιαρχου.

The woodcut may be compared with Spon's engraving of a Corinthian column at Mylasa. A panel or tablet, similar to that here represented, states that it was erected by the people in honour of their benefactor Menander, the son of Euthydemus. (See Spon, *Voyage*, tom. i. p. 275.) Probably this is the "single fluted column" which Mr. Fellows saw at Mylasa. We may suppose that each column, or a sum of money as an equivalent, was contributed to the erection of the temple at Labranda by the person recorded on the panel.

The "city" mentioned in the inscription was no doubt Mylasa, to which Labranda belonged as a κωμη, or village. The temple seen by Mr. Fellows was probably erected on the site of the "ancient temple of Jupiter" (Διὸς νεὼς ἀρχαῖος), of which an interesting account is given by Strabo (lib. xiv. cap. 2. §. 23.). That this building was more modern, might be concluded not only from the architecture as described by Mr. Fellows, but also from the form of the ω (Ш) in the word στεφανηφορων (see above, No. XXIX.), and from the term Archiatros (*chief physician*), a title not in use before the time of Nero*. The word σπειρα, which I have translated the "*base*," is not explained in this sense in the Lexicons, nor, I believe, is it so used in any extant author. But the curious and valuable architectural inscription brought from Athens proves that it denoted the base of an Ionic or Corinthian column. See Walpole's Memoirs on European and Asiatic Turkey, pp. 586, 601.

The epithets applied to Tryphænete prove that females took part in the exercises of the gymnasium.

* Ackermann's Preface to Aretæus, inserted in Kuhn's edition and treatise, Erläuterung der vornehmsten Medicinalgesetze bis zum xiii. Jahrhundert; also Henry Meibonius in Comm. in Marc. Aurel. Calliodori archiater. comitis. p. 13. No. 2.

APPENDIX B.

The Corn-drag.—Page 70.

Paul Lucas noticed this method of threshing near the Sea of Marmora. He has represented in an engraving both the instrument itself and the mode of drawing it by oxen. He describes the method of arming it with gun-flints, and of making it heavy by causing persons to sit upon it. (*Voyage dans la Grèce, l'Asie Mineure*, &c., tom. i. ch. 24. p. 182.)

This is the *tribulum* mentioned by Virgil (*Georg.* i. 164.), and described in the following terms by Varro (*De Re Rustica*, i. 52.): "Id fit e tabulâ lapidibus, aut ferro asperatâ, quo imposito aurigâ, aut pondere grandi, trahitur jumentis junctis, ut discutiat e spicâ grana." The prophet Isaiah alludes to it, chap. xli. 15: "Behold, I will make thee a new sharp threshing instrument having teeth."

Chips of Fir-wood used for giving light.—Page 140.

This use of fir-wood, cleft or torn into strips, and especially of the *root* of the tree, is well known, and is described in an instructive essay lately published by Mr. Arthur Aikin, "On artificial light from solid substances, and the manufacture of candles*." But the account here given by Mr. Fellows from his own observation, enables us to form a much more exact and accurate idea of the practice. When compared with the passages referred to by Mr. Aikin, and with those which I shall now cite from Theophrastus, it appears to me to warrant the inference that this method of obtaining artificial light has prevailed in Asia Minor for nearly 3000 years.

* Transactions of the Society of Arts, 1839, vol. liii. pp. 4, 5.

According to Theophrastus the tree best adapted for yielding *torch-wood* (δᾴς) was the Πεύκη, which is still called πεύκος by the Greeks of Asia Minor, and is the *Pinus maritima* of Linnæus. Theophrastus says that the roots were particularly resinous, and also the heart of the trunk. He speaks of the torch-makers of Mount Ida (οἱ περὶ τὴν Ἴδην δᾳδουργοὶ), an expression which both proves the early prevalence of this custom in Asia Minor, and shows that a distinct, and probably a numerous class of persons were employed in this occupation. The process is described as follows. When the pine (πεύκη) had attained to its full maturity, the torch-maker (δᾳδουργὸς) cut out a piece from the trunk near its base. The consequence was an accumulation of turpentine in the vicinity of the wound. After the lapse of twelve months the portion thus impregnated was cut out, and divided into suitable lengths. This was repeated for three successive years, and then, as the tree began to decay, the heart of the trunk was extracted, and the roots were dug up for the same purpose. (*Hist. Plant.*, lib. i. cap. 6. § 1.; lib. iii. cap. 9. § 3.; lib. x. cap. 2. §. 2, 3.) Theophrastus also mentions a diseased state of the pine, when from the excess of turpentine the whole trunk became torch-wood (ὅλον γίνεται δᾴς. *Hist. Plant.*, lib. iii. cap. 9. § 5.); and in conformity with the preceding observations, he remarks that this tree survives the operation of being cut for torches (τὰ δ' οὐδὲν πάσχει, καθάπερ ἡ πεύκη δᾳδουργουμένη. *Hist. Plant.*, lib. iv. cap. 16. § 1. ἡ δὲ πεύκη καὶ δᾳδοκοπουμένη σώζεται. *De causis Plant.*, lib. v. cap. 16. § 2.).

These statements show the precise meaning of the Homeric word δαΐς, in Attic Greek contracted into δᾴς· It meant either *torch-wood* considered in the mass, or a lath or strip of such torch-wood made to be used as a candle or a flambeau. Dorville has given this explanation in his notes on Charito, lib. v. cap. 9. These pieces of resinous pine-wood are even now called δᾳδία by the Greeks of Mount Ida. (Sibthorp and Hunt in Walpole's *Memoirs*, pp. 120. 235.)

We read in the Odyssey (σ. 309.) that the suitors of Penelope, wishing to have a dance after nightfall, heaped three brasiers with wood, and from time to time inserted into it *torches*, i. e. pieces of fir-wood impregnated with turpentine, as above described, and thus adapted to illuminate the apartment (*καὶ δαΐδας μετέμισγον*). In the palace of Alcinous (Od. η. 100–102.) a more ingenious and elegant arrangement is adopted:

> Refulgent pedestals the walls surround,
> Which boys of gold with flaming torches crown'd;
> The polish'd ore, reflecting ev'ry ray,
> Blazed on the banquet with a double day.
>
> *Pope's Translation.*

With this account of torches and torch-wood we may compare the account which Mr. Fellows afterwards gives of the mode of obtaining *fire-wood* (Chap. IX. pp. 257, 258.). This is based upon the same circumstance, the tendency of the resin or turpentine to accumulate and exude wherever an incision is made in the fir-tree. After repeated incisions, and the application of fire and the axe, the tree "at last falls, borne down by a heavy gust of wind." To the same primitive and tedious method of felling trees intended for burning, Theophrastus, speaking of the natives of Ida, appears to allude when he says, "that after these things the tree, being decayed, falls in consequence of the under-cutting, by the force of the winds*."

Napkins embroidered with gold.—Page 153.

This species of Oriental luxury was known also to the ancients. In the Life of Alexander Severus, written by Lampridius, we read, that although that Emperor took great delight in good linen, he objected to having it ornamented with gold, because he considered that the excellence of linen con-

* Μετὰ δὲ ταῦτα διὰ τὴν ὑποτομὴν ἐκπίπτειν τὸ δένδρον ὑπὸ τῶν πνευμάτων σαπέν. *Hist. Plant.*, lib. x. cap. 2. § 7.

sisted in being soft and smooth, whereas the insertion of gold made it both rough and rigid.

We passed much snow, and were visited by a storm of small pieces of ice, of broken forms and transparent.—Page 166.

I once witnessed the same appearance and in circumstances very similar. I was crossing the elevated plain which lies between Aix-la-Chapelle and Cologne. The weather was intensely cold, the ground covered with snow, and the sun shining brightly. I was struck by the brilliant flashes of light reflected from the snow both in falling and as it lay upon the ground. Having alighted to examine it, I found that it was a variety of snow, differing from the beautiful stellated forms which have been delineated by Hooke in his Micrographia, and more recently by Scoresby in his Account of the Arctic Regions, and consisting of thin parallelograms of ice about half an inch long, and with angles of 60 and 120 degrees.

Springs of fresh water rising in the sea.—Page 184.

I am not aware that any other traveller has noticed the "curious effect" here described, which must be attributed to the difference in the refraction of light in passing through fresh and salt water.

The frequency of submarine freshwater springs on the northern coast of the Mediterranean Sea is very remarkable. I have met with the following instances in addition to that here recorded.

1. The copious spring in the gulf of La Spezia is well known. It often rises to a considerable height above the surface of the salt water. In this case also the rock is a recent calcareous tufa or breccia.

2. In the gulf of Taranto. "At the distance of two hundred

yards from the mouth of the Galesus, two powerful freshwater springs, called *occhi,* rise in the sea, and bubble up to its surface with sufficient strength to drive away any boat that floats over them. I was told that they may be seen in calm weather gushing from two black caverns at the bottom of the water." (The Hon. Keppel Craven's Tour through the Southern Provinces of the Kingdom of Naples, p. 181. See also Baron Riedesel's Travels, translated by Forster, p. 180.)

3. The inhabitants of the ancient Aradus, the Arvad of the Old Testament, obtained water in case of a siege by the following method. Their city was crowded together upon an island situated at a short distance from the northern extremity of the coast of Phœnice. In the strait they discovered a spring of clear water rising from the rock of limestone. Their expedient was to go to the spot in a boat with a leaden bell-shaped instrument having a small hole at the top, round which was fastened a leathern pipe. They let down the instrument upon the spring. At first sea-water was forced up; but after a little while they obtained the spring-water in whatever quantity they desired. (Strabo, lib. xvi. cap. 2. § 13.)

The fine bay of Phineka.—Page 214.

The modern name Phineka is little changed from the ancient Phœnicus. Livy mentions "portum Phœnicunta" (lib. 37. cap. 16.). According to Stephanus Byzantinus, this was also the name of an island, perhaps one of those mentioned by Mr. Fellows. Livy speaks of the cliffs which overhung the town. Phœnicus (i. e. Φοινικοῦς, contracted for Φοινικοεις,) would signify *a place abounding in palm-trees* (φοινικες); so that the name agrees most remarkably with Mr. Fellows's account of the number of palm-trees still growing there.

Wine flavoured with the Fir-apple.—Pages 234, 235.

Compare the remarks of Dr. Sibthorp and Lord Aberdeen in

Memoirs relating to European and Asiatic Turkey, edited by Walpole, Lond. 1818, p. 235.

Eggs of the ostrich an emblem of faith.—Page 241.

In an ancient inventory of the relics, &c. belonging to Durham Cathedral, and in other documents of the same kind, repeated mention is made of *Griffin's Eggs.* May not these have been ostrich eggs, valued during the middle ages on the principle here explained?

Howling of hired women at funerals.—Page 241.

See the preceding Remarks on the Greek inscription, No. VI., (page 314,) which is a law enacted to regulate the practice.

"Whether the horses of the ancient Greeks were shod."—Page 242.

Mr. Bracy Clark has shown that they were not, but that great care was taken to harden the hoofs. See his valuable Essay on the Usages of the Ancients respecting Shoeing the Horse, 2nd edit., London, 1831, 4to.

Milk of sheep, goats, and buffalos generally used.—Page 242.

The ancients also used the milk of sheep and goats only; the use of cows and oxen was chiefly for the plough and other agricultural work.

Musical instruments.—Page 253.

The "flute," as here delineated, was called *αυλος* by the Greeks, *tibia* by the Latins. The "guitar" is probably the χελυς or χελωνη of the Greeks, the *testudo* of the Latins. A good representation of an Egyptian guitar is given in Denon's *Voyage*, plate lv. No. 27.

Chirping of the "Gryllus."—Page 273.

This must no doubt have been the Τεττιξ or Cicada, so well known from the mention of it by Homer, Anacreon, and Virgil, and so much the object of favour among the Athenians.

Thermal waters of Hierapolis.—Pages 283, 284.

Appearances exactly like those here described present themselves at the baths of San Filippo in Tuscany. See Edinburgh Philosophical Journal, 1820, vol. ii. pp. 290—300; Lyell's Principles of Geology; De la Beche's Geological Manual, p. 136.

The thermal waters of Hierapolis are mentioned by numerous ancient authors, who are referred to by Cellarius, Ant. Orbis Notitia; by Mannert; and by the commentators on Stephanus Byzantinus. It appears that the ancient inhabitants erected fences around their fields and gardens merely by leading the hot water in channels so as to deposit the incrustation in the proper lines of direction.

INDEX.

NAMES OF PLACES

MENTIONED IN THE JOURNAL,

AS PRONOUNCED BY THE PEOPLE, AND AS WRITTEN BY THE ROYAL GEOGRAPHICAL SOCIETY.

As pronounced by the people.	As written by the Royal Geographical Society.	As pronounced by the people.	As written by the Royal Geographical Society.
Acruicooe	Akhúr-kőï.	Boodoór	Búrdúr.
Acsá	Ak-hisár.	Boodroóm	Búdrúm.
Adramít	Adramit.	Booják	Búják.
Alaysoón	Aghlásún.	Boonábassy	Bunár-báshí.
Allah-shehr	Alá-shehr.	Brúsa	Bŭrúsah.
Altuntash	Altúntásh.	Bulladán	Búluwádín.
Aneghoól	Aïnehgól.	Caracooe	Kará-koï.
Arracooe	Ará-kőí.	Cassabá	Kasabah.
Asalook	Ayá-solúgh.	Castellorizzo	Castello Rizo.
Atália	Antáliyah.	Castledá	Kastel-tágh.
Báffy	Báfí.	Catchíburloo	Gechi-búr-lú.
Báker	Bákir.	Chánly	Chánlé.
Bállook	Báluk.	Channákálasy	Chanákkal'ah-sí.
Beahráhm	Beïrám.	Chétme	Chetmeh.
Beérmargy	Bérmarj.	Cousk	Cousk.
Béiramitch	Beïrámícheh.	Criscool	Kĭriskúl.
Bérgama	Berghamah.	Crissa	Kĭrísah.
Bijikly	Bijik-li.	Dávre	Davreh.

As pronounced by the people.	As written by the Royal Geographical Society.	As pronounced by the people.	As written by the Royal Geographical Society.
Delíktash	Delik-ṭásh.	Káraboóna*c*ooe	Ḳará-bunár köï.
Demelheér	Demelheh.	Karaváren	Kará Váren.
Dil	Dil.	Kásrukhan	Khosreu Khán.
Dollomón	Ṭálamán.	Keméreh	Kemereh.
Dooaslán	Duuáslán.	Kiacooe	Ḳayá kóï.
Doorr*á*	Durrah.	Kir'kagatch	Kirḳ-ághách.
Doósler	Dúsler.	Kiz'zlejik	Ḳizil-jiḳ.
Doovér	Duvah.	Konsk	Kóshk.
Dumb*á*ri-ovasy	Dunbáh-ovah-sí.	Koógez	Kógez.
Enáe	Enáï.	Kooník	Kunik.
Ersek	Hersek.	Koósdervent	Kiz-dervend.
Esky Hiss*á*	Esky Ḥiṣár.	Koot*á*ya	Kútáhiyah.
Esky Stámbool	Eski Stán búl.	Léfky	Lefkeh.
Fórnas	Phúrnas.	Mácry	Maḳri.
Gébsy	Gebiseh.	Mánser	Maghnísá.
Ghiáourcooe	Janker-cháï.	Mellássa	Milásah.
Ghúmbat	Ghumbát.	Moóla	Mughlah.
Goojcivák	Gújaḳ.	One-óenoo	In'öní.
Goózel hiss*á*	Gúzel ḥisár.	Oóscooda	Uskudar.
Hágicooe	Ḥájí köï.	Palláttia	Palaṭiyá.
Hallil Elly	Ḳhalíleh-lí.	Phin'eka	Finekeh.
Hoola	Húlah.	Sandookleé	Sandúḳ-lí.
Iakly	Y Ayáḳlí.	Sansóon	Ṣánṣún.
Idín	Aïdin.	Sara cooe	Saráï kóï.
Iny	Ineh.	Shéblac	Chiblák.
I'smeer	Izmír.	Sichanleé	Sichán-lí.
I'smid	Izmíd.	Sohoót	Sugúd.
Isnic	Izník.	Sokay	Sokeh.
Kákava	Kakavah.	Sóma	Sómah.

As pronounced by the people.	As written by the Royal Geographical Society.	As pronounced by the people.	As written by the Royal Geographical Society.
Soósa	Susah.	Tékrova	Tekroveh.
Sparta	Ispártah.	Tj*á*den	Cháden.
Stámbool	Stánbúl.	Vasilichia	Vasilikia.
St*a*rus	Stárros.	Vizierkhán	Vezír-khán.
Tam'book kalasy	Pambúkkaláh.si.		

THE END.

LONDON:

PRINTED BY RICHARD AND JOHN E. TAYLOR,

RED LION COURT, FLEET STREET.

SD - #0014 - 190521 - C0 - 229/152/22 - PB - 9781332164424